A Genealogical History of the French and Allied Families

A Genealogical History of
the French and Allied Families

REV. ATCHISON QUEAL
Father of the Author

LUCY FRENCH QUEAL
Mother of the Author

A Genealogical History of the French and Allied Families

BY
MARY QUEAL BEYER

PRIVATELY PRINTED AT CEDAR RAPIDS IOWA
BY THE TORCH PRESS FOR MARY QUEAL BEYER
1912

Of this de luxe edition of the Genealogical History of the French and Allied Families there were two hundred copies printed, this copy being number

COPYRIGHT, 1912, BY
MARY QUEAL BEYER

THE TORCH PRESS
CEDAR RAPIDS
IOWA

DEDICATED TO THE LOVING MEMORY OF MY FATHER AND MOTHER, REVEREND ATCHISON QUEAL AND LUCY FRENCH QUEAL, BY THE AUTHOR

Those who do not treasure up the memory of their ancestors, do not deserve to be remembered by posterity
  EDMUND BURKE

FOREWORD

The study of genealogy has been for some years on the increase Many causes have contributed to this. Among them are the patriotic societies whose membership in part at least depends on descent from revolutionary stock. The increasing tendency to reach for baubles in American society causes many a quest for proof of kinship with those in England who have the right to use insignia by heraldic authority Not a few engage in the search of family history believing that somewhere in the East or in Europe is a fortune lying unclaimed awaiting its rightful heir And then there are those whose traits of mind and special tastes lead to this kind of writing for the mere love of the semi-mysterious, ever elusive information, lying just beyond reach, the attainment of which is the goal of an aspiration smaller, though no less sincere, than is that of him who explores uncharted seas and sciences

This beautiful book is due neither to a need for proof of patriot or Pilgrim lineage, to a desire of display, nor to the hope of fame or fortune.

Mary Queal Beyer has deeply loved her immediate ancestry She has even deeper love for her living kin by blood and marriage. She has put her thought in printed fact rather than adulation. In the form of a book she has recited a family record, and challenged her descendants to measure up to a standard high and firm and fixed in the affairs of home and country.

It is my pleasure as the chief administrative officer of the State Historical Department of Iowa at Des Moines, to have witnessed the faithful labors of Mrs Beyer amongst the books and references in our collections I have observed the really wonderful collection of fam-

FOREWORD

ily data she has gathered into her hands, and I may say into her mind, and the fidelity, patience, and industry she has given to the preparation of these for publication

The family and friends of Mrs Beyer may assure themselves she has prepared for them a work no one else could have done They are the beneficiaries of a lavish hand and loving heart. They have had made for them a lasting memorial such as is not within the power of painter or of sculptor to conceive, and thus she has classed herself with genius.

This beautiful book will be held and prized generations after its author has laid it down forever Its spirit speaks of her in eloquence she has devoted in words to others alone This word of her I feel is due

EDGAR R HARLAN,
Curator State Historical Department of Iowa, Des Moines, Iowa

AUTHOR'S PREFACE

When I began this work, my only thought was to leave to my children the results of my research. Family records preserved in letters or in the pages of diaries kept by those who have long since been crowned, have yielded much of interest to the people of the present day, and have created a desire to put these records in some tangible form for the use of future generations.

Much time has been spent in research with the hope of adding to the stock of information already possessed, and while the energy thus expended has been rewarded beyond all expectation, yet the work is far from complete, and many errors have doubtless crept into these pages.

It is to be hoped that the future generations of these families will make as enviable a record as have those who silently follow each other through these pages. While none have climbed to dizzy heights of fame, yet none have brought shame or disgrace for a heritage to the generations unborn, so this history will stand as the life record of plain, honest common people.

I wish at this time to make acknowledgement to Mrs Lucy French Stoner of Cambridge, Massachusetts, Dr S H French of Amsterdam, New York, and Seward H French of Binghamton, New York, for the very efficient help rendered in verifying statements and copying court records; to Mrs Nellie Pendell of Binghamton, New York, for the loan of the account book kept by Samson French; and to Mrs Jennie McElyea Beyer of Ames, Iowa, who has been my invaluable assistant in the compilation of this history.

I wish to make special mention of the Iowa Historical and Genealogical Library which I consider one of the best that any seeker of information along these lines of research can visit; and lastly of my husband, Jackson Beyer, who has rendered the publication of this volume possible.

MARY QUEAL BEYER

CONTENTS

THE FRENCH FAMILY	21
THE INGALLS FAMILY	229
SEAWARD GENEALOGY	249
THE QUEAL FAMILY	274
THE BEYER FAMILY	343
THE COOPER AND ENGELBECK FAMILIES	363
THE ARMITAGE AND BEARD FAMILIES	368
INDEX	371

ILLUSTRATIONS

Rev. Atchison Queal and Lucy French Queal . .	*frontispiece*
Site of Meeting House in Cambridge	31
Site of Home of Lt. William French, Cambridge, Massachusetts	31
Faneuil Hall	36
Tablet on Billerica Common, where First Meeting House stood	42
House now standing on Farm owned by Lt. William French .	49
Old South Burying Ground, Billerica, Massachusetts . .	49
Division of Estate of Lt. William French (fac-simile of Original Document)	57
John and Sarah Estabrook French and Son, Benjamin . .	63
House built by John French, 1720	70
Bullet Molds used in Revolution	70
Gun, Bullet Molds, and Camp Kettle used by Ebenezer French	70
State Historical Building of Iowa	90
Burying Ground at Southwick, Massachusetts . . .	101
Dr. S. H. French	107
Home of Dr. S. H. French	107
Dr. Lucius French and His Home	111
Catalogue of Descendants of Samson and Lusannah French .	118
Photograph made from Account Book kept by Samson French .	121
Portion given to Thomas by His Father, Samson French .	128
Family Record kept by Samson French . . .	137–141
Polly Temple, Wife of Thomas French, Jr. . . .	145
Thomas French and Three of His Children . . .	146
Rear View of Old Mill House (built in 1810) . . .	149
Home of Thomas French	149
Old Grist Mill on Castle Creek	149
Mary French Smith	160
Samson French's House at Decatur	160
Samson French House, built in 1857, Morrow County, Ohio .	165
Demit from Masonic Lodge given Samson French in 1833 .	166
Lottery Ticket held by Samson French	169
Thomas, John, Oscar, Martin, Alva, and Calvin French .	170
Sampler made by Elizabeth Seaward	173

ILLUSTRATIONS

Needle Book made by Elizabeth Seaward	174
Lucy French Stoner	186
Certificate of Service given O. L. R. French	191
Pass given to Alva French	191
Discharge given Alva French from Squirrel Hunters	196
Certificate of Service given Squirrel Hunters	199
Seward H. French	200
Calvin D. French at Time of Enlistment	210
After Escape from Andersonville	210
Thomas, John, and Oscar French	217
Martin M., Alva C., and Calvin D. French	218
Section of Lucy Ingalls's Wedding Veil	226
Eliza Ballou Garfield	233
Children of Stephen and Lucy Ingalls Seaward	243
Direct Descendants of Henry and Sybil Ingalls	244
Asa Palmerlee and Lucy Seaward Palmerlee	257
Smith B. Queal	267
Cottage of Geo. W. Queal, Long Beach, California	267
William N. Queal	271
Anna Queal Starkweather	272
Trunk brought by Robert Queal from Ireland in 1797	275
Worcester, New York, showing South Hill	276
William C. Queal	280
House built by William C. Queal in 1847 at Worcester, New York	288
House where Atchison Queal died in 1859	288
Fac-simile of Letters Patent issued to Atchison Queal	295
Discharge from Service given to Hedding H. Queal	301
Hedding Queal	302
John H. Queal	305
Five Children of William C. and Mary Graves Queal	311
Old French School House at Decatur, New York, where Reverends Atchinon Queal, William G. Queal, and Luke C. Queal each preached His First Sermon	312
Lot in Maple Grove Cemetery where Sixteen of the Queal Family are buried	317
Captain Paul A. Queal	324
Adam Beyer	338
Jacob Beyer Homestead	338
Jackson Beyer	342
Mary Queal Beyer	343
Home of Author at Des Moines, Iowa	344

ILLUSTRATIONS 19

Parsonage at Fly Creek, New York	347
Church at Fly Creek, New York	347
Mrs. Jennie McElyea Beyer	348
John Hedding Beyer	351
Harmon Engelbeck	355
Caroline Engelbeck	356

THE FRENCH FAMILY

THE name French is supposed to have originated in France, appearing first in England soon after the Norman Conquest, being noted in the list of those who fought with William the Conqueror at the battle of Hastings. Records in Yorkshire, England, show the name as early as 1100, and later on it appears in the west and north, being found in North England and Scotland. During this time the name was variously spelled Franceis, de Frenssh, le ffrensh, Frenssh, Frensche, Frensce, Franche, Freynch, the earliest notice of the surname French, as it is used today, appearing in 1252 [1]

The first generation of this branch of the French family of which there is any authentic record, dates from the death of Thomas French, which occurred at Weathersfield, County Essex, England, in 1599

First Generation

THOMAS[1] FRENCH the elder, of Weathersfield, County Essex, England, died 1599. In his will he mentions wife Bridget, three children and grandson John, son of Thomas, and gives to the poor of Halstead, Essex; of West Wratting, Cambridge, Snetisham, Norfolk, Little Birdfield and Arkesden, Essex
- I. Thomas, married Anne
- II. Mary, married John Collin
- III. Elizabeth, married John Meade

Second Generation

THOMAS[2] FRENCH (Thomas[1]), of Halstead, County Essex, England, died January 27, 1613, leaving wife Anne, six sons, and several daughters
- I. Thomas, married a Miss Wood.
- II. John

---

[1] County Records of the surnames of French in England by A. D. Weld French.

III. Edward.
IV. Robert.
V. William.
VI. Francis.
Also several daughters.

Third Generation

THOMAS³ FRENCH (Thomas,² Thomas¹), of Halstead, County Essex, England, married a daughter of —— Wood.
  I. William, born March 15, 1603; married Elizabeth ——.
 II. Francis, baptized June 29, 1606.
III. Jerrymya, baptized November 21, 1607.

Fourth Generation

LIEUTENANT WILLIAM⁴ FRENCH (Thomas,³ Thomas,² Thomas¹), born March 15, 1603; married Elizabeth, surname not known, about 1623. To them were born:
    I. Francis, born in England, 1624; came with parents in ship "Defence"; removed to Milford, Connecticut, about 1650, and four years later was one of the settlers in Derby, Connecticut. He married April 10, 1661, Lydia Bonnnell of Milford. To them were born nine children. Francis French died February 14, 1681. Lydia Bonnell French died April 1, 1708.
   II. Elizabeth, born in England, 1629; married Robert Eliot of Dedham.
 III. Mary, born in England, 1633; baptized when between two and three years of age at her father's "joyning"; married Jonathan Hyde, and died May 27, 1672, at the birth of her son Joseph, who was her twelfth or fourteenth child.
 IV. John, born in England, 1635; married June 21, 1659, Abigail Coggan, daughter of Henry of Barnstable. She died April 5, 1662. John married (second) July 3, 1663, Hannah, daughter of John Burrage of Charlestown. To them were born two children:

1. Hannah, born in Billerica January 20, 1664; married August 3, 1685, Dr John Kittredge To them were born five children, they being the progenitors of a long line of medical men, through their sons John and Jacob Simeon, the grandson of John, was the father of eight sons, all of whom were physicians.
2. Abigail, born in Billerica December 6, 1665; married Benjamin Parker. To them were born one son and three daughters
Abigail died March 13, 1728.

Hannah, second wife of John French, died July 7, 1667
John French married (third) January 14, 1668, Mary, daughter of John Rogers To them was born one child

3. Mary, born in Billerica March 4, 1670; married Nathan, son of Daniel Shed To them were born nine children Nathan Shed died June 18, 1736 Mary Shed died August 21, 1740.

Mary, third wife of John French, died June 16, 1677
John French married (fourth) January 16, 1677 (or 1678), Mary, daughter of Francis Littlefield of Woburn, and widow of John Kittredge of Billerica To them were born six children:

4. John, born in Billerica May 15, 1679
5. Elizabeth, born in Billerica July 24, 1681; married Thomas Abbott
6. William, born in Billerica November 26, 1683; died April 21, 1685.
7. Sarah, born in Billerica September 15, 1685; married —— Flint, of Charlestown After his death Sarah married April 5, 1710, Joseph Frost. To them were born three sons and one daughter
8. William, born in Billerica August 8, 1687; married Mehitable Patten To them were born eight children:
    a William, born January 25, 1713; married Tabitha —— To them were born eleven children, by name:

Jonathan, William, Joseph, Tabitha, Benjamin, Nehemiah, Mehitable, Ephraim, Mehitable (second), Stephen, Betsey.
- b. Elizabeth, born in Billerica April 3, 1716; married Ephraim Kidder. To them were born nine children. Elizabeth died November 30, 1755.
- c. Mehitable, born in Billerica August 29, 1718; married John White.
- d. Nathaniel, born in Billerica February 2, 1721; married Elizabeth Frost. To them were born eleven children, the names of three being known to the author — Nathaniel, Joel, and William, the last named being born March 27, 1753, and claimed by his descendants as the first martyr to the cause of American independence.
- e. Jonathan, born in Billerica May 28, 1724; died June 20, 1725.
- f. David, born in Billerica May 28, 1724.
- h. John, born in Billerica May 27, 1730; married Mary, daughter of Jacob French; he married (second) Priscilla Mace. John was the father of eleven children.

9. Hannah, born in Billerica February 18, 1693; married Jonathan Richardson. To them were born one daughter and three sons. Jonathan died August 13, 1720. Hannah married (second) February 15, 1726, Benjamin Frost. To them was born one daughter. Hannah died September 12, 1769.

Mary, fourth wife of John French, died in 1719.

John French was a colonel in the militia, and was often in the town's service. He was wounded by the Indians in an assault on Quaboag in 1675. He died in October, 1712.

- V. Sarah, born in Cambridge in March, 1638; married Jonathan Peake.
- VI. Jacob, born in Cambridge March 16, 1640; lived in Billerica

on the "east road" near the home of his brother John. His house was one of the garrisons of 1675, and was probably the same building which according to Hazen's *History of Billerica*, was occupied by James Fletcher in that year. He was a sergeant in the militia. He married September 20, 1665, Mary, daughter of Richard Champney, ruling elder of Cambridge church. To them were born ten children:[1]

1. Jacob, born in Billerica February 20, 1667; died 1700.
2. William, born in Billerica July 18, 1668; married Sarah Danforth May 22, 1695. To them were born twelve children:
    a. Jacob, born in Billerica May 16, 1696, married May 29, 1722, Elizabeth Davis. To them were born eight children. Elizabeth died February 3, 1738. Jacob married (second) May 19, 1741, Sarah Brown. To them were born four children. Sarah died August 16, 1765. Jacob married (third) November 19, 1766, Mrs. Mary Curtis, who died September 19, 1769.
    Jacob French died March 7, 1775.
    b. Joseph, born in Billerica January 26, 1698; died February 13, 1698.
    c. Sarah, born in Billerica December 29, 1698; married Nathaniel Whittemore. Sarah died August 15, 1734.
    d. William, born in Billerica January 25, 1701; married January 22, 1727, Joanna Hill, who died January 17, 1769. William married (second) November 27, 1770, Mrs. Mehitable Mooar. William was the father of eleven children. He died April 9, 1776.
    e. Jonathan, born in Billerica January 25, 1703; died March 9, 1728.
    f. Elizabeth, born in Billerica April 3, 1705; married February 3, 1730, Josiah Crosby. Elizabeth died

---

[1] From chart prepared by Rev. H. Martin Kellogg — a descendant of Jacob French.

November 27, 1739. The husband's death occurred a few years later.

g. Ebenezer, born in Billerica August 5, 1707; married August 27, 1729, Elizabeth Hill. To them were born nine children. Elizabeth died March 26, 1786. Ebenezer died December 31, 1791.

h. Mary, born in Billerica October 7, 1709; married January 16, 1730, Benjamin Manning. To them were born eleven children.

i. Nicholas, born in Billerica September 5, 1711; married June 5, 1744, Priscilla Mooar (born June 12, 1724). To them were born nine children, by name: Timothy, Priscilla, Nicholas, Isaac, Lucy, Sarah, Jonathan, Sarah (second), David.
Priscilla Mooar French died February 18, 1784.
Nicholas French died August 20, 1796.

j. Lydia, born in Billerica April 29, 1714; died August 2, 1731.

k. Esther, born in Billerica May 16, 1716; died July 7, 1736.

l. Samuel, born in Billerica May 21, 1718; married Elizabeth Barron. To them were born ten children, by name: Mary, Isaac, Elizabeth, Esther, Sarah, Samuel, Lucy, Oliver, Samuel (second), Silas.

3. Mary, born in Billerica, October 6, 1669; died November 12, 1669.

4. John, born in Billerica October 6, 1670; died December 3, 1670.

5. Joseph, born in Billerica May 5, 1673; died September 25, 1676.

6. Jabez, born in Billerica September 16, 1674; died at birth.

7. Mary (second), born in Billerica March 5, 1676; married December 13, 1695, Jonathan Baldwin. To them were born three sons and two daughters.

FRENCH AND ALLIED FAMILIES 27

    8   Hannah, born in Billerica October 23, 1677; died at birth

    9   Elizabeth, born in Billerica June 8, 1679; married William Manning To them were born nine children

    10   Sarah, born in Billerica March 7, 1681; married Thomas Baldwin To them were born seven sons and one daughter. Sarah died June 16, 1761

Mary Champney, wife of Jacob French, died April 11, 1681
Jacob French married (second) Mary Convers of Woburn
To them was born:

    11   Abigail, born in Billerica April 20, 1686; died March 29, 1687

Mary Convers French died June 18, 1686
Jacob French married (third) Mary ———, who was drowned June 9, 1709
Jacob French married (fourth) Ruth ———, who died November 6, 1730
Jacob French was the father of eleven children He died May 20, 1713

VII   Hannah, born April 12, 1641; died June 20, 1642

VIII   Hannah (second), born February 16, 1644; married John Brackett September 6, 1661. To them were born nine children.

Hannah French died May 9, 1674

IX.   Samuel, born December 3, 1645, died July 15, 1646

X   Samuel (second), born about 1647 or 1648; married Sarah Cummings (born January 27, 1661), the marriage taking place December 28, 1682

Samuel French died November 4, 1727 A complete genealogical record of Samuel (second) French, from whom the author is descended, will be found in this volume, following the history of his father, Lieutenant William French

Elizabeth, wife of Lieutenant William French, and mother of the before mentioned ten children, died March 31, 1668.

On May 6, 1669, Lieutenant William French married (second) Mary, daughter of Thomas Lathrop and widow of John Stearns of Billerica. To them were born four children.

XI. Mary (second), born April 3, 1670; married Nathaniel Dunklin. To them were born twelve children.

XII. Sarah (second), born October 29, 1671; married Joseph Crosby of Billerica May 6, 1691.

XIII. Abigail, born April 14, 1673; died April 13, 1674.

XIV. Hannah (third), born January 25, 1676; married John Childs of Watertown October 5, 1693.

From one of these fourteen children of Lieutenant William French, Alice French (Octave Thanet), the author, of Davenport, Iowa, is descended.

Lieutenant William French died November 20, 1681, aged seventy-eight years.

In the winter of 1634, the Defence sailed from Hartwick,[1] for the New World, but the ship being driven back on account of bad weather, the journey for the time being was abandoned, and it was not until August 10, 1635, that this vessel finally embarked upon the voyage that was to land her passengers on the shores of the then almost unknown continent. The Defence, being old and unseaworthy, sprung a leak in the first storm encountered, which exposed those on board to such great danger that they were about to return to port. However, they finally succeeded in repairing the damage and continued their journey, encountering many storms during their thirty-four days upon the sea, came in sight of land October 2d, and the following day, October 3, 1635, landed at Boston. Thomas Bostacke of London was master of the ship. Among the passengers is found the name of William French, his wife Elizabeth, and four children, they being the first of this family to set foot on American soil.

William French was born in Halstead, County Essex, England, March 15, 1603, and married Elizabeth, surname not known, about 1623, her age being given as thirty or thirty-two in the record in the customs house, London, England.

On reaching Boston, William French purchased property and set-

---

[1] This seaport was at the mouth of the Stover in Essex, having a spacious and safe harbor.

tled in the Newe Towne, called New Town or Newtown until May 2, 1638, when the General Court "Ordered That Newtowne shall henceforward be called Cambridge,"[1] and no other act of incorporation is found on record. His home was on the westerly side of Dunster street, about midway between Harvard Square and Mount Auburn street, the site now being occupied by a bank. He bought this property in 1639 and sold it to William Barrett June 10, 1656, after his removal to Billerica.

The following deed was given at that time, the original being on file in the East Cambridge court house:

WILLIAM FFRENCH DEED TO WM BARRETT

To all people to whome this present writeing shall come to be seen or Read, Know ye that I Wm ffrench of Cambridge in the county of Middlesex in New England Taylor, ffor and in consideration of fifty pounds sterling to me the said William ffrench before the ensealing & delivery of these presents, well and truly payd by William Barret of the same place Taylor, the receite whereof I the said William ffrench do by these presents acknowledge, and therewith to be fully sattisfied and payd, and thereof of every part and parcell thereof do clearly and absolutely acquitte, exonerate, and discharge the said William Barrett, his Heyres, Executours, Administratours, and every of them for ever by these presents have granted, bargained, aliened, enfeoffed and confirmed, and by these presents do fully, cleerely, and absolutely grant, bargaine, and sell, Alien, enfeoffe, and confirme, unto the said William Barrett, his Heyres and Assignes for ever, my now Mansion house scittuated in Cambridge before named with about halfe a rood of land adjoyneing to the same and planted with fruite trees, and bounded with Water Street east, Daniel Kempster South, Abraham Morrill West, Steeven Day North, Also a Barne and out house standing on the east side the Highway with about Halfe a rood of land adjoyneing thereto, and bounded with the aforesaid street West, William Bordman north, and the Swamp east and South, with all the Towne rights and priviledges, for wood, timber, commonage or otherwise to the said house apperteyning or in any wise belonging, To Have & to Hould the said Messuage and Tenement, and other the premises, and every part and parcell thereof, with all & singular their appurtenances, unto the said William Barrett his Heyres and Assignes forever, to his and their only propper use and behooffe. And I the said William ffrench do covenant, promise, and grant for me,

---

[1] Paige's *History of Cambridge*

my Heires, Executors, Administrators, Assignes by these presents, that I the said William ffrench have good right, full power, and lawful Authority to grant bargaine, & sell the said Dwelling house, and barne and yards, and orchard thereto apperteyneing, with all other the appurtenances and priviledges thereof, And that the said William Barrett his Heyres & Assignes shall and may at all times, and from time to time for ever hereafter, peaceably and quietly, Have Hold, occupy, possesse & enjoy the said Bargained premises, and every part, and parcell thereof, with their and every of their appurtenances, without any lawfull lett, trouble, Eviction, Expulsion, suite, molestation, Disturbance, contradiction, or Deniall of me the said William ffrench, or of Elizabeth my Loveing wife, or either of us or by any other manner of wayes or meanes whatsoever haveing any lawful right or interest therein. In witness whereof I the said William ffrench, as also Elizabeth my wife, have here unto put our hands and seales, this tenth day of June. In the year of our Lord God One thousand six hundred fifty and six.

Signed, sealed, and Delivered	WILLIAM FFRENCH
in the presence off	and a seale
John Steedman	ELIZABETH FFRENCH
Thomas Danforth	her X marke
	& a seale annexed

This deed of sale was acknowledged by William ffrench and Elizabeth his wife, this Xth of 4th mo 1656.

[1] Entered and Recorded, January 3th, 1656.

By THOMAS DANFORTH Recorder

On the west side of Dunster street at the north corner of Mount Auburn street the first meeting house was built, and the following inscription may be seen today on the granite corner stone of the building now standing on the lot:

Site of the First Meeting House in Cambridge   Erected A. D. 1632.

This meeting house was a plain simple structure built probably of logs and had a thatched roof, the congregation presumably being called to worship by the beating of a drum.

Acknowledgment is hereby made to Mr. Perrin, treasurer of First Church, Cambridge, for the privilege of looking through the church records and copying such portions as were desired. Here was found the following entry:

---

[1] The first month of the calendar year at that time was March.

Site of Meeting House in Cambridge

Site of Home of Lt. William French, Cambridge, Massachusetts

William French and Elizabeth his wife, both members in full communion. Their children — Elizabeth now Eliot and now joyned at Dedham. Mary baptized in England between two and three years old at her father's joyning. John baptized by Mr Hooker in Cambridge. Sarah, Jacob, Hannah, born and baptized in this church.

This church, originally Congregational in doctrine, but since 1829 Unitarian, subscribed to the following covenant:

We whose names are underwritten do solemnly acknowledge Jesus Christ to be the Son of God and the Savior of the world, as he is represented in the New Testament, and as his disciples we do now express our earnest desire and intention to live a holy, religious and useful life, after the example and in the spirit of our Lord. We do also purpose to walk with the church while we have opportunity in a regular attendance on Christian ordinances in the promotion of Christian truth and charity, and in the exercise of those acts of Christian fellowship and affection, which the relation in which we stand seems to us to demand. It is usual for those who become members of the church to sign their names to this covenant or to signify their assent to it to the pastor, or in case of his absence, to the deacons. If any individual should decline from conscientious scruples to sign or assent to the covenant, the pastor has in such a case a discretionary power to dispense with the observance of this form.

Some of the authority vested in the church at that time may be gleaned from the following extracts taken also from the records of First Church:

In 1639, "John Stone and his wife were admonished to make biger bread and to take heede of offending by making too little bread hereafter." It seems that they were brought before the church to answer to the charge of cheating.

Alexander McKenzie of this church wrote "an epitaph upon the deplored death of that supereminent minister of the gospel," Mr. Jonathan Mitchell:

> Here lyes the darling of his time
> Mitchell expired in his prime
> Who four years shorte of forty seven
> Was found full ripe and plucked for heaven
> Was full of prudent zeal and love,
> Faith, Patience, Wisdom from above;
> New England's stay, next age's Glory.

> Angels may speak him; Ah! not I
> (Whose worth's above hyperbole)
> But for our loss, wert in my power
> I'd weep an everlasting shower.

Governor Belcher says of Thomas Dudley, who was deputy governor and later governor of Massachusetts in Winthrop's time:

> Here lies Thomas Dudley that trusty old stud.
> A bargain's a bargain and must be made good.

[1] Under date of April 4, 1636, a record is made of the men who were "purchasers and have proprieties in the fresh pond meadow and their quantitie of acers; with an agreemente made by jointe consente att those Lotts Drawinge." Among the names appears that of William French, who drew five acres.

Again, under date of September 21, 1639, "John Sill: Bought of William ffrench one house with garden and back side in the towne to ye creeke west Captaine Cooke, South Robart sst east Mrs. Glouer north." Under the same date, "Edmond Ffrost Bought of Thomas Bloggett one house garden Backside in Water Street William ffrench North east, Edmond Auger South, Nathaniel Sparrowhawk Northwest Water street southeast."

"William French Impr. in the towne one dwelling house with about half a rood of ground. Nathaniel Sparrowhawk west, Katharine Hadden South waterstreet east. William French six acr. & halfe more or lesse, William Man east Christopher Cane west Charlestowne lyne north, comon south."

August 15, 1646, "Andrew Stevenson bought of William Ffrench four acr. of land more or lesse in the new west field Gregory Stone Southeast, Roger Bancroft northeast, highway southwest and northwest."

December 10, 1646, "Itm. Bought of William ffrench in the lotts beyond Menotomy six acres & halfe."

In the year 1537 King Henry VIII granted a charter to the Honorable Artillery Company of London. A century later some members

---

[1] From *Proprietor's Records of the Town of Cambridge.* Printed by order of the city council, under the direction of the city clerk, Cambridge, 1896.

FANEUIL HALL.
Headquarters of the Ancient and Honorable Artillery Company of Massachusetts as it appeared in 1742 — Seal

FRENCH AND ALLIED FAMILIES

of that company who had settled in Boston, wishing to organize a military company similar to the one in England, presented a petition to Governor Winthrop asking for a charter. The request was at first denied, the council considering it "dangerous to erect a standing authority of military men," but finally a charter was granted March 13, 1638. This company was to be called "The military company of the Massachusetts." The company was organized on the first Monday in June, 1638, and elected Robert Keayne, who came in the Defence with William French in 1635, to be captain. Fifty-seven new members were recruited during that year, each one of whom was vouched for by two members, and we find William French as one of the fifty-seven, he being vouched for by Colonel George Cooke and Joseph Cooke. The name of the company was later changed, not by any action of its own, but by reason of its age and honor. Captain Keayne called it the "Artillery Company" and the "Great Artillery Company." Since organization it has been the custom to have sermons preached annually to its members, and from 1708 to 1738 the sermons were delivered before the "Honorable Artillery Company." The sermon of 1738 was preached before the "Ancient & Honorable Artillery Company" and from that year until the present time all sermons have been preached to them under this title.

The first headquarters of the company was in a building that stood on the site of the old state house, at the head of State street, Boston. This building was destroyed by fire in 1711, but a new building was at once erected which stood until 1747, when it was also destroyed by fire. However, the company had moved to Faneuil Hall in 1746, where they still have their headquarters.

The Boston *Herald* of October 15, 1910, contained the following

ANCIENTS OFF TO SEE KING

FOUR MEMBERS LEAVE TO NOTIFY GEORGE V OF HIS ELECTION

A number of members of the Ancient and Honorable Artillery company assembled at the South station at 1 P. M. yesterday, to witness the departure for London of Capt John D Nichols, Lieut. Francis H Appleton, officers of the company, and Col. Sidney M. Hedges, its former commander. . .

The committee goes to present to King George a certificate of honorary membership in the organization. They sail from New York today on the Armenia.

William French was made junior sergeant of the Ancient and Honorable Artillery Company in 1643, first sergeant in 1646, and ensign in 1650. The ranks of this historic organization are recruited from all parts of the United States in much the same manner today as at these earlier dates, their membership being limited to one thousand, the present list numbering five hundred fifty. At the time of his death (1681) William French was holding the office of captain in an artillery company in Billerica.

According to *Records of the Colony of Massachusetts Bay*, Volume II, page 186, General Courte of Election held March 26, 1647, John Winthrop was chosen governor. Under date of May 26th, in the records of the court is the following entry:

In answer to the request of ye towne of Cambridge the corte doth allow and confirm Willi. French lieft of that company and Edmond Winship ensign.

Volume III, page 109, May 26, 1647:

In answer to ye petition of ye towne of Cambridge for ye courts acceptation and confirmation of Wm French as ye lieft of ye military company there. Ye petition was granted and ye pson approved of and confirmed in ye place of both.

It appears from the records that William French was recommended by petition to the General Court for lieutenant October, 1645, but another man received the appointment.

It is interesting to note that November 15, 1637, was the date of the order establishing the college at Newetowne, just a few months before the order came changing the name from Newetowne to Cambridge, March 13, 1638 (or 1639). The college was to be called "Harvard," in honor of the Rev. John Harvard, who endowed the institution with half of his estate, variously estimated from eight hundred to sixteen hundred pounds, together with his entire library. Towns also contributed various sums to this college, record being made of Ports-

FRENCH AND ALLIED FAMILIES

mouth, New Hampshire, contributing sixty pounds annually for seven years; Dover, thirty-two pounds yearly, Exeter, ten pounds yearly. It is an historical fact that the first commencement exercises of Harvard College were held in the First Meeting House on Dunster street, Cambridge

About this time a printing house was established in Cambridge, and the first blank printed was the freeman's oath William French was made a freeman March 3, 1636; that is, he became possessed of civil rights; in fact, became a citizen

That property owners were amenable to certain laws with respect to their live stock is shown by the following excerpt:

FROM CAMBRIDGE RECORDS
(In list of fines)

Brother ffrench for 2 hogs at one time & one at another, and 2 at another without a keeper is fined 1£.

Cambridge is also distinguished as the place "where the first Protestant mission to the heathen began; the first sermon in a heathen tongue was preached there, and the first translation of the Bible by an Englishman into a heathen tongue was made at this place; and lastly, the first Protestant tract in a heathen language was printed there." The heathen referred to in this extract were the Indians, who were numerous in this locality at that time, and were receiving religious instruction from John Eliot

As the colony of Massachusetts grew, one town after another was taken away from the Cambridge territory, and Billerica is noted in 1655 as a colony by itself, the first appearance of the name being in 1653 This settlement was first known as Shawshine, which in the Indian vocabulary is said to mean smooth — glassy The pioneers however preferred the more familiar name of Billerica, in memory of the old town in Essex, England, from whence many of them are supposed to have come; for in 1650 reference was made by residents of Woburn to lands "on the east side of Billerica," and a petition from the inhabitants to the General Court in 1654, asking for a further grant of land, especially requested that the settlement might have the name "Billericay" In 1655 the inhabitants again petitioned the General Court, requesting "immunities and freedom from all publick rates and charges of Cambridge," and that the land might belong entirely to them for "ye better encouragement and carrying on publick charges that will necessarily fall out." An agreement was accordingly made between the town of Cambridge and the progressive inhabitants of this young settlement, and on the 29th of May, 1655, the court confirmed the arrangement and granted the petitioners' request. The names of those who signed the proposition on the part of the new town were: "Ralph Hill Sen'r, John Sterns, Willm pattin, George ffarley, Ralph Hill Jun', John Croe, James Parker, John Parker, Jonathan Danforth, Henry Jeifts, Willm Chamberlin, and Robert Parker," who were the "present Inhabitants." These men and women who laid the foundations of Billerica were a community that sought and held to such elements as could be well molded together — a sturdy, loyal, honest, God fearing people.

Imagine if you will, one of those beautiful Indian summer days when the foliage on the trees has not lost its brilliant autumnal coloring; a gently rolling country traversed by streams, the landscape divided into small fields, each surrounded by stone fences or rather walls as they are called, their somber gray color a fitting background for the green of the pines and the brilliant hues of the foliage; well constructed roads winding along under the shade of apple trees bearing their burden of luscious fruit; comfortable, spacious, and beautiful homes on either side of the one main street with the town hall and church standing near the center, and you have a glimpse of the Billerica of October, 1910, the place to which William French removed after leaving Cambridge in 1653, to make a home for his dear ones. At that time roads were only paths in the woods, no fences were built, and only about twenty-five families were living in the town. The families had increased to forty by the year 1660, a number of these having come from Cambridge.

In matters pertaining to education, little is noted after the first settlement of the country as receiving the immediate attention of the French family. In 1642 the selectmen were enjoined to "have a vigilant eye over their brethren and neighbors to see first that none of them

TABLET ON BILLERICA COMMON
Where first Meeting House stood, erected 1663

shall suffer so much barbarism in any of their families as not to endeavor to teach by themselves or others, their children and apprentices so much learning as may enable them perfectly to read the English tongue." The penalty was twenty shillings for each neglect. The same act required parents to "give religious instruction to their children and apprentices and bring them up in some honest lawful calling, labor or employment, either in husbandry or some other trade profitable for themselves and the commonwealth, if they will not or cannot train them up in learning to fit them for higher employment." Billerica could not at once meet this requirement, but "1 March 5, 61, The Townsmen doe agree yt Lieftenant Will French and Ralph Hill senior doe take care and examine the several families in or Towne whether there children and servants are Taught in the precepts of Religione in reding and Lerninge there Catechism."

In 1658 the Rev. Samuel Whiting was chosen minister and he remained with his people for fifty-six years. During the first few months of his ministry it is supposed that the preaching services were held in private homes, but in 1659 the inhabitants agreed "that there shall be a meeting house built; this winter follinge; thirty foote longe: and twenty and four foot wide. and twelve foot high and the studs to be twelve foot asunder; the sids and eands shall be covered with bords: and the Roof with thatch."

The meeting house was erected according to these plans in the winter of 1660, and a suitable allotment of land for the benefit of the church was reserved. It was built under the direction of John Parker, one of the most honored of citizens, and among the items of expense we find where fifteen shillings were paid "to henry Jefts for briks 300 for ye ministers chimley." The building of a house for the minister and the raising of his salary, brought a heavy common expense on the community, and under date of July 15, 1659, is found where "Lieut. Wm. French was chosen comitioner for making the cuntry rate and caring in a duplicate to ye shire meeting and George Farley and Jonathan Danforth is joyned with him for this work."

The church was regularly organized April 27, 1663, "when ye

counsel of elders and messengers from other churches" were present, but not until November 11th of the same year was the ceremony of ordination performed, and the young Harvard graduate solemnly installed after the simple but impressive manner of the Puritan faith.

The Reverend Mr. Whiting had a large parish, for it extended from Concord and Acton to the Merrimack and Andover. His people heard two sermons each Sabbath, and they were not short ones either. The modern sermon would have been as much of a surprise to these people as the railroad, telegraph, or daily newspaper. It was at church that the people received not only spiritual food, but much of the intellectual and social stimulus needed was here given. The young pastor satisfied this demand with honor and credit to himself. He baptized the children and buried the dead; but probably did not often perform the marriage ceremony, for the early fathers thought it smacked too much of popery for the minister to marry them, so they went to the magistrate instead, for the performance of the marriage vow. People came for miles to hear the gospel preached, and in consequence some suitable arrangement was necessary for the care of their horses. The following extract from Hazen's *History of Billerica* will show how shelter was provided:

> The towne doe give leave that Ralph Hill Sen'r, George Farley, Will Ffrench, Ralph Hill Jun'r and John Parker, and such other persons as make use of their horses to Ride to ye meeting: shall have liberty to make sum housing or housings to sett up for horses from time to time without molestatione; and to sette up ye saide houseing below the Hill between the meeting house and Goldinge More's barn, or in some other place convenient for them.

In 1661 the problem of seating the people in the church was settled, and it was agreed that "ye towne doe apoynte Lieut. Wm French, John Parker, Ralph Hill Sen'r and Will Tay to sett in the Deacon's seat; and also the towne do appoint & impower these four men joyned with Mr. Whitinge to appoint the rest of the inhabitants and proprietors belonging to the town there several places where they shall sitt in the meeting house according to their best discretion." The method far into the next century was to seat according to age and the amount of rates paid, giving to age the preference. Deacons were seated in front of the pulpit and their wives with the widows. The list of those who were to have "pues" was governed by the amount of real and personal tax they were to pay. Among the twenty-two tax payers thus entitled to a sitting, we find the name of William French. Rank, wealth, and social standing too were factors determining where people should sit, and there was ample room for jealousy on this subject.

The question of providing financially for the pastor was arranged in the following manner

> At a town meeting 16 da 6 mo 1658 We do agree to give to Mr. Samuel Whiting Jun'r (our minister) that house which is now upon ye township comfortably finished for him and his heirs if he continues amongst us durng his life But if he shall remove from amongst us, then the said house with all the accommodations of the same shall return again to the towne to be at their dispose, or if Mr Whiting shall dye with us, then the towne shall have the refuseing of the said house and all other accommodations aforesaid belonging to the same if Mrs Whitinge do sell ye same
>
> 2 We promise to give to him ye sume of fourty pounds per year for his maintenance for the first two years of his settling with us, and for the third year fifty pounds, and for the fourth year sixty pounds, and for afterwards we do promise to ingage to better his maintenance as the Lord shall better our estates
>
> 3 We do Joyntly p'mise to cary at or owne charge from year to year so much of the pay (as doth amounte to twenty pounds) as shall be brought in to him in wheat or other graine or porke, to deliver the same either at Mistick Mill or at Charlestowne, which Mr Whiting shall apointe and to deliver the same at such prizes as such pay shall or doth at such times pass fro man to man unless Mr Whiting and the Towne shall make any other agreement concerning the same
>
> 4 We do promise to p'vide his firewood & to bring it home to his house from year to year at our own charges
>
> 5 We do promise to fence him in a paster for to keape his horse in as convenient as we may
>
> Ult. for his acomodations, we do promise to laey to ye said house a ten acre lot, for his house lot and twelve acres of meadow, with other accomodations convenient to the same, i e to grant to him all other divitions of lands and meadows with other lots of ye like quantity

The persons subscribing to the premises, who were then the inhabitants, were:

Ralph Hill Sen'r	John Parker
Willm French	James Parker
John Rogers Sen'r	Willm Tay
George Farley	Willm Chamberlin
Wm Pattin	John Trull
Sam'l Chamm	James Patterson
John Sternes	John Marshall
Jonath. Danforth	John Shildon
Ralph Hill Jun'r	Henery Jeiffs
	John Baldwin

It speaks well for the courage and faith of nineteen men that they were ready to assume the responsibility of such action, by signing this document, and also for the minister that he was willing to make his home in this little wilderness.

In 1679-80 the roof of the meeting house was shingled and a gallery put in, and this building continued to be used for church services until 1692 when it was replaced by a new structure. The old church was sold to the contractor for forty pounds to be used as a town hall and school house after it had served the community as a place of worship for fifty years.

The first record of tithing men appears October 8, 1677, when the town was divided into five parts, the groups being in neighborhoods. George ffarley, tithing man, had seven families in his care, one of whom was Lt. Wm ffrench.

From the original book containing the first records of the church, which book is still preserved in the vault of the Town Hall at Billerica,[1] was gleaned the following:

A Church book belonging to chh of Christ in Billerica given to said chh by ye persons hereafter named who gave the sums affixed to each of their names to pay for it.

Deac'n Joshua Abbott	£ 0 " 5 " 0
Deac'n Wm Stickney	0 " 5 " 0
Deac'n Sam'l Whiting	0 " 5 " 0
Capt'n Thos Kidder	0 " 5 " 0
Lieut Jacob Danforth	0 " 5 " 0
Lieut Daniel Stickney	0 " 4 " 0

[1] From records kept in Town Hall, Billerica, copied by the author October 14, 1910.

Wm French	0 " 4 " 0
Christ'er Osgood	0 " 5 " 0
Benj Lewis	0 " 3 " 0
John Tarboll	0 " 1 " 0
	2 "10 " 0
Lawful money	
175	0 " 6 " 0

The following record of births, marriages, and deaths is given in the book referred to as having taken place in William French's family while residents of Billerica The record is incomplete as it gives to the daughter Sarah the dates belonging to Abigail whose name is not mentioned

Elizabeth wife of william ffrench dyed	31 – 01 – 68
lieut Wm ffrench and Mary sterns widdow joyned in marriage betor Captain Gookin	06 – 03 – 69
Mary Daughter of Lt Wm & Mary ffrench borne	03 – 02 – 70
Sarah Daughter of Lt Wm & Mary ffrench borne	14 – 02 – 73
and departed this life	13 – 02 – 74
Hannah Daught'r of Lt Wm & Mary ffrench was borne	25 – 11 – 76
lieut Wm ffrench dyed (being in his year 78)	20 – 09 – 81

In 1667 an act was passed to prevent "the profaneness" of turning the back upon the public worship before it is finished and the blessing pronounced Towns were directed to erect a "cage" near the meeting house and in this, all offenders against the sanctity of the Sabbath were confined

That William French must have been one whose judgment was respected, and whose authority was recognized in church affairs, is evidenced by the fact of his appointment to discipline people He was also given authority under date of October 18, 1659, to marry persons in the "towns of Billiriky and Chelmsford", was appointed to sit in the deacon's seat in 1661, and in 1662-63, record is made of his having contributed to the support of the minister to the amount of one pound ten shillings, the salary for the year amounting to seventy-one pounds one shilling eight pence

Dec 23, 1662, The Towne did agree ye Lieut Wm French and George ffarley as a committee in the Towns behalf, shall treat with Ralph Hill sen'r about a piece of land half an acre for a buring place.

The result was that about a year later Ralph Hill Sr. gave to the town about half an acre of land for the burying place, on condition that "the town shall fence all against it next unto his own land from which this half acre shall be taken."

This was the origin of the Old South burying ground, and it is a matter of record that Ralph Hill died within a week after giving this land for a "burying place," his own body doubtless the first to be laid in this cemetery, since which it has been enlarged at two different times. The oldest stone (1686) to be found bears the name of John Rogers, but more than thirty who bore the name of French rest here, and this is undoubtedly the last resting place of Lieutenant William French and his wife Elizabeth, although there are no stones to mark their graves, nor the grave of Ralph Hill.

The women of that day must have been after Paul's own heart, for no record is made of any part taken by them in church affairs, which is probably accounted for, by the fact that Shepherd in his *Autobiography* says: "A man may speak and prophecy but not women; a company of men may make a church, and so receive in and cast out of the church, but not women, though professing saints."

Not alone in respect to affairs of church did William French devote his time and energy, but in matters pertaining to the welfare of the general public did he show his interest, for record is made of his being chosen deputy "for this town for the next general court and no longer," December 17, 1660, and two days later he was in his seat at Boston, the first deputy from Billerica to the General Court. He was also the first representative from Billerica in 1663-64.

The first record made of the appointment of selectmen or "Townsmen" as they were frequently called, was in 1660 when John Parker, Lieutenant Wm. French, Ralph Hill Sr., Thomas Foster, and Jonathan Danforth were chosen selectmen for "ye yere inseiunge," and on January 28, 1661, Lieutenant Wm. French was chosen by the freemen of the town to carry the votes for nomination of magistrates and county treasurer.

House now standing on Farm owned by Lieutenant William French at Billerica

Old South Burying Ground
Billerica, Massachusetts

FRENCH AND ALLIED FAMILIES

A careful survey of the ancient records of land grants in Billerica, shows that the present villages of Bedford, Carlisle, Tewksbury and North Tewksbury, Dunstable, Merrimac, and Litchfield are all located on land which belonged originally to this town. Large grants of land were made to the governors of the colony and to the church, so that only about two-fifths of the whole town was free and common land open to the occupancy of settlers. The land for settlement was divided into what they called "ten acre lots" as shares. Each "ten acre lot" consisted of one hundred thirteen acres of upland and twelve acres of meadow, and carried with it the right to all "town privileges" after additions and divisions of town and meadow. It is interesting to note that Lieutenant William French held two of these shares, amounting to two hundred fifty acres. Another instance is recorded where he drew at the first division seventeen shares, at the second, sixteen, and at the third, twenty-two shares.

Under date of August, 1661, Lieutenant William French signed an agreement that Jonathan Danforth should have one thousand acres of land; and again record is made of ten acre rights to the heirs of Lieut. Wm. French, when they received ninety-three acres as the result of such division. Still another record is found where they received forty-five acres from the fourth range west of the first and second ranges.

The farm where William French had his home was what was known in that locality as part of the Dudley farm east of the farm of Ralph Hill Sr., toward Indian Hill, as the hill north of Nutting's pond was called.

In December, 1660, "At a meeting at Luifteut French's the major part of ye Townsmen did agrei yt Will Browne should wait sum time for the disposing of his acomidations yt was granted him by the Towne in reference to the getting of his charges yt he had himself, or by such other person as the Towne shall approve on, by his procuring or otherwise procured by the Towne; it was also yielded to the saide Will Browne that it sholde be propounded to the towne and move to another vote whither Simon Crosby shall injoy the Bargaine solde to him by the saide Will Browne, whether the saide Simon shall injoy the same notwithstanding the vote yt is paste by the towne already, or whether he shall not injoy it." The result was in favor of Simon Crosby for in the future he appears as a citizen.

A glimpse of the pioneer side of life is shown under date of July 9, 1661, when "It is ordered that what person soever shall kill a wolfe or wolves shall have for every wolfe killed and brought to the constable accordinge to law, he shall have for every wolfe Twenty Shillings, which shall be payd by the constable then being in the towns behalf — provided that either English or Indian shall make proof to the constable or selectmen that it was killed within the boundes of our Towne."

At a county court held at Charlestown December 21, 1680:

> This court being informed that Lt Wm French of Billerica is by Gods hand thorow impotency & weakness unfitt to governe his Domestick concrnes. At the request of his friends Deacon Thompson & his sonne Jacob ffrench, are impowred to assist his wife, in the ordering & disposeing of his estate, so as may best conduce for the supply of his family.

ffreeman Sworne.

Mr Thomas Sheppard	Tho. Prentice sen'r
Thomas Prentice Jr	Jno ffuller sen'r
Jonathan ffuller	Joshua ffuller
Jacob Hurd	Ebenezer Wiswall
Samuel Ballard	Jno Prentice
Jno. Chadwick	Hen Greene
Mr Thos. Cheavers	Pelatiah Smith

That the close of a life so full of activities and good deeds for his country and fellow men should be saddened by the clouding of his mental faculties during these later years, seems full of pathos. Only eleven months elapsed between the decree of the court providing proper guardianship, and the death of Lieutenant William French, which occurred November 20, 1681. The following is an exact copy of his will still on file in the probate court at East Cambridge, Massachusetts:

The last Will and Testam^t of
Wm ffrench of Billerica
aged about seaventy & six years

FRENCH AND ALLIED FAMILIES

I William ffrench being weak in body yet of a disposing mind do make my last Will and Testament as followeth

And in the first place I do committ my soul into the hands of God my Creator and gracious redeemer, and my body to ye Earth to a decent buriall in the hope of a glorious resurrection to eternall life

And in reference to ye good things of this life yt the Lord hath graciously lent me, I do thus dispose of them, and in the first place I do will that all my just debts be discharged with the charge of the funerall as speedily as conveniently may be, and whereas I have already given to all my children that have been already married their portions I only add to them as followeth To the Eldest son of John French, to Wm the son of Jacob French, to Elizabeth ye daughter of Richard Ellis, to Jonathan ye son of Jonathan Hides, to ye eldest daughter of Jonathan Peake, to Marah ye daughter of Jno Brackett, which are all my grandchildren, to each p^{r}son afors^d twenty shillings, to be pd to each of them as followith, to those two yt are already married, within one year after my decease and to ye othr within one month after yr marriage And for ye remainder of my whole estate that I shall dy seized with I do give unto my beloved wife and to those children born to me by her, to be divided to each at the discretion of or hond County Court after my deceas ffinally I do nominate and and empowr my beloveed wife & my son Jacob ffrench to be my executors of this my Will, as witnesseth my hand and seale hereunto this fift day of June in the year of o^r Lord God one thousand six hundred seaventy and nine, & in ye thirty first year of o^r Souveraign Lord King Charles ye second

WM FFRENCH and seale

Signed & Sealed
  in p r sence of
    Sam ll Whiting Junr
    Jonath Danforth, Sen
20-10-81 Jonathan Danforth sen^r m^d oath in Court to the abovs^d will.

J R. C

Allowed

  20 10 81
    To ye dratching of ye children 006–13–04
    To ye widdow ⅓ ye remaind^r
    To ye widdow ye remaind^r ⅔ equally
To be set out by Lt Jonath Danforth, Joseph Thompson & Josiah Converse to each his p^t & ye widdow to have ye benefitt of ye childrens portions for ye bringing up & education until they come of age to choose ye Guardians

T D R

An Inventory of the Estate of Lt. Wm. ffrench of Billerica who deced 20. Nov^b, 1681, being his 78 year of his age.

Imp r. In the parlor, one feath r wth its furniture	005–00–00
Warming pans 3s. Smoothing Iron: 12d. old chairs & cushions 5s. old Chest, box trench^{ry} 7s. 4d.	000–16–04
Trammels, Tongs, ffireshovel, slice fire fork 11s. 9d. Looking glass 2s. In pewter 1l. 6s.	001–17–09
In the Parlour Chamb Two flock beds with their furnitures. His wearing apparel 01l. 16s.. Table cloth napkins 11s. pillow beers 6s. chest box 7s.	003–00–00
In yarne 1l. 4s. wool 9s. 2 hat brushes 18d. Scales & weights 12d. sconces 12d.	001–16–06
In the Sellers in Syder & wooden wares 3l. 14s. many old tubs 4s.	003–18–0
In the Leantoe Chambs old Cobirons, 3s. frying pan, 3s. old Iron 5s. hay spades 18d. Gridirons 3s.	000–15–6
In brass 2l. 10s. Iron potts 12s. 2 spits 3s. old Muskett & Gun barrell 12s. brass mortar 3s.	004-00–00
Ax & wedges 7s. 6d. 2 chains 10s. horse harnes 10s. Hoops & boxes 10s.	001–17–6
In corne 9l. 8s. Cartshod wheels span shackle pan, rope plow, old shares yoke	014–18–0
fflax seed, 5s. grindstone 5s. Scythes 6s. how 2s. harrow-tines 2s. 6d. Sickles 18d.	001–2 –0
old adds. 12d. Skillet frame 12d. Hows 2s. Hooks 16s. hay hooks & hay spades 2s. old augres 12d.	

FRENCH AND ALLIED FAMILIES

short saw 3s.	00–11–0
Saddle, bridle 10s. hamer 12d. measures 12d gooses, Pinsers marrow holl. 2s. 6d	000–14–6
6 swines 6l. one mare 2l. neat cattle wth provision lay^d in for them 25l.	33–00–0
In John Sterns Homstead remaining due	20–10–0
House & barne homstead Meadows & outlands	104–00–0
	200–15–1

More the Estate is credito^r

By Nathaniel Taye	000–12–0
By Deacon Josiah Convarse	017–00–0
By Samuel Sternes	008–05–9
By Isaack Sternes	005–00–0
	231–12–10

The Estate is Debto^r

To ye Revd Sam l Whiting 4l 19s To Zach. Shed 13s.	005–12–00
To Nath. Tay mony 5s 6d To Joseph Walker 9s. 9d mony	000–15–03
To Tho ffoster sen 12s 8d. To Simon Crosby mony 3s 6d	000–16–02
To John Rogers sen 4s 6d To Priscilla Rogers mony 3s	000–07–06
To Mr Davise of Charlestown 8s 6d. to Widd Cutlar 13s	001–01–06
To Nath Hancock To Golden More	
To the constable for ye last years Rates	
To Nath. Hill money 22s To Tho Pattin 5s	001–07–00
To Jacob ffrench upon book 1l 5s 9½d to him on bond 15s 8d.	002–01–05½
To Sam ll Sterns for wages 6l more he demands 3l.	009–00–00

To lt. Randall Nicolls 30 sh. To Capt. Hamonds lady 10s.	002–00–00
To old Mr Parker his estate of Boston 8s. to ffr More of Camb. 6s.	000–14–00
To John Lewistone 5s. To Tho. Dutton jun r 4s. 3d.	000–09–03
To Sam ll Sterns 3l. 10. To Tho. Sterns 14s. 6d. both on ye acct of their father John Sterns deced	004–04–06

   Billerica 6. 10. 81. apprised by vs.
     JONATHAN DANFORTH SEN R
     PATRICK HILL

8. 10. 81. Mary ffrench executrix
to ye estate of Lt French her
deced Husband appeared in
Court & m^d oath to ye abovs^d
Inventory.

    J. R. C.

A division of the estate was made "according to the order of ye Hon'd County Court at Cambridge Dec 20, 1681 by Jonathan Danforth Sen'r, Joseph Thompson, Josiah Converse," which record was filed January 6, 1687. "The inventory of sd estate given in said court did amount to with debts 0231£, 12s., 10d."

"The debts due from said estate entered in ye inventory with ye legacy given by said will and the charge of ye division and of courts for confirmation did arise to   53l.–08s.–00d.
The estate to be divided was   182l.–04s.–01d.
the order of ye court being that ye estate shall be divided to ye widdow one third part of ye whole estate, and to ye three children ye remainder two thirds equally.

The division of ye estate according to ye first inventory given into court was as followeth.

To the widdow one third part which was	60l.–14s.–6d.
To Mary ffrench now Mary Sharp	40l.–10s.–00d.
To Sarah ffrench	40l.–10s.–00d.
To Hannah ffrench	40l.–10s.–00d.
	182l.–04s.–10d.

A DIVISION OF THE ESTATE OF LT. WM. FRENCH
Fac-simile of Original Document

The division of ye estate is as followeth

To Mary ye eldest daughter, of the homestead twenty acres of upland, lowland and swampland, with four acres of meadow land partly lying within it and joyning to it with half ye dwelling house and half ye barne, (the east end of both) it is bounded Northward by Wm Chamberlin Sen'r fence & by ye division of Sarah ffrench eastward by Henery Tuffs southward by ye highway and Hannah ffrench westward ye north line & about one hundred & five pole long, and forty seven pole wide at east end. (There is contained within it 3 or 4 (4) acres of meadow land, that pertains to Wm Chamberlaine Sen'r according to ye bounds of it formerly set out to him) this containes about one half of ye orchard, and half liberty of passage upon all needful occations this part of ye other division to his meadow and of use of ye highway that lyeth between this and ye west division, and is to allow like liberty upon this land on ye north side of it for Sarah ffrench her heires or assignes to go (cart ox or horses) to the east division of this lot, all of which upland and meadow, orchard and housing, was accounted at 30 and 4 pounds

	34l –00–00
She has received more of the estate in moveables	6l –10s.–00
To Sarah ffrench ye 2d daughter 40 acres in ye old common field at	06l –00–00
To 4 acres in mill swamp according to ye records of it at	12l –00–00
To 3 acres division in mill swamp granted to ye estate in 1685	04l –00–00
To one acre in prospect meadow according to ye record of it at	01l –00–00
To 14 acres of ye homestead at ye east end with liberty to pass upon Mary's land to it, at	14l –00–00
To so much due from Daniel Champney Cambridge	03l –10–00
	40l –10–00

To Hannah ffrench ye west end of ye homestead, bounded by pond meadow west, by Henery Jeifts on ye south, by Wm Chamberlaine north, with halfe ye orchard, ye orchard is bounded on ye east end by meadow according to an old maple tree marked in ye line of division of ye farm lots and so runs northward in a direct line to ye S. W. corner post of Wm Chamberlaine's meadow. The N of orchard runs according to a heap of stones laid in ye highway (being about 28 pole wide at sd Highway) and so run eastward to ye meadow thro ye orchard by a dwelling house and half ye barn, ye west end of both; and as for land about ye house it runs southward from ye midle of ye house to ye dividing line of ye orchard and 16 foot northward of the centre of sd house to ye highway & for ye barne half ye yard before it as now it stands to divide against ye midle of ye barn and 16 foot northward of ye centre of ye barn and so to ye highway on each side of ye barn, apprised at

	22l. 00s.–00d.
also five acres of pond meadow by it at	15l. 00s.–00d.
and in part of Daniel Champneys debt	03l. 10s.–00d.
	40l. 10s.–00d.

Billerica   6   10 m   1687
Apprised and divided by us
The widdows part was set out in goods & chattels & debts & twenty pounds that was due and set out to her from ye estate of her first husband John Stearns deceased of witness that we consent to this division. We have set to our hands and seals.

    her
MARY X DUNKLIN
    mark

    her   her
HANNAH X child   SARAH X CROSBY
    mark   mark

The only literary production extant from the pen of William French is the following tract, written by him to a friend in England, and may be found in Volumes III, IV, *Third Series of the Collections of the Massachusetts Historical Society.*

STRENGTH OUT OF WEAKNESS

The best news I can write you from New England is, the Lord is indeed converting the Indians, and for the refreshing of your heart, and the hearts of all the godly with you; I have sent you the Relation of one Indian of two yeares profession, that I took from his owne mouth by an Interpreter, because he cannot speak or understand one word of English.

The first Question was:

Q   How did you come first to any sight of sinne
A   His answer was, Before the Lord did ever bring any English to us, my Conscience was exceedingly troubled for sin, but after Mr Mayhew came to preach, and had been here some time, one chiefe Sagamon did embrace the gospel, and I hearing of him, I went to him, and prayed to

him to speak something to me concerning God, and the more I did see of God, the more I did see my sinne, and I went away rejoycing, that I knew anything of God, and also that I saw my sinne

Q I pray what hurt doe you see in sinne?
A Sin, sayeth he, is a continuall sicknesse in my heart
Q What further evill doe you see in sinne?
A I see it to be a breach of all Gods commandments.
Q Doe you see any punishment due to man for sinne?
A Yea sayth he, I see a righteous punishment from God due to man for sinne which shall be by the Devills in a place like unto fire, not that I speak of materiall fire (saith he) where man shall be for ever dying and never dye
Q Have you any hope to escape this punishment?
A While I went on in the way of Indianisme I had no hope, but did verily believe I should goe to that place, but now I have a little hope, and hope I shall have more.
Q By what means doe you look for any hope?
A Sayth he by the satisfaction of Christ. I prayed the Interpreter to tell him from mee that I would have him thinke much of the satisfaction of Christ, (and so he told him) I prayed him to returne mee his Answer.
A I thanke him kindly for his good counsell, it doth my heart good, sayd he, to heare any man speake of Christ
Q What would you think if the Lord should save you from misery?
A If the Lord, said he, would save me from all the sinne that is in my heart, and from that misery, I should exceedingly love God, and saith he, I should love a man that should doe me any good, much more the Lord, if he should doe this for me
Q Doe you think that God will doe you any good for any good that is in you?
A Though I believe that God loves man that leaves his sinne, yet I believe it is for Christ's sake
Q Doe you see that at any time God doth answer your prayers?
A Yea sayeth he, I take everything as an Answer of prayer
Q But what special answer have you notice of?
A Once my wife being three days and three nights in labour, I was resolved never to leave praying till she had deliverance, and at last God did it, and gave her a sonne, and I called his name Returning, because all the while I went on in Indianisme, I was going from God but now the Lord hath brought mee to him back againe

By this time the Captaine Gookinge came to us, and he asked him this question —

Q What he would think if he should finde more affliction and trouble in Gods wayes than he did in the ways of Indianisme.
A His answer was, when the Lord did first turne me to himselfe and his wayes, he stripped me as bare as my skinne, and if the Lord should strip mee as bare as my skin again, and so big Saggamore should come to mee, and say, I will give you so big Wampom, so big Beaver, and leave this way, and turne to us againe: I would say, take your riches to yourself, I would never forsake God and his wayes again.

This is a relation taken by myself.

WILLIAM FRENCH.

Fifth Generation

SAMUEL[5] FRENCH (William,[4] Thomas,[3] Thomas,[2] Thomas,[1]) the tenth child of William and Elizabeth French, was born in Cambridge, Massachusetts, about the year 1648; removed with his parents to Billerica in 1653, and later went to Dunstable. He married Sarah, daughter of John Cummings Sr., December 24, 1682. She was born January 27, 1661. To them were born eight children:

I. Sarah, born in Dunstable February 7, 1684.
II. Samuel, born in Dunstable September 10, 1685; died November, 1757.
III. Joseph, born in Dunstable March 10, 1687; died September, 1735.
IV. John, fourth child of Samuel and Sarah Cummings French, was born in Dunstable May 6, 1691. The name of his wife and date of his marriage is not known. To them were born:
   1. John, born March 1, 1719.
   2. William, born October 18, 1721.
   3. Hannah, born April 29, 1724.
   4. Eleazer, born October 12, 1726.
   5. Elizabeth, born April 29, 1729.
   6. Ebenezer, born May 31, 1731; married Sarah Proctor of Acton; married (second) Susannah Hamblet of Nottingham, N. H. To them were born:
      a. Charlotte, born August 13, 1774; married Isaac Woods.

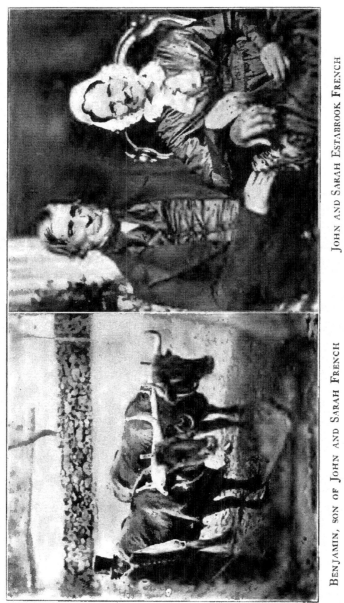

Benjamin, son of John and Sarah French   John and Sarah Estabrook French

b   John, born March 17, 1778; married Sarah Estabrook. To them were born:
   aa. Susan, born ———; married Moses Crockett She died November 12, 1846
      bb   Jefferson, born ———; married Elizabeth Spaulding. To them were born:
      Sarah Elizabeth, born ———, married John Russell
      Charles Jefferson, born ———, married Rosella Pike To them were born two children
      John William, born ———; married Mary Jane Venner To them was born one son
      Edward Beecher, born ———; married Emily Underwood; married (second) Mrs Luthera Jackman
      Henry S , born ———; married Annie Thompson To them was born one son
      George M , born ———; married Eliza Pierce. To them was born one daughter.
      Francis Lyman, born ———; died in infancy
      Lewis Morton, born ———; married Mrs Susan Hosmer
c. Sarah, born ———; married David Barnard To them were born·
   aa   Sarah F., born ———, married A. Hamilton Leppere To them were born three children
   bb   Louisa M.
   Sarah Barnard died January 21, 1866
d   Rhoda, born ———; married Jefferson Caldwell To them were born·
   aa. Harriett N.
   bb   Myra A
   Rhoda Caldwell died December 2, 1837
e. Ebenezer, born ———; married Sarah R French To them were born:

aa. Sarah R., born ——; married Samuel Hall.
bb. Susan C., born ——; married Wallace Peabody.
cc. Mary E., born ——. Mary sailed in 1874 for India as a missionary. Her health failed and she returned after two years.

Ebenezer died March 3, 1857.

f. John H., born ——; died April 3, 1831.
g. Mary D., born ——; died February 13, 1817.
h. Mary D. (second), born ——; married Joseph Barnard. To them were born:
   aa. Joseph Morton, married Nettie Bisemore. Joseph died in 1879.
   bb. Charles Frank, lost at sea.
   cc. Chandler, died in infancy.
   dd. Henry.
   ee. Eudora, died in 1856.
   ff. Howell.
   gg. Adelgitha, died in 1858.
   hh. Naamah.
i. Benjamin, born ——; married Sarah E. Holmes. To them was born:
   aa. William L., married Addie Cummings. To them were born three sons and one daughter.
j. William, born ——; married —— Eliza Wright. To them were born:
   aa. Anna E., married —— Anderson. To them was born one son, Kenneth French.
   bb. Ellen W., married Andrew Bates. To them were born two sons. Author of poem, "Eleazer French's Arm," which appears at close of this generation.
   cc. Mary G., married W. Luzerne Lovejoy. To them was born one son.

####### FRENCH AND ALLIED FAMILIES

    k   James M , born ——; married Jane A Fowler. To them were born.
        aa   Walter H. M.
        bb.   Estella J
        cc   Cordelia J.
    l   Samuel A , born ——, married Mary E Parks To them was born:
        aa   Sadie, born ——
7   Sarah, born October 6, 1733.
John, fourth child of Samuel and Sarah Cummings French, bought land of his father in 1714; of Henry Farwell in 1721, and a part of the Brattle farm in 1732 Date of his death is not of record

  V   Ebenezer, born in Dunstable April 7, 1693; date of marriage not known; was the father of one son, Ebenezer, born October 27, 1723 Ebenezer (senior) was killed by the Indians September 5, 1724, at Naticook Brook, New Hampshire.
  VI   Richard, born in Dunstable April 8, 1695
  VII.   Alice, born in Dunstable November 20, 1699; married subsequent to 1719 Nathaniel Woods (born in Groton October 19, 1694), son of Nathaniel Woods He was a sergeant in Lovewell's third expedition and on the day of battle was in command of the fort Their home was in Groton
  VIII   Jonathan, born in Dunstable February 1, 1703 or 1704; married Jane, surname not known, and died November 17, 1757. In his will there is no mention of children. He left his property to Oliver Woods, a son of his sister Alice

Dunstable was granted by Massachusetts and was a part of that province until 1741, when a revision of the province line transferred the greater part of the original grant to the jurisdiction of New Hampshire Just what time Dunstable was settled is not known Grants of land were made in 1659 and farms are of record there before the year 1673, the township originally embracing more than two hundred square miles In 1673 a grant of one thousand acres was made to the Ancient and Honorable Artillery Company of Boston, and upon this land today stands the most densely populated part of Nashua, New Hampshire. This was known as Artillery Farm.

Dunstable received its name as a compliment to Mrs. Mary Tyng, who came from Dunstable, England, the name coming from "Dun" a hilly place and "staple" a mart or place of public traffic.

It is not known in what year Samuel French came to this community, but among the first settlers are found the names of Rev. Thomas Weld, Joseph Wheeler, John Blanchard, Jonathan Tyng, Cornelius Waldo, Samuel Warner, Obadiah Perry, Samuel French, Robert Parris, Thomas Cummings, Isaac Cummings, Joseph Hassell, Christopher Temple, John Goold, Samuel Gould, John Lollendine, Christopher Reed, Thomas Lund, Daniel Waldo, William Beale, Samuel Beale, John Cummings, Robert Usher, Henry Farwell, Robert Proctor, Joseph Lovewell, and John Lovewell, Jr.

The search for the history of Samuel French has been somewhat puzzling. Even the date of his birth is uncertain, but it was probably in 1648 as has been stated, when his mother was about forty-five years of age. He married Sarah Cummings December 24, 1682, being at that time about thirty-four years old. Men as a rule in those days married young, and it is supposed that an earlier marriage must have taken place, for the will of his father made in 1679 states: "And whereas I have already given to all my children that have been already married their portion, I only add as follows:" and the document makes no mention of son Samuel. The theory is that Samuel married in his younger days and may never have had children, or they may have died.

Dr. S. H. French of Amsterdam, New York, who has rendered invaluable service in the compilation of this history, writes in regard to this matter:

> For many years I have thought that Sarah Cummings was a second wife, and that Samuel French had been married before. I once wrote to Dr. John M. French of Milford suggesting this, and in his reply he said it was a new idea to him, but he rejected it for the reason that there was no record of the marriage and death of such a person. Now I am willing to admit without

Gun, Bullet Molds, and Camp Kettle used by Ebenezer French

House built by John French, 1720
Bullet Molds used in Revolution

question all the records, but am not willing to believe that no births, deaths, or marriages failed of being recorded through neglect or accident Take the case of the second Sampson His father told him he was born in Dunstable and gave him the date I believe the first Sampson *knew when and where* his son was born, and that he told the truth, and yet there is no record of such a birth in Dunstable.

Fox gives Samuel French as one of the early settlers of Dunstable, but his name is not on the petition to have the town incorporated in 1674, and probably not one-half of the petitioners lived in Dunstable at that time

The same year that he married there were thirty-five proprietors or persons who owned land in Dunstable. Of these only fourteen lived there, the others residing in Boston, Salem, Cambridge, and other places Two years later he helped to found a church in Dunstable of seven male members, each land owner pledging himself to pay the minister fifteen shillings a year for every thirty acre "house lot" he owned When Samuel French married Miss Cummings he was evidently living in Dunstable and his father-in-law, John Cummings, was registered as a land owner

About four years before Samuel married Miss Cummings his father, William French, made his will Some time before this date Samuel had received his portion.

That he was a land owner is known, for he gave to his son John a deed to a part of his farm in 1714, under the reign of Queen Anne The house that John French built on this land is still standing, being used (in the fall of 1910) as a storehouse for apples. This house contained about five rooms, but only the frame of the original structure remains, it having been re-roofed and patched up with old boards A visit to this farm in October, 1910, reveals the fact that it is still kept in the French family, William L French being owner and proprietor

He has in his possession the old camp kettle, bullet molds and musket which his ancestor, Ebenezer French, son of John French, used in the Revolutionary War He relates the story of how his great-grandfather, Ebenezer French of Dunstable, being on guard one evening with this musket in his hand, thought he saw a pine tree moving Determined to take no chances in the matter, he fired and an Indian fell The iron dish in the picture is one in which the grandfather of William L French baked his bread, fried his meat, and cooked his potatoes

When the great-grandfather of William L. French was discharged from the Revolutionary army at Sacketts Harbor, he was paid in Continental money and while walking home stopped to get his breakfast, which consisted of one potato, a small piece of ham, and some corn bread, for which he paid forty dollars ($40.00) in Continental currency. The chair in the picture was used in the home by the great-grandmother

From the *History of Dunstable* (Fox) we learn that Deacon Samuel French, who came from Billerica to Dunstable and built the house still standing close to the state line (the one just described), was probably the first innkeeper of the town, for at the town meeting held May 23, 1732, among other bills the following appears, and by vote of the meeting was allowed and ordered paid to the heirs:

The town of Dunstable Dr to Samuel French (Dec'd)	
1725 to dining the Selectmen & Meals	0l – 8s –0d
Ditto in ye year 1726 6 meals	0 – 6 –0
for Rhum & Cyder had at Mr Wm Lunds (for the Selectmen)	0 –12 –6
Going abt to take the Invoice 4 days	0 –16 –0
Total	2 2 6

On August 15, 1726, Samuel French deeded to his son, Samuel French Jr, a tract of land consisting of thirty acres more or less, for sixty pounds

DEED

SAMUEL FRENCH TO SAMUEL FRENCH JR

To All Christian People to whom this present Deed of Sale Shall Come Samuel French of Dunstable in the county of Middlesex in New England Husbandmen Sends Greeting Know ye that I the Said Samuel French for and in Consideration of the sum of Sixty Pounds money to me in hand before the executing & delivery of these Present well and truly paid by Samuel French Jr of said Town and County Yeoman The Receipt whereof I do hereby acknowledge and thereof and of every part thereof for myself my heirs Exeucs and Admins do acqunt and discharge him the Said Samuel French Jr his heirs and assigns forever by these Presents Have given granted bargained Sold aliened conveyed and confirmed and by these Presents do freely fully and absolutely give grant bargain sell alien Convey and confirm unto him the sd Samuel French Jur his heirs and assigns forever a

Distinct parcel of upland situate lying and being in the township of Dunstable on the west side of Merrimack River bounded as follows viz beginning at the north East Corner it being a pine Tree on merrimack River Bank from thence bounded by william Lund up to the highway or common road of passing to a great Rock from thence Southerly by the Common Road of passing to the Said Samuel French Junrs own land and on all other points bounded by the Said Samuel French Jurs own Land it being by Estimation Thirty acres be the same so much more or less as also all the Divisions in the Common or undivided Land in Dunstable aforesaid belonging to this Thirty acre Right which is to be laid out after the Date of these Presents together with all the Rights Libertys Profits Priviledges & appurtenances thereunto belonging and all the Estate Right Tittle Inheritance Possession Claim & demand of me the said Samuel French of in and to the same and every part thereof. *To Have And To Hold* all and singular the above granted Premises with all the appurtenances thereof unto the Said Samuel French Junr his heirs and assigns to Heir and their own Sole proper use Benefit and Behoofe forever and I the Said Samuel French for my self my heirs execus and admins do covenant Promise and Grant to and with the Said Samuel French Junr his heirs and assigns that at the time of the Execution and Delivery of these Presents I the said Samuel French am the true Sole and only lawfull owner of all the aforegranted and bargained premises having in myself full power good right and lawfull authority to Sell and dispose of the same in manner as aforesaid and that the said Samuel French Junr his heirs and assigns shall and may from Time to Time and at all Time forever hereafter have hold use occupy possess and Enjoy all the above granted premisses to the said Samuel French Junr his heirs and assigns against the lawful claim and Demand of all and every person and persons whomsoever In Witness whereof the said Samuel French hath hereunto sett his hand & seal this Second day of July in the year of our Lord one thousand seven hundred & twenty six and in the Twelfth year of King George's reign.

               SAMUEL FRENCH & Seal

Signed sealed and delivered in presence of us Abraham Taylor John Med at Dunstable August 15th 1726 The above named Samuel French personally appearing acknowledged the above written Instrument to be his voluntary act and Deed forever.   ELEAZR TYNG JUR pd
Midsx Gt Camb January 8th 1729

          Read & Entered by Ira Foxcroft
                Reg.

The ecclesiastical affairs of the town are somewhat shrouded in mystery The people seem to have had no settled minister during their many wars, but a meeting house was completed in 1678, built probably of logs Mr Thomas Weld was employed at as early a date as May 1, 1679, as minister, and a "thirty acre right," consisting of about six hundred acres was granted for a "ministerial lot" to encourage the ministry In December, 1682, the town "let out to Goodman Akers to cut ten cords of wood for two shillings a cord, country paye, and Sargt Cummings is to cart the same for two shillings a cord same paye " This was probably for Mr Weld, who had been married a short time previous. In 1683 a second meeting house of larger size and better finish was built at a cost of approximately three hundred or four hundred dollars This church was organized the year following, and consisted of six male members — John Blanchard, John Cummings Sr, Samuel French, Obadiah Perry, Jonathan Tyng and Cornelius Waldo Mr Thomas Weld was ordained minister on December 16, 1685

The following is the covenant of this church ·

> We covenant with our Lord and with one another, and we do bind ourselves in the presence of God, to walk together in all his ways according as he is pleased to reveal himself unto us, in his blessed word of truth, and do explicitly profess to walk as followeth through the power and grace of our Lord Jesus Christ
>
> We avouch the Lord to be our God and ourselves to be his people in the truth and simplicity of our spirits
>
> We give ourselves to the Lord Jesus and the word of his grace, for teaching, ruling and sanctifying of us in matters of worship and conversation, resolving to cleave unto him alone for life and glory, and to reject all contrary ways, canons, and constitutions of men in his worship
>
> We promise to walk with our brethren with all watchfulness and tenderness, avoiding jealousies, suspicions, backbitings, censurings, provocations, secret risings of spirit against them, but in all cases to follow the rule of our Lord Jesus Christ, to bear and forbear, to give and forgive as he has taught us
>
> In public or in private, we will willingly do nothing to the offence of the church, but will be willing to take advice for ourselves and ours as occasion may be presented
>
> We will not in the congregation be forward either to show our own gifts or parts in speaking, or scrupling or there discover the weakness and failings of our brethren, but attend an orderly call thereto, knowing how much

the Lord may be dishonored and his Gospel and the profession of it slighted by our distempers and weakness in public.

We bind ourselves to study the advancement of the Gospel, in all truth and peace both in regard to those that are within and without, no ways slighting our sister churches, but using their counsels as need shall be; not laying a stumbling block any, no, not the Indians whose good we desire to promote, and so to converse that we may avoid the very appearance of evil

We do hereby promise to carry ourselves in all lawful obedience to those that are over us in church or commonwealth knowing how well pleasing it will be to the Lord that they should have encouragement in their places, by our not grieving their spirits through our irregularities

We resolve to approve ourselves to the Lord in our particular callings, shunning idleness as the bane of any state, nor will we deal hardly or oppressively with any, wherein we are the Lord's stewards Promising also unto our best ability to teach our children the knowledge of God, and of his holy will, that they may serve him also, and all this not by any strength of our own, but by the Lord Jesus Christ whose blood we desire may sprinkle this our covenant made in his name

On October 4, 1797, every inhabitant was ordered to "bring half a cord of wood to Mr Weld by the first of November or forfeit five shillings for each neglect" This contribution was in addition to his salary as minister, the price of the wood then being about one dollar per cord, making an extra tax on the membership of fifty cents each In 1699 this wood rate was increased and assessment made according to the financial ability of the inhabitants, who were required to furnish the minister nineteen cords The "minister rate" assessed upon all the inhabitants was about fifty dollars, this probably being the amount of his salary The population at this time possibly did not exceed one hundred twenty-five, twenty heads of families contributing to the "wood rate" — one of whom was Samuel French.

In 1700 it was voted to "glaze" the meeting house, which was done at a cost of one pound, one shilling, and six pence, these being the first window lights in their church

The manners and customs of that time were very different from those of the present day, as may be gathered from the following expense account of the funeral of James Blanchard, who died in 1704, he being a farmer in fair circumstances:

	£ s d
Paid for winding sheet	0–18–0
Paid for coffin	0–10–0
Paid for digging grave	0– 7–6
Paid for the use of the pall	0– 5–0
Paid for gloves (to distribute at the funeral)	1– 1–0
Paid for wine, segars and spice (at the funeral)	1– 5–9
Paid to the Doctor	0–14–9
Paid for attendance, expenses etc.	1–17–5
	6–19–5

The minister received the title of "Mr" not "Rev." for this was considered an "innovation of vanity" upon Puritan simplicity. In 1699 the term "Mr" was not yet applied to common people, the appellation between neighbors being Goodman and Goodwife or Goody. Adams's *Annals of Portsmouth* gives some of the curious customs and Puritan laws of the age.

For example: It was voted under date of September 25, 1662, that a cage be made or some other means invented by the selectmen to punish such as sleep or take tobacco on the Lord's day out of the meeting in the time of the public exercise. Ten years later it was voted that if any shall smoke tobacco in the meeting house at any public meeting he shall pay a fine of five shillings for the use of the town.

1642. By a law of Massachusetts no freeman was allowed to vote in town meeting nor sit as a deputy in the General Court unless he were a church member. On September 8, 1642, this law was dispensed with as to the towns in New Hampshire.

1648. Delusion respecting witchcraft appeared, Margaret Jones of Charlestown being the first to be convicted and executed.

1649. Wearing of long hair was condemned as sinful. Dancing at weddings was forbidden.

In 1666 William Walker was imprisoned a month "for courting a maid without the leave of her parents."

In 1675 "there is manifest pride appearing in our streets" and also "superstitious ribbands used to tie up and decorate the hair." These things were forbidden under severe penalties, the men being forbidden to "keep Christmas" because it was a "Popish custom"

May 21, 1688, Samuel Goold is chosen dog whipper for the meeting house Fox says "What were the duties of this functionary we are not informed so far as is implied in the name. It stands alone, without precedent or imitation The choice is recorded with all gravity among other dignitaries of the town, and the office was doubtless in those days a serious and real one and no sinecure, unless we suspect our grave forefathers of a practical joke." The office might have been created for the purpose of giving a shiftless man something to do, and it might not have made him a living, as, leaving Dunstable, he moved to Chelmsford, where we find in the history of that village that Samuel Goold and his wife were the only paupers, that town contributing eight shillings a week to their support This was in 1720

So strict were these people in the observance of the Sabbath that "John Atherton was fined 40 shillings for wetting a piece of an old hat to put into shoes where they had chafed his feet when marching."

Those who neglected to attend church for three months were publicly whipped In Harvard College students were whipped for grave offenses in presence of students and professors in chapel, and prayer was offered before and after the infliction of the punishment.

Prayer at funerals in New England formed no part of the service previous to 1685, and no sermon was preached — the burial being silent

Before 1689 no person could vote or be elected to office until he had been made a freeman of the commonwealth This might be done by the General Assembly or the county court, but only upon evidence of his being a member in good standing of some congregational church — not congregational as understood today; rather some public worshiping body of Christian people

Samuel French must have been a potent factor in the Indian hostilities which almost constantly engaged the attention of the settlers, for record is found of his having been credited with military service at the garrison at Marlborough, October 19, 1675, three pounds; and again another record is made of service at Chelmsford, July 24, 1675, three pounds, eight shillings, and six pence.

During King William's War, which began in 1689, an attack on Dunstable was planned but averted, owing to information given by two friendly Indians, and companies were sent in defense of the town. On the evening of September 2, 1691, the Indians suddenly appeared and murdered five of the inhabitants, and on the 28th two more became the victims of their atrocities.

This locality was also associated with another tragic event in history: In April, 1697, Mrs. Hannah Dustin, on her way to Boston in company with Mary Neff and a boy, passed through Dunstable in a canoe, they having been taken captive by Indians at Haverhill, Massachusetts, and carried to the mouth of the Contocook River in New Hampshire, where they succeeded in escaping by killing their captors, who were in a drunken stupor. This is regarded as one of the most remarkable and heroic deeds on record, with Hannah Dustin as the celebrated heroine of colonial days.

In point of population, Dunstable was at this time the smallest township in the province, and but for the indomitable perseverance and courage of five men — Major Jonathan Tyng, Lieutenant Samuel French, John Lovewell, Samuel Whiting, and the Rev. Mr. Weld — must have been abandoned. The Indians still continuing their hostilities, another garrison was established for the defence of the little settlement, which was manned December 25, 1702, by a company of soldiers, one of whom was Samuel French.

On the night of July 3, 1706, a party of two hundred seventy Mohawk Indians suddenly assaulted a garrison house in which Captain Pearson of Rowley and twenty of his troopers, who had been ranging the woods, were posted. The door having been left open and no watch appointed, the soldiers were surprised. John and Elizabeth Cummings, who had gone out to milk the cows, were fired upon, the latter being killed, while the former, with a gunshot wound in his arm, escaped to the woods, where he remained in concealment during the night. After a bloody fight the Indians were routed. It was here that Samuel French and his family were garrisoned at this time.

These garrison houses were surrounded with palisades — a wall of stone or timber — rising to the roof In the wall there was a gate of heavy plank, secured with iron bolts, port-holes were made in various places and the underbrush was cleared away from the vicinity in order that the approach of the enemy might be seen To these garrison houses the inhabitants would remove when the alarm was sounded throughout the settlement that the Indians were lurking near. Such occasions as these were undoubtedly the inspiration for the poem, "Grandmother's Aprons," written by Eleanor French Bates, and published in the *Patriotic Review*

GREAT-GRANDMOTHER'S APRONS

Safe in the heart of a meadow, away from a woodland nook
Which else might shelter a warrior, and near to a favoring brook
They built the stout old blockhouse, to guard from a painted foe,
And there dwelt great-grandmother, two hundred years ago.

The Indian tribes were rising, and fast through the woodpaths came
Many a maid and matron of slender but dauntless frame,
And grandmother ran to welcome, and offered them of her best,
But first she tied on an apron she took from an oaken chest

With faltering feet came a mother, her baby but ten days old,
And grandmother went to meet them and brought them into her fold
She comforted little children — she tied on an apron first —
And gave them porridge for hunger and a piggin of milk for thirst

She cooked the pork and potatoes which made up the homely fare,
And hospitality entreated the gathering neighbors to share,
She spread sweet straw and cornhusks for the refugees to rest,
Nor did she forget an apron, all fresh from her oaken chest

She went with the boys to the meadow to help drive up the kine,
She took her turn at watching for an Indian scout or sign,
And, absently donning an apron (for thus doth the legend go),
She cleaned and loaded the muskets — dames of her day did so

But when came the sunny morning, each heart was warm with cheer,
For safe were the hardy settlers — no red men had come anear —
And when she untied four aprons, one from above another,
No one was more astonished than dear, brave, great-grandmother!

Conditions of peace did not prevail until the treaty of Utrecht, April 11, 1713, which continued for a period of eleven years, or until 1724, when hostilities were again renewed, during which time Lieutenant Ebenezer French, son of Samuel French, was killed by the Indians on September 5, 1724. Of the men who lost their lives at this time, eight were buried in one grave in the old burying ground at Little's Station. Their gravestone, which still stands, is marked "Memento Mori. Here lies the body of Mr Thomas Lund who departed this life Sep 5, 1724, in the 42d year of his age. This man with seven more that lies in this grave was slue all in a day by the Indians."

From *Soldiers in King Philip's War* we find that the towns assumed the payment of the wages of their own soldiers to their families at home — they thus receiving sure and immediate aid, and the towns being credited to that amount upon their colonial rates or taxes. In this manner the families were supported.

During these terrible years when one war followed so closely on another, and the rumors of threatened invasions by the Indians proved only too true, is it any wonder that, owing to the exposed situation of the settlers, by the year 1696 fully two-thirds of them had abandoned their homes and the state had been obliged to remit fifty pounds in taxes to the town for those who had deserted it? That this period of depression continued for some years is shown from the fact that in 1701 the General Court gave twelve pounds toward the maintenance of the minister in Dunstable, after it had been shown to them how the settlers had been obliged to leave their homes as the result of the devastation due to the Indian wars. It certainly is hard for us in these days of peace and prosperity, to realize the terrible scenes through which our ancestors were compelled to pass. It is a matter of history that no colony suffered as did this one from Indian wars. Belknap says: "Every man who was forty years of age had seen twenty years of war. Such continued dangers and hardships, although affording no good school for cultivation and refinement, furnished a race of hardy soldiers and sterling patriots for the times that tried men's souls." They lived constantly in dread of the lurking foe — much of the time shut up in garrisons, living on the most frugal fare, loaded muskets in their hands whether they ventured forth in the field to work or to attend divine worship Surely these pioneers were of the stuff of which heroes are made, and they laid a good foundation for this wonderful republic

That Samuel French was wounded in some of the numerous engagements occurring in his lifetime is known, owing to a statement found in Vol IV, of the *Provincial Papers of New Hampshire.* From *Journal of the House*, under date of April 28, 1726.

> Voted That Samuell French be allowed and paid out of the publick Treasury eight pounds, Sixteen Shillings, in full of all Demands on his Accompt for Doctor Halls curing him of a Shot wound & Diet & Lodging the said Sum being in full for all Demands
>
> JAMES JEFFREY
> Clr Assembly

Under same date

> Allowed Sam'l French out of the Treasury eight pounds sixteen shillings to discharge his acct. for cure of a gunshott.
>
> JAM JEFFREY assem.

[1] The date of the death of his wife is not known, but that of Samuel French is given as having occurred in November, 1727

There were many traditions among the early settlers of Massachusetts, among others, that there had been gold coin buried in different places throughout the land Every family owned a "divining rod" and there was much seeking and digging, with little or no success There was said to be a "spell" upon the gold, so that if a person should speak when searching, the pot of gold would disappear forever. It is related that one midnight the "divining rod" of John, son of Samuel French, and some others who had assembled with him, leaned toward a certain spot; so they dug in silence and the spade at last hit against an iron pot Ebenezer, son of John, then but a lad eight years of age, had followed them unseen, and when he heard the ring of the metal gave a shout of victory Alas! the pot of gold disappeared forever from the land of the French families

---

[1] Stearn's *Thirty Dunstable Families*

ELEAZER FRENCH'S ARM

(Eleazer French lost an arm at the battle of Bunker Hill, and picking it up, bore it as a trophy from the bloody field.)

When dwelling on the heroes of field, redoubt and trench,
Shall we not tell the story of young Eleazer French?
    With fowling piece and powder horn
    Under the clear June starlight borne,
    They labored till the early morn
        On Bunker's honored height;

Long hours the pick and shovel plied,
And each who, weary, stepped aside,
Found eagerly his place supplied
    Throughout the summer night.
No stouter hearts of stronger frame
Were there, with patriot fire aflame,
Than those from Dunstable that came
    To battle for the right.

And when th' invading force was met,
With powder grime and bloody sweat,
The farmers' flintlocks paid the debt
    They owed to Howe's great guns.
Muskets of old-time minute men!
Ye told the story once again,
How tyrants doubt and falter when
    Assemble Freedom's sons.

Full soon they heard the bugle call
And saw the young Eleazer fall,
Where sped the British cannon ball
    Upon its path of harm.
"Fall back! keep safe from further ill!"
They shouted; he, unconquered still,
Quoth stoutly, and with steadfast will,
    "No! not without my arm!"

The severed limb all bleeding lay,
But he who fought that glorious day,
Took it upon his anguished way

        And left no trophy there,
    Racked with fierce pains and bitter qualms,
    Fainting, and stunned with war's alarms,
    Bravely he bore off both his arms
        To show what soldiers dare

O ye who sing our heroes of parapet and trench,
Fail not to tell the story of brave Eleazer French!
                      ELEANOR W. F BATES

MARY'S SAMPLER

The silks are dim and faded that once were bright and gay,
The blue has turned to creamy white, the pink has changed to gray;
Long time the web has hid within the attic's farthest nook,
Wrought more than ninety years ago by Mary Estabrook.

Upon the old stone door-step, when summer days were long,
She sat and marked her letters, peradventure sometimes wrong,
And if she took some stitches out to put them in again, —
Dear little Mary, did you long to drop your needle then?

Or if the days were sultry, she took her pretty work,
And sat beneath the butternuts where cooling shadows lurk,
Twin trees were they, of ample girth, and Mary loved them well,
Perchance a tribute leaf or nut upon her sampler fell

In Mary's quaint old garden, sweet-williams, pinks and phlox
Grew side by side with balsams, prince's feather, four-o-clocks;
Tall tiger lilies stood alone, stiff poised on stately stem,
Near where the poppies spread their bloom, each one a glowing gem.

The beauty of the blossoms slipped into Mary's soul,
And in the centre of her web she stitched a curious scroll,
A twisting vine of varied green, with here and there a rose,
Or else it is a strawberry — perhaps — but no one knows

Cross stitch and over and over, the sampler grew apace,
Three times she marked the alphabet upon its homespun face,
And when the letters were too few to finish out the line,
She made a row of tiny trees, with foliage thick and fine

If any little maidens now live in that fair town,
One wonders if they ever take a square of linen brown,
And patiently work day by day, design upon design,
As once did "Mary Estabrook, of Sudbury, aged nine!"

ELEANOR W. F. BATES [1]

Sixth Generation

JOSEPH[6] FRENCH (Samuel,[5] William,[4] Thomas,[3] Thomas,[2] Thomas[1]), third child of Samuel and Sarah (Cummings) French, was born in Dunstable March 10, 1687. He married Elizabeth, daughter of John Cummings Jr., and Elizabeth Kinsley Cummings, about 1711, she dying April 30, 1751. To them were born:

I. Joseph, son of Joseph and Elizabeth Cummings French, was born July 28, 1713; married Bridget ——. To them were born:

1. Isaac, born May 26, 1734; died August 4, 1753.

Bridget French died October 29, 1735.

Joseph married (second) Elizabeth ——. To them were born:

2. Joseph, born November 1, 1739; married March 3, 1768, Sybil Richardson. To them were born four children.
3. Josiah, born June 27, 1741; died in infancy.
4. Josiah (second), born June 17, 1743.
5. Thomas, born May 4, 1745.
6. Elizabeth, born March 6, 1746 or 1747.
7. {Bridget, born August 30, 1749.
8. {Mollie, born August 30, 1749.

Elizabeth French died January 20, 1753.

Joseph French married (third) Rebecca ——. To them were born:

9. Susannah, born October 16, 1757.
10. Theodore, born June 6, 1759; married Rhoda Danforth (born April 22, 1769) October 4, 1781. To them were born five children.

Theodore married (second) Caty (Honey) Lovewell

---

[1] Published some years ago in *The Youth's Companion*.

FRENCH AND ALLIED FAMILIES

(born in Dunstable March 2, 1759) February 3, 1791
To them were born three children
Rebecca French died March 21, 1776
(Captain) Joseph French died April 21, 1776.

II. Elizabeth, second child of Joseph and Elizabeth (Cummings) French was born ———, 1715; married Captain John Cummings (born January 14, 1698) in 1736 To them were born:

1 Olive, born May 15, 1738; married Captain Leonard Butterfield (born in Dunstable November 17, 1740). To them were born five children:
   a. Leonard, born February 28, 1772.
   b. Olive, born April 19, 1773.
   c John, born December 1, 1776.
   d Sarah, born May 5, 1779
   e. Catherine, born January 18, 1781
2. Rebecca, born August 4, 1740; married Asahel Wyman May 28, 1761
3 Elizabeth (Betty), born May 28, 1744, in Dunstable; married November 27, 1766, Jacob Jewett (born in 1745) of Hollis, New Hampshire To them were born eight children:
   a James, born August 22, 1767
   b John, born July 2, 1769
   c. Jacob, born June 14, 1770
   d David, born August 16, 1773
   e Elizabeth (Betty), born October 15, 1775.
   f. Lucy, born August 9, 1777
   g Ralph Winslow, born December 8, 1779
   h Leonard, born October 2, 1787
4. Easter, born August 21, 1745; married January 11, 1767, Jonas Butterfield (born September 12, 1742) To them were born:
   a Rebecca, born in Dunstable October 1, 1768
   b Jonas, born in Dunstable May 24, 1773

c. Esther, born in Dunstable April 12, 1778.
   d. John, born in Dunstable April 16, 1780.
 5. Molly, born August 1, 1747; married Joseph Fletcher (born June 18, 1752). To them were born:
   a. Molly Cummings, born September 15, 1773.
   b. Isaac, born November 23, 1784.
   c. Elizabeth Underwood, born February 24, 1790.
   d. Catherine, born May 6, 1792.
   e. Lucinda, born November 26, 1795.
 6. Lucy, born June 6, 1748; married April 30, 1772, Abijah Wright.
 7. John Jr., born January 13, 1753.
 8. Katy, born October 21, 1755.
Captain John Cummings, husband of Elizabeth, died August 15, 1770.
Elizabeth died July 2, 1793.

III. Sampson, born July 28, 1717; died July 19, 1785.
IV. Josiah, born February 24, 1723; died January 28, 1742.
V. Thomas, born June 29, 1724.
VI. Benjamin, sixth child of Joseph and Elizabeth (Cummings) French, was born July 6, 1726; married January 8, 1751, Molly Lovewell (born May 26, 1732). To them were born:
 1. Benjamin, born December 11, 1752; died October 29, 1776.
 2. Esther, born January 7, 1754; married Dr. Allin Toothaker; married (second) Timothy Taylor.
 3. Mollie, born October 18, 1756.
 4. Katherine, born August 19, 1758.
 5. Augustus, born June 16, 1760.
 6. Betsey, born January 16, 1762.
 7. Charlotte, born September 21, 1763; married July 12, 1779, James Cummings (born in Dunstable July 12, 1757). To them were born four children. James died September 6, 1840. Charlotte died September 27, 1787.

FRENCH AND ALLIED FAMILIES

    8. Frederick, born September 26, 1766; married December 30, 1790, Grace Blanchard. To them were born five children Grace died February 6, 1845 Frederick died March 28, 1824.
    9. Thomas, born August 7, 1768; married Elizabeth Blanchard January 7, 1796. She died May 4, 1843. Thomas died May 3, 1846
   10 Lucy, born November 7, 1769
   11. Bridget, born January 14, 1772

Molly Lovewell French died December 17, 1774

Benjamin French married (second) Mary Cummings February 1, 1776

He died December 15, 1779

VII. Samuel, born July 14, 1728; died January 11, 1730
VIII Samuel (second), born August 10, 1730.

Tradition speaks of two other sons of Joseph and Elizabeth French, David and Ebenezer by name, the latter of whom kept a tavern in the valley of the Merrimac The incident relates that while trading with the Indians for furs, on refusing to give them more rum when they had already drank freely, he was murdered by them in a spirit of revenge

It is a matter of history that in 1706, when Joseph French was about nineteen years of age, he with his father, mother, brothers, and sisters, took refuge in the garrison house of his uncle, John Cummings John and Elizabeth Cummings were the parents of four sons and four daughters Joseph's cousin Elizabeth (born January 5, 1687) being about the same age as himself, their close association and companionship ripened into something deeper and more tender, and about 1711 they were married and established a home of their own It was Elizabeth's mother, known as Goody Cummings, who was killed by the Indians, and her father wounded by them, when the garrison was surprised on the night of July 3, 1706 These were certainly cruel days, and it is hard for us to realize what must have been the suffering of these people, surrounded as they were by danger and death Not until 1713 were the doors of the garrison thrown open and peace assured, and it was during this year that the first child of Joseph and Elizabeth was born.

That the colony of Dunstable was in almost continual warfare during the life of Joseph French, is shown by the following petition addressed to the Governor and Council of Massachusetts, under date of May 20, 1725:[1]

> The petition of the Selectmen of Dunstable Humbly Sheweth: That whereas your Honors hath found it necessary to order Col. Tyng and his men into the woods on the sad occasion of Capt. Lovewell's defeat, we are extremely exposed and weak by reason of so many of our fighting men being cut off last summer, and so many killed now in the Province's service. We would beg leave to represent to your honors our case as very sad and distressing having so many soldiers drawn out, and our inhabitants reduced to so small a number by the war. Several families have removed, and more are under such discouragement, not daring to carry on their planting or any other business that they fully design it. We hope your Honors will take our deplorable circumstances into your compassionate consideration, and order such measures to be taken for our defence & support until our men return as you in your wisdom shall think fit. And your Petitioners, as in duty bound will ever pray. (Signed)
>
> SAMUEL FRENCH
> JOSEPH SNOW   } Selectmen
> JOSEPH FRENCH
> JOHN LOVEWELL
> JOHN FRENCH
> JOHN CUMMINGS
> JOHN CUMMINGS JR.
> NATH'L CUMMINGS
> JONATHAN CUMMINGS
> JONATHAN COMBS

John Lovewell also sent in a petition at the same time for help to defend his garrison, stating that unless assistance came he must leave it to the enemy. These petitions were granted and a guard of twenty-five soldiers was posted in the town.

Joseph French was chosen on March 31, 1719, to make coffins "where there be need for the year ensueing." Friendly Indians lived in this community and it is probable that this vote referred to them,

---
[1] Fox.

State Historical Building of Iowa, where much of the Data for this Volume was obtained

as there was a charge made by him not long after "for Jacob Indians coffin 7s."

The selectmen and other persons in the employ of the town at this period charged five shillings per day for their services.

January 16, 1717, it was voted in Dunstable that "Henry Farwell and Seargt Cummings are to endeavor to get a minister as soon as they can, and see after Mr Weld's place (the old parsonage) to buy it if it be to be had Also Joseph French was to entertain the minister."

The amount of taxes raised from 1726 to 1733 for the general expenses of the town, including the support of the minister, varied from two hundred fifty to four hundred dollars per year So scattered were the inhabitants that no school was kept in the town until 1730 'In 1749,[1] the town voted to have a school for eight months of each year. One teacher was employed and the school was kept in four places in the town, alternately Soon after, the French war began and no other record of school is found until 1761. When a settlement contained fifty families, they established a school; when one hundred families, they established a grammar school

Joseph French was a man of influence in the community, a selectman, and an extensive land owner The house where he lived was eight rods north of the state line after the change in boundary, he owning about five hundred acres of land in this locality He died intestate in 1735, leaving a large estate to his wife and children.

JOSEPH FRENCH'S INVENTORY

An inventory of all Singular the Estate Real & Personal of Mr Joseph French Late of Dunstable Dec'd

His Apparel

	£
Impr. to a coat and Laccoat	6– 0–0
To another coat and Laccoat	1– 0–0
To a Great coat	3– 0–0
To a Laccoat coat 16 / one pr Breeches 16 /	1–12–0
2 pr Stockins @ 12 / one pr hose @ 10 /	1– 2–0
1 hat @ 15 / one shirt @ 1£ /	1–15–0

---

[1] Fox

Household stuff & Utensils

7 pr sheats @ £7 6 Table cloths @ 1" 2"	8– 2–0
6 Towels @ 9 / one bed and furniture 1. 7" 10"	7–19–0
To one bed more & Furniture @ 5" 10"	5–10–0
One Brass Kettle & Skillet @ 5" 10" 12 plates @ 17	6–10–0
Six platters @ £2–0 one bason & 2 porringers 10 / wing glass	2–10–0
To one Quart pot 7 / one mugg 2 / peper box 1/6	0– 9–6
To two glass Bottles 2/ andirons & frying pan £1–12	1–14–0
Tongs and fire pail 12/ Box iron & heaters 5/ pothook 2/	0–19–0
a Gridiron 2/ to a Tramel 6/ fifteen chairs £2 /	2– 8–0
A Chest 7 / 2 Tables @ £1 — chest of drawers £1	2– 7–0
Lining wheel @ 11 / wollen wheel @ 4	0–15–0
Iron pott @ 17 / Brass Spurrs @ 3/	1– 0–0

Husbandry Tools &c.

to Saddles @ £1" 16 / one Gunn @ £1" 10 / one axe @ 12/	3–18–0
two Scyethes @ £1–4 / Broad ax £1– Grindstone /	2–14–0
a Broad hoe @ 6 / cart & rigging @ £2–12–0	2–18–0
Two Draught chains @ £1–16 horse traic @ 10/	2– 6–0
One Yoake Staple and ring @ 6/ one Slead @ 10 /	0–16–0
To Carpenters Tooles @ 12 / coopers tooles @ 18	1–10–0
Joyners Tools @ 10 / Iron crow @ £1–10	2–00–0
to Old Casks £1– Looking Glass 5 /	1–05–0
one plow @ £1– Breaking up plow @ £ 2	3–00–0

Stock &c

To One pr Oxon @ £18 pr Stears coming 3 year old £6–5	24– 5–0
To one red cow @ £6–10 / Brown cow @ £5–10	12–00–0
To two Brindle cows @ £12 one horse @ £12	24–00–0
one mare @ £10– two calves @ £3 — —	13–00–0
26 Sheep @ £15–10– to 8 Swine @ £13	28–10–0
2 Steares four years Old @ £10 — one red heifer @ 5–10	15–10–0
to a Brown heifer Coming four years Old @	4–15–0
To three heifers @	6–00–0
To one Red and White cow @	6–00–0

Brought over	208–16–0

FRENCH AND ALLIED FAMILIES

In Dunstable
Real Estate

To the Homestead Buildings &c. @	920–00–0
To a piece of Swamp Called Half moon @	50–00–0
To a farm at Nisitisseth of 400 acres	190–00–0
In Nottingham 200 acres @	240–00–0
The sixth part of a farm called Davenport	60–00–0
In Groton to about one hundred acres meadow upland	70–00–0

Total £1738– 6–0

The above inventory was made and apprized for the subscribers ye 29th of Sepr 1735 - ZACCHEUS LOVEWELL
JOHN FRENCH
HENRY FARWELL JR

The administratrix makes mention of common rights and undivided lands, also a piece of meadow lying in Nottingham, about six acres, and another piece in said town, about three acres

Elizabeth French, administratrix, exhibited an inventory on oath before Jon Remington, J. P. Records in court house in East Cambridge, October 17, 1910

February 16, 1736 Widow gave bond as guardian to Sampson, Benjamin, and Samuel, who only are under age Widow content with her third and with the whole distribution So is the eldest son.

ELIZABETH FRENCH'S BOND

Know all men by these Presents
That we Elizabeth French widow of Joseph French Husbandman — both of Dunstable in the County of Middlesex in the Province of the Massachusetts Bay in New England, are holden and stand firmly Bound and Obliged unto Jonathan Remington Esq his Successor or Assigns in the full Sum of one thousand Pounds To be paid unto the said Jona Remington his Successors or Assigns in the Office of Judge of the Probate of Wills and for Granting Letters of Administration on the Estate of Persons Deceased in the said county of Middlesex. To the true Payment whereof, We jointly and severally bind our Selves and our several respective Heirs Executors and Administrators, firmly by these Presents Sealed with our Seals; Dated the Sixteenth Day of February Anno Domini 1736

The accounts of debts and credits of the estate of the late Joseph French of Dunstable Deceased which the administrator viz Joseph French son of the deceased, and Elizabeth French widow of the Deceased have charged themselves withall viz Debts Due to the Deceased at his death which they find Received.

	£ s d
From Timothy Adams two Pounds	2– 0–0
From John Richardson two Pounds	2– 0–0
From Samuel Searls one Pound	1– 0–0
John Tayler one Pound ten shillings	1–10–0
More Fifteen pounds eighteen shillings	15–18–0
From Peter Powers five Pounds	5–00–0
More five shillings	0– 5–0
	236– 3–6

and desireth allowance for debts paid which was due from the deceased at his death which the sd administrator have since Paid and discharged to the several creditors.

	£ s d
to Colonel Eleazer Tyng	0– 5–0
to Mr Nathaniel Prentice (nine pounds & three shillings)	9– 3–0
to Mr Prentice Six Pounds sixteen shillings & three	6–16–3
to James Parham Sixteen pounds five shillings	16– 5–0
to Thomas Harwood Two pounds eight and nine Pence	2– 8–9
to Capt Blanchard three Pounds	3– 0–0
more	
to Capt Blanchard	19– 0–0
to Sam^{ll} Huston Three Pounds five Shillings	3– 5–0
to Jonth Barron one pound one shill & sixpence	1– 1–6
to hugh Nawhan ten shillings	0–10–0
to John Blanchard fourteen shillings	0–14–0
to Tyler & Hancock three pounds, three shillings	3– 3–0
to Benj. Gould one pound four & sixpence	1– 4–6
to Jon'a Cummings ten shillings	0–10–0
to Thomas Chamberlain six pounds seven shillings and three pence	6– 7–3
to Saml Robe sixteen shillings	0–16–0
to Capt Parker Twelve pounds ten Shillings	12–10–0
to Jona Snow ten shillings	0–10–0
to Thomas Pollard one pound four shillings	1– 4–0
to the widow Curtis Twenty five Pounds	25– 0–0
to Mr Walton	0– 5–0
to " Jabez Davis	00– 6–0
to " James Dutton	00– 3–0

to " Jacob Pierse	00- 2-10
to Capt Blanchard	00- 2-6
to the three men prizing the Estate	2- 5-0
to Entertaining the Prizors three days	1- 4-0
entertaining the first apprizors	1- 0-0
to Thomas Chamberlain	1- 6-0
X Thos Barrett	6-10-0
X Mary Waters (for funerals)	35- 7-7
X Benjn Alford for 6 Gallons of Rum	2-14-0
X Mr Lemmion for Funerals	27- 6-5
X Thomas Barrett	6- 0-0
For the apparel used in the Family (all save one suit apprized at 6ll)	8- 9-0
P'd for admnr 7/6 Inventory	
To the admnr for their troubles & journeys	8- 0-0
Framing this acct in part 3/ examining & allowing 5	0/ 8-0
Recording to copy	0-12-0
Capt Jno Hall of Medford by grandson	11-12-0
& fees supposed to be 28/	1- 8-0

The acct of Eliz. French & Josf French late of Dunstable in the county of Middlesex Dec'd Intestate

The said accountants charge themselves with the estate of the said Dec'd specified in an Inventory thereof by them exhibited into the Probate office for sd county on the   Day of
                amounting to

viz Real Estate	Personal	£208-16-6
and they now add — (ex on the other side)		
and the said amounts to over allowance in their discharge as follows — viz		
38 Gravestone about		6-15-0½
pd Daniel Dickey		10
copy of Inventory		4
	Amt	247- 3-1
To the widow for her Privilege	30ll	279- 3-1

not to be recorded till it be known
whether the Fees for sending the execution
be 2£ more or less

                        Middlesex October 18, 1739

Eliz & Jos French presented the foregoing & made oath that the same containing a full and true acct of their admnr on the said Dec'd Estate to pay as they have proceeded therein — the same having been examined & vouchers produced for the most of the articles therein contained.

I allow thereof

JONN REMINGTON Jpro

Seventh Generation

SAMPSON[7] FRENCH (Joseph,[6] Samuel,[5] William,[4] Thomas,[3] Thomas,[2] Thomas[1]) was born in Dunstable, New Hampshire, July 28, 1717. But little is known regarding his early history, not even the name of the first wife having been found, due no doubt to the fact that the records of Dunstable from 1733 to 1746 were lost; but he must have married during this time, as his son Sampson was born September 15, 1742, the following record being found in an old account book kept by his son Samson Jr., and now owned by one of his descendants — Mrs. Nellie Pendell of Binghamton, New York. The same account book speaks of other children — David, Aaron, and Jonathan. For his second wife he married Sarah Clement, March 7, 1748 (or 1749), the record of this marriage being found in *Vital Records of Haverhill*. His father died in 1735 when he was but nineteen years of age, and in the probate court of East Cambridge, Massachusetts, is found the following bond filed under date of February 16, 1736, by his mother, Elizabeth Cummings French:

BOND

The condition of this obligation is such That if the above bounden Elizabeth French, nominated and allowed to be guardian unto her child Sampson French a Minor in the 19th year of his age, son of Joseph French — late of Dunstable in the county of Middlesex, Dec'd, and do well and truly Perform & Discharge the Trust and office of Guardian unto the said Minor and that in and by all things according to Law; And shall render a plain and true Acompt of her Said Guardianship upon oath and all and Singular Such Estate as Shall come to her hands and possession by virtue thereof, and of the Profits and Improvements of the Same so far as the law shall charge her therewith (when she shall be thereunto Lawfully required) and shall pay and Deliver what and so much of the said estate as shall be found remaining upon her Acompt (the same being first examined and Allowed of by the Judge or Judges for the time being, of the Probate of Wills &c. within the county of Middlesex foresaid) unto the Said Minor when he

shall arrive at full Age or otherwise as the Said judge by his or their decree or Sentence pursuant to Law Shall Limit and Appoint; Then this obligation to be void, otherwise to remain in full force.
Signed Sealed & Delivered in Presence of us
SAM'L DANFORTH
JOSEPH BEAN

            her
         ELIZABETH X FRENCH
            mark
         JOSEPH FRENCH

This record was made on the back of the bond.

 Sampson French
  Guard n Bond
   Fees pd for 3 Bonds
        18/
          to Judge pd

February 16 1736
The miners election of his Guardian wanting
          Judge pd
Sampson to signifye under his Hand this
choice of his Mother —

From records in East Cambridge probate court house, in the division of the property of Joseph French is found the following real estate, set off to Sampson:

 We have also divided and set off to Sampson French the second son of ye said dec'd a tract of land containing about one hundred and thirty acres in ye township of Nottingham, bounded the westerly by Merrimack river southerly by land of Joseph Snow Easterly by part of ye sd Dec'd land, the dividing line beginning at an heap of stones lying in the northerly line of Joseph Snows land — from thence running northerly to a white oak marked, so on the same course to an heap of stones lying in ye southerly line of Oliver Colburn land, also one twelfth part of a farm called Davenports farm lying in sd Nottingham @ £223-10-0 ye whole

That Sampson French had inherited some of the business sagacity of his father in accumulating property to add to that which had been given him, is shown by a careful perusal of the Town Papers of New Hampshire

 In the list of the proprietors of the township called South Monadnock No. One, and of the lotts by them Respectively drawn (as sett against each persons names) in said Township — W^M DOWNE
                  Prop^{ers} clerk.

Sampson French drew No. 9, range 1; No. 10, range 1; No. 9, range 5. Under the charter of Peterborough Slip, 1750, at a meeting held at Portsmouth, June 16, 1749; and also under date of 1752 Sampson French drew land, the acreage not being given. In 1751 he owned two shares in land sold to John Hutchinson in meeting held at Portsmouth.

The township of Richmond was granted on February 28, 1752, to Joseph Blanchard and others in 71 shares. The plan describes a tract of land of the contents of six miles square, and Sampson French was one of the proprietors. Under date of January 1, 1753, we find him one of the grantees of the Duplex charter, and on December 27, 1753, one of the grantees of Brattleborough. In 1772 a petition of the proprietors of Walpole for equivalent grant — a township of six miles square on the east side and adjoining the Connecticut River, with the names of seventy-five grantees attached, the list including the name of Sampson French, his name also appearing among the ninety who signed the petition to have the Province divided into two counties.

It is noted in these records where, on account of trouble with the Indians, the grantees of Richmond had been unable to comply with the conditions of the grant and asked an extension, that said request was granted by the governor and council June 11, 1760, and among the proprietors of the above named grant is given the name of Sampson French. Further record is made of his having been connected with land grants in Dupplin and Boyle, New Hampshire, and also, under date of June 16, 1749, that he purchased land from John Mason soon after his marriage to Sarah Clement.

August 31, 1747, the Reverend Samuel Bird received a call to settle in Dunstable, and soon after was ordained as pastor. He was to be paid "100 ounces of silver coin Troy weight, sterling alloy, or the full value thereof in bills of public credit," which amounted to about one hundred dollars yearly, provided "that he preach a lecture once in three months at least in this town" and "visit and catechise the people" — and it was finally so decided in 1748.

At a meeting held in Dunstable March 2, 1746, the name of Sampson French appears as one of the qualified voters in the papers relating to the settlement of this man as minister in their church For some reason not given, his ministry was not acceptable to all the people of the town, for on August 31, 1747, at a meeting held for that purpose, the following vote was proposed.

> Whereas the Church of Christ in this town of Dunstable in the Province of New Hampshire on the 6th day of July last, made choice of the Rev Samuel Bird for their Pastor and Teacher, and having presented their vote to this town with a desire that this Town would concur with them in their choice, and make choice of said Mr Samuel Bird for the settled minister of this Town Now therefore be it voted and agreed that the said church's choice be concurred with, and that the said Mr Samuel Bird be chosen for the settled minister of this town.

Voted in the affirmative by thirty-two men — one of whom was Sampson French The negative motion was:

> We the subscribers Inhabitants and Free holders of the town of Dunstable hereby Desire and Impower Joseph Blanchard Capt Joseph French (an older brother of Sampson) and Mr Jn Butterfield or either of them in our names and behalf to Represent to the Gen'l Assembly of this Province the unreasonableness and illegal proceeding of Sundry of the inhabitants of Dunstable in their town meetings the Summer past, and particularly the town meeting July sixth 1747, and the votes at the adjournment of that meeting, and all votes Relating to the choice or Settlement of Samuel Bird as the minister of this town, and pray that they be made void or Otherwise Relieve us in the premises.

There were nineteen men who voted this negative petition

Finally, a petition was presented to Governor Benning Wentworth, and to the representatives in General Assembly, signed by twenty-nine men, stating that the choice of Samuel Bird as pastor and the settlement of his salary was not legal, and asking that the vote taken at that meeting be declared null and void, or to grant the petitioners "Such other Relief as you shall see meet and reasonable " In the House of Representatives May 13, 1748, the following record was made:

> Voted that the prayer of ye annexed petition be granted & that ye meetings mentioned in s'd Petition be & hereby are declared illegal null and void
> D. Pierce chr

In Council May 14, 1748.
The above vote of the House read & concurred
                              THEODORE ATKINSON Secy.
In Council May 17, 1748 Consented to
                              B. WENTWORTH.

This church fight took on party shape, laying the foundation for political differences. It is interesting to note that in estimating the strength of the two factions and their consequent right to vote either for or against the settlement of the pastor, they took an inventory of their yearly income as freeholders. The invoice of the property of the people opposed to Mr. Bird amounted to five hundred eighty-three pounds, while that of his friends only reached the sum of one hundred ninety-three pounds. The revenue accruing from the real estate owned by Sampson French at this time was ten pounds, and the record shows him to have been on the losing side. Mr. Bird was a "New Light,"[1] afterward called Methodist, and it is probable that the differences of opinion among the people can be ascribed to this fact.

While things seemed quiet on the surface, yet for many years they had two meeting houses and no minister in Dunstable; but finally one meeting house was purchased and converted into a dwelling house. In 1761 a town meeting was called to see what doctrine they would support and it was decided to take the doctrines contained in the New England confession of faith, and accordingly a minister was invited to settle with them, providing he would fulfil the duties of a pastor according to the doctrines set out, which again caused the old party differences to arise, and the invited pastor refused to accept the call. For nearly twenty years these differences continued to exist, until finally the town ceased to have anything to say in church affairs.

A meeting was held at the home of Jonathan Lovewell in Dunstable in the "province of New Hampshire," March 30, 1748, of the inhabitants qualified to vote in the choice of town officers. The town officers consisted of five selectmen, who were to be assessors, one constable, two tithing men, two surveyors of highway, two field drivers,

---
[1] Fox.

BURYING GROUND AT SOUTHWICK, MASSACHUSETTS, WHERE SAMPSON FRENCH IS BURIED

two fence "vewers" (one of whom was Sampson French), and three hog constables Twenty men were present at this meeting, seventeen of whom elected themselves to office

This settlement was so harassed by the Indians that the majority of the settlers deserted their homes, and those who were left were too poor to maintain public officials, so that from 1692 to 1768 they had no representatives at the General Court

The old French War broke out in 1755 and from the muster rolls of 1758 is gleaned:

> Return of the Men enlisted for his Majesty's Service within the Province of the Massachusetts Bay in the regiment whereof John Osgood Jun Esq is Colonel to be put under the immediate command of His Excellency Jeffry Amherst, Esqr General and Commander in Chief of His Majesty's Forces in North America for the Invation of Canada.

Following this, twenty-eight names were listed, including that of Sampson French, under date of March 28, 1757 (former expedition 1757), resident of Haverhill and age forty In the same list is found the name of Sampson French Jr, enlisted under date of April 6th from Haverhill, age seventeen, and like his father, had been in a former expedition to Lake George in 1757. Rather an unusual thing for a father and son to be in the same company in the same war. That the father continued in service is evidenced from finding his name on the muster roll of Captain Joseph Smith of Rowley from April 8 to December 12, 1760, also on the muster roll of Captain Edmund Mooers Company, "entered Nov 2, 1759, to Jan 5, 1761 "

The date of the second marriage of Sampson French has been recorded in these pages, and some time after 1761 he removed to Hampden county, Massachusetts, where he died at Southwick, Tuesday, July 19, 1785, aged sixty-eight years

Fox says: A picture of Dunstable as it was before the Revolution, and of the manners and customs, opinions and feelings, doings and sayings of the inhabitants, would be highly interesting To sketch such a picture would require the hand of a master, as well as materials which can now hardly be obtained. A few facts and anecdotes must serve instead.

Slavery was then considered neither illegal nor immoral. Several slaves were owned in this town; one by Paul Clogston. She was married to a free black named Castor Dickinson, and had several children born here, but before the Revolution he purchased the freedom of his wife and children. Slavery in New Hampshire was abolished by the Revolution.

In those days it was customary to drink at all meetings, whether of joy or of sorrow. The idea which was long after in vogue — "to keep the spirits up by pouring spirits down" — seems then to have been universally prevalent. Even at funerals it was observed and in the eyes of many it was quite as important as the prayer. The mourners and friends formed themselves in a line, and an attendant with a jug and glass passed around and dealt out to each his or her portion of the spirit, and the due observance of this ceremony was very rarely omitted. It has been said that sometimes "one more thirsty than the rest," after having received one "portion," would slily fall back from the line under some pretext or other and reappear at a lower place in season to receive a second portion."[1]

Expense of raising a meeting house — about 1740:

Also allowed to Sundry Persons for Provisions & Drink at the raising the meeting house the sums following.

	£ s d
To Joseph Blanchard for Rum & Provisions	2-15-3
To The Rev Mr Thomas Parker	2- 0-0
To Sam'l Colburn	1- 1-6
To Jonathan Chamberlain for a salmon	0- 4-6
To Archebald Stark for a Salmon	0- 9-0
To William Tarble	0- 6-0
To Peter Russell	0-13-6
To Henry Farwell & Joshua Converse	0-15-6
To Benjamin Thompson Esq.	1- 1-0
To Captain Thomas Tarble	1- 6-11
To Capt. William Lawrence	1-16-3
To Captain Jona Bowers	0-18-6
To Capt. Josiah Richardson	1-17-0
To the Rev. Willard Hall	1- 0-0

---

[1] This is stated on the authority of Mrs. Kidder, wife of the Rev. Mr. Kidder, an eye witness.

Stephen Peirce	0- 6-0
Had of William McClinto for Raiseing	
6 glls of Rhum at 18s p Gll	5- 8-0

In 1702 selectmen agreed with Widow Noble "to beate ye Drom and sweepe ye Meetting house for one year for which they will receive two pounds and five shillings "

In 1703 it was voted "to build pewes in ye meeting house where ye plank seats now stand "

It was voted that persons should be seated in the meeting house according to their age and estate, and that "so much as any man's estate is increased by his negroes that shall be left out "

If a man lived on a hired farm, or had obtained his property by marriage with a widow, such property was reckoned at only one-third the value it would have possessed had the man obtained it by his own industry.

Eighth Generation

¹ SAMSON ⁸ FRENCH JR (Sampson,⁷ Joseph,⁶ Samuel,⁵ William,⁴ Thomas,³ Thomas,² Thomas ¹) was born in Dunstable, New Hampshire (now Massachusetts), September 15, 1742 He married Lusannah Root (born September 20, 1752) at Southwick, Massachusetts To them were born:

I   Josiah, born December 22, 1768; married Lucinda Parker

II   Sarah, born November 15, 1770; married Nathaniel Lee To them were born a numerous family of sons and daughters They lived for many years at Chenango (now Glen Castle), Broome county, New York Sarah Lee died in Illinois, aged over eighty years

III.   Thomas, born February 13, 1773; married Polly Hiscock about 1793.

IV   Rebecca, born December 23, 1774; died May 19, 1776

V   Ira, born February 24, 1777; died December 11, 1778

VI.   Submit, born December 14, 1778; married Festus Morgan February 20, 1800, who died September 23, 1800; eight days after his death a son was born to them at the home of Submit's

---

[1] The spelling of the name Sampson was changed in this generation by Samson Jr

father. She married (second) Phineas Merchant, by whom she had sons and daughters. The family lived many years in Otsego county, New York; afterwards at Glen Castle, where Submit (French) Merchant died.

VII. A daughter, born June 3, 1780; died June 12, 1780.
VIII. Lucy, born June 2, 1781; married Michael Tuttle. To them were born:
    1. Lois, born ———; died when fourteen years of age.
    2. A son.

Michael Tuttle was drowned August 21, 1816, while bathing in the Connecticut River.

IX. Clement, born September 1, 1783; married Elizabeth Hawks (born in 1786) in 1803. To them were born:
    1. Franklin, born January 29, 1804, at Deerfield, Massachusetts; married Sally Johnson, in 1827; married (second) Olive Pope February 25, 1830. To them were born two children — a son and daughter. He married (third) Phebe LaMoree, March 20, 1834. To them were born five sons, one of whom died in infancy.
    2. Ira, born September 19, 1805, at Rodman, New York, married May 28, 1829, Hepsibah Lyon. To them were born three children:
        a. Aaron, born March 29, 1831.
        b.
        c. } Twins, who lived but a few hours.

    Ira French married (second) Sally Harrington May 21, 1834. To them were born two children:
        d. Dwight, born May 13, 1835. He has a son, W. K. French, a pharmacist in Worcester, New York.
        e. Salphronius H., born July 16, 1837.

Salphronius H. French, physician, surgeon, and banker, was born at Castle Creek, New York, July 16, 1837, a son of Ira and Sally (Harrington) French; was educated at the Binghamton (New York) Academy, and commenced the study of medicine with his uncle, Dr. S. H. French, at Lisle, New York, in 1857. He attended

Dr. S. H. French

Home of Dr. S. H. French at Amsterdam, New York, built nearly forty years ago

the College of Physicians and Surgeons in New York City for one year, and was graduated from the Albany Medical College in 1859 He began the practice of medicine at Slaterville, New York, in February, 1860, but in December, 1861, entered into partnership with his uncle in Lisle, continuing until July, 1862, when he joined the One Hundred and Ninth New York Volunteers as assistant surgeon, with the rank of first lieutenant. Discharged from the service in 1864 because of ill health, he returned to Lisle, remaining until 1871, when he removed to Amsterdam, New York, where he has since resided Dr. S H French was one of the founders of the Amsterdam Savings Bank and has been its president since it was opened for business in 1887 He has for many years been president of the Amsterdam Free Library, and a trustee of the First Methodist Church He was for several years health officer of Amsterdam, and is a consulting physician of the Amsterdam Hospital. On October 28, 1868, he married Mary A Hurd of Colesville, Broome county, New York Their only child, Charles E. French, was graduated from Princeton University in 1894, and is treasurer of the Amsterdam Savings Bank Doctor French's address is 40 Church street, Amsterdam, New York

  Sally Harrington French died in July, 1837.

  Ira French married (third) Delia Brooks July 12, 1838 To them were born six children

  f. Francis, born June 12, 1839.
  g Mary, born December 9, 1840
  h. Ellen, born December 2, 1842
  i. Lucy, born April 24, 1845.
  j Jane, born June 2, 1847
  k Emma, born March 23, 1851.

3. Root, born February 27, 1807; married Amanda Spencer May 16, 1830 To them were born three children — two sons and one daughter — the eldest son dying at seventeen years of age

Root French was a man of uncommon energy and industry, but few men being his equal in physical endurance In all his business transactions he was strictly honest; was generous to the needy, and ready to extend the hand of kindness to those in affliction. He united with the Baptist church in early life, remaining a consistent member until his death, which occurred September 5, 1866.

4. Ebenezer Smead, born at Zoar (now Charlemont), Massachusetts, April 8, 1810; married Anna Seward. To them were born:

   a. Lucius, born February 2, 1832. Graduated in medicine at Pittsfield, Massachusetts, in December, 1853; located in Hyde Park, Pennsylvania, February 15, 1854; moved to Lisle, Broome county, New York, in 1858; went west in 1861, locating in Anamosa, Iowa. In September, 1862, was appointed first assistant surgeon of the Thirty-first regiment, Iowa Volunteers, which position he resigned June 9, 1863, on account of illness. Married Ellen Cook December 29, 1864, and removed to Davenport in March, 1865. To them was born one daughter — Nellie, born December 10, 1865; married John H. Whitaker September 4, 1901, at Davenport, Iowa. Ellen Cook French died December 11, 1865. April 25, 1867, Dr. Lucius French married (second) Agnes Norval.
   Dr. French was prominent in his profession, being a member of a number of medical associations. He died September 10, 1910, at his home in Davenport, Iowa.

   b. Hepzibeth, born September 16, 1833; died April 19, 1885.

   c. Olive, born November 20, 1835; married Chas. Wood September 23, 1859; died in Binghamton April 22, 1900. One daughter, Rose, born July 2, 1864, married Allen Spencer.

   d. Betsey, born February 9, 1838; married Henry Martin Stanford March 22, 1857. One daughter,

Dr. Lucius French and His Home in Davenport, Iowa

FRENCH AND ALLIED FAMILIES

Rosa Olivia, born October 25, 1859, died March 25, 1862

e Mary, born August 4, 1841; married Isaac Howland June 20, 1866 To them were born·
    aa. William, born March 6, 1871, died April 10, 1873
    bb Frank, born April 17, 1874
    cc Nellie, born May 29, 1877; married Frank Pendell She is the fortunate owner of the account book kept by Samson French to which reference has been frequently made in these pages.

f Orin, born September 23, 1844; died October 23, 1844.

g Carson, born August 21, 1853; married Mina Keeler January 1, 1876; graduated in medicine at Bellevue, New York City, March 14, 1887. Practiced medicine at Lisle, Broome county, New York Is now living at Chenango Bridge, New York

At an early age Ebenezer French manifested a strong mechanical taste, occupying much of his time in constructing pop guns, bows, arrows, and handsleds As he grew older his mechanical genius was directed to experimenting with the construction of shot guns and rifles, and although never given any educational advantages along mechanical lines, yet it was said of him that he could shoe a horse, make a butcher knife, or construct a wagon.

After his marriage, he entered into an agreement with his father to remain at home and manage the affairs of the farm, which arrangement proved so satisfactory that no change was made during the life time of his parents Ebenezer French and his wife were both members of the Methodist Episcopal church, he being for many years superintendent of the Sunday school at Glen Castle, New York

    5 Salphronius Henry, born at Zoar August 26, 1811; married October 6, 1834, Cynthia Harrington They adopted a daughter, Augusta E., who married James Squire

Dr. S. H. French, of Amsterdam, New York, writes the following sketch of his uncle, Dr. S. H. French, of Lisle, New York:

Salphronius Henry, fifth and youngest son of Clement and Elizabeth French, was born at Zoar, now Charlemont, Massachusetts, August 26, 1811, and in 1814 went with his parents to Chenango, Broome county, New York. During his early life he was much afflicted with rheumatism, which condition of health led his father to give him an opportunity to attend school, where sufficient taste for books and thirst for knowledge was developed to lay the foundation for his future professional career. When fifteen years of age he entered a select school in Binghamton, New York, where he pursued his studies with great industry for four summers, paying his expenses by working in gardens, etc., and teaching school in the winter season. In October, 1830, when nineteen years of age, he began the study of medicine, and the following spring an opportunity was afforded to further pursue his work in the office of his uncle, Doctor Hawks of North Adams, Massachusetts, which offer was gladly accepted, as his resources were limited to his own exertions. In 1832, he attended a course of lectures in the Berkshire medical institution of Massachusetts, from which school he graduated in December, 1833. After receiving his diploma he found he had not sufficient funds to carry him home, so sold a book and trunk to raise the necessary amount for the journey. The severe struggle with poverty and adverse circumstances, the lessons of economy, and the self-reliance gained during that struggle, were of priceless value in after life.

Shortly after reaching home he formed a partnership with Dr. P. B. Brooks of Lisle, Broome county, New York, which continued for two years. Doctor Brooks removed to Binghamton and Doctor French (who had been away for a few months) received so urgent a request from the citizens of Lisle, that he returned and resumed his practice, continuing in this place until incapacitated by disease.

Doctor French joined the County Medical Society in 1834, of which organization he was president during the years of 1842, 1850, and 1852. He was elected a delegate to the State Medical Society in 1846, and in 1850 was made a permanent member of the organization; was also a member of the American Medical Association He enjoyed a large practice, and while keeping fully abreast with his profession in the reading of medical books and journals, yet found time to become a proficient student in botany and geology, which studies he pursued as a form of recreation About twenty young men received their elementary medical education in his office, some of whom have risen to distinction in the profession

In political belief Doctor French was a Whig, and was elected to the legislature by that party in 1846. He was possessed of strong convictions along temperance lines, and never sacrificed his opinions in behalf of any candidate for office

In early life, Salphronius French became convinced of the truths of the Christian religion, and was for years a faithful, consistent member of the Methodist church

Captain Frank Landers, to whom the following certificate was given, is now a resident of Webster City, Iowa, and Dwight French, justice of the peace who acknowledged the document, was the older brother of Dr S H French of Amsterdam, New York

> I do hereby certify that I am still treating Frank E Landers of the Sixteenth New York Battery for various ailments, and that he is unable to travel or perform any military duty.
> Lisle January 12th 1864   S H. FRENCH M D
> Sworn and Subscribed before me this 12th day of January, 1864
>   DWIGHT FRENCH
>   Justice of the Peace

About two years after his marriage, Clement French [1] started with his family for the wilderness country of Sandy Creek, New York After a tedious journey they arrived in the month of March at Harrison (now Rodman), New York, where he purchased fifty acres of land and erected a log cabin, which was the birthplace of his sons, Ira and Root In the meantime his father, who had removed to Zoar (now Charlemont), Massachusetts, wrote to Clement urging his return, which request he complied with, and here his sons Eben-

---
[1] From *Outlines of the Genealogy of the French Family*, written in 1875, by Dr S H French (fifth son of Clement and Elizabeth French) of Lisle, N Y

ezer and Salphronius were born. About this time a company — composed largely of Boston people — had purchased a large tract of land lying west of the Chenango River and north of the Susquehanna. This tract — still known as the "Boston Purchase of Ten Townships" — was being rapidly settled, and the glowing descriptions to which Clement listened, together with an enterprising spirit, caused him to again seek a home in the forests of New York. He soon had an opportunity to purchase fifty acres of land on Castle Creek, six miles north of Chenango Point (now Binghamton), where he and his family, after a journey of two hundred miles, arrived on June 1, 1814. The location was a lonely one, but one wagon passing his dwelling during the first year of his residence in that place. The years of 1815 and 1816 are memorable in history as cold seasons, severe and repeated frosts occurring every month in the year, and as a result no corn was raised during this time and but few potatoes, so that the food was necessarily scanty and plain. The nearest school was two and a half miles distant; thus the smaller children were entirely debarred from its benefits. The third summer of their residence in this place a school district was organized, and Clement French's wife was employed to teach the school, their stable having been prepared for that use.

In 1818 Clement sold his farm to his father, Samson French, and purchased for six dollars per acre a tract lying one and one-half miles distant, on which land he built a cabin in the spring of 1819. With the help of his sons he succeeded in paying for this farm and purchased more land adjoining. Although by occupation a farmer, he devoted rainy weather and evenings to cooper work and the making of shoes, the story being related of his having made a pair of shoes on his eightieth birthday.

In religious faith Clement French was a Methodist; he was a firm supporter of the temperance cause and of the various benevolent and charitable institutions of his day.

Clement French died in October, 1865; his wife Elizabeth died November 1, 1864.

X. Clara, born September 7, 1785; died March 6, 1786.

CATALOGUE OF THE DESCENDANTS OF SAMSON AND LUSANNAH FRENCH
Written by Ezra Williams

XI   Clara (second), born February 22, 1788; married Harry Tuttle, brother of Michael Tuttle. Clara died February 28, 1839

XII. Julia, born August 25, 1792; died May 29, 1793

XIII Charlotte, born January 10, 1795, married Ezra Williams September 12, 1814, at Northampton, Massachusetts To them were born six children, the names of three being known
1. Daniel, born November 14, 1815; died May 26, 1816
2 David.
3 Arthur

Charlotte French Williams died in Washington, D C, in 1853, and some of her descendants now live in Philadelphia, Pennsylvania. Ezra Williams (husband of Charlotte) was born May 31, 1790 He moved with his family to Westford, Otsego county, New York, where they resided for seven years, going from thence to Detroit, Michigan, from which place they removed to Washington, D C, in 1845 He was a man of good business ability and was engaged in many pursuits in his earlier life Was made a judge and sat on the bench while in Detroit He was an extraordinary penman, being employed for many years as a clerk in the office of the secretary of war at Washington, D C, which position he held at the time of his death, which occurred during Lincoln's administration He wrote "A Catalogue of the Descendants of Sampson and Lusannah French," a photograph of which appears in this volume

The "Account Book" of Samson French Jr contains the following reference to this family· "My daughter today — Williams — with her two sons, David and Arthur, and they arrived here on Saturday Sep. 29, 1832, about 10 of the clock, and left here on Monday at 8 of the clock and I parted with them for last time & I never expect to see them anymore so farewell."

Samson French Jr was born in Dunstable, New Hampshire,

September 15, 1742. He married at Southwick, Massachusetts, in 1768 Lusannah Root who was born September 20, 1752. The date of his mother's death is not known, but his father remarried when he was six or seven years of age. Samson French Jr. enlisted when sixteen as a soldier in the army during the "Old French War." He served during two campaigns, a portion of the time being under General Amherst, helping to reduce the walls of Louisburg. The rest of the time he was engaged in batteauxing (boating) on the Mohawk River, carrying supplies to the soldiers at Fort Stanwix (now Rome).

Dr. S. H. French says: "There is a tradition that the second Samson went to war on account of friction between him and his step-mother. Whether this be true or not, it is certain that his father went to war at the same time, and she must have been a mighty uncomfortable woman if they preferred the war up near Newfoundland to the war at home."

When about twenty years of age Samson Jr. returned to Dunstable and soon after with his father removed to Hampshire county, Massachusetts, where he married Lusannah Root in 1768.

From a letter written to Dr. S. H. French, at Amsterdam, New York, by J. M. French, of Milford, Massachusetts, is made the following extract:

> Regarding the age of Sampson [Samson] Jr., I find upon looking up the matter a second time that this list was taken from the muster rolls of 1758 and that the date of enlistment was April 6th of that year, while the "1757" referred to the date of a former expedition in which he was also engaged; at least so I understand it. That would make him sixteen, as you said you had before supposed. As to his lying, while I agree with you that it is "a thing no French ought to do," yet when we consider that as I now think *he only lied* one year; and further the *he lied in a good cause* — namely that he might be accepted as a soldier to fight the enemies of his country (there was no cowardly sneaking out of the fight — I couldn't have borne that) I am inclined not indeed to justify but surely to excuse him.

An extract is here given from a letter received by the author from Dr. S. H. French of Amsterdam, New York, to whom an appeal had been made for information concerning the early history of Samson French Jr.:

182

I was told by my Father I was born in New hamshire in the town of Dunstable on the 15 day of September in the year of 1742 & this day the 15 of September in the year of 1832 I Call my Self ninety years of age & that by my self and I have my Self

Photograph made from Account Book kept by Samson French Jr.

FRENCH AND ALLIED FAMILIES 123

You ask about the military history of our early ancestor, born 1742 In 1776 he was about thirty-four years old, his son Thomas about three years old, and his son Clement not yet born Sampson was the only one who could have taken part in the Revolution, and he did not, for the reason that he was at heart a Tory He did not take up either side actively, but said he thought the war was a mistake and King George's government good enough My father told me he was drafted twice and each time furnished a substitute, which he could have done as he had considerable property Some one ought to have punched this particular Sampson in those days, but he was six feet tall and had a red hot temper, so he escaped. But there is something to be said for our Sampson As we look at it now, a man to be patriotic in 1776 must be willing to help destroy the regular government In 1861 it was considered patriotic to support and defend the regular government My own experience leads me to think that serving in the army as a soldier intensifies and renders more permanent attachment to and respect for a regular government Now our Sampson enlisted in the British army under General Amherst and served in the war between England and France before the Revolution Perhaps this experience helped color his later opinions

The census of 1790 gave Southwick a population of eight hundred forty-one, and the name of Samson French appears first in a list of five chosen for selectmen in 1792, he also being numbered among the earliest settlers of that town The village contained one hundred twenty-three houses, which sheltered one hundred forty-eight families Philadelphia was the capital, and George Washington president of the United States Eight days were consumed in making the journey from New York to Washington, so a little idea can be gained of the condition of the country at this time This census gives Samson French as having two males over sixteen years in his family. These must have been Josiah and Thomas, one under sixteen, which was Clement, and five females — his wife and four daughters then living making this number It is quite gratifying to note that the number given in the census corresponds exactly with the family record, for the people of that day objected to the taking of the census, for they imagined that it was a scheme for increasing their taxes, so were cautious in giving data to census enumerators They also objected on religious grounds — a count of the inhabitants being considered a mark of divine displeasure. However, the census was probably taken to find out the military strength of the country, and was given with considerable accuracy, due no doubt to the fact that if any inhabitant failed to give a true account he would forfeit twenty dollars — one-half of which went to the assessor, the other half to the United States government.

The census of 1790 forms a unique inheritance for the nation, for each of the states concerned thus has a complete list of the heads of families in the United States at the time of the adoption of the Constitution. The first census act was passed at the second session of first Congress, and was signed by President Washington March 1, 1790. Nine months were allowed to complete the enumeration; seventeen marshals had charge of this census; number of assistants estimated at six hundred fifty; total population at that time as turned in by the enumerators, 3,929,214; entire cost of the census, $44,377. The Union at this time consisted of twelve states. There were no roads; bridges were unknown.[1]

The records in the court house at Springfield, Massachusetts, contain a number of transfers of property between the years 1771 and 1798, bearing the signature of Samson French Jr. and Lusannah French. Perhaps the one contained in Vol. 37 is the most unusual, owing to the signatures of the daughters being affixed as witnesses to the document:

> Samson French of Northampton in county of Hampshire for £480, deeded tract to Warham Edwards of Southwick, containing about eighty (80) acres with house and barn.
> Dated Oct–30–1798. Signed sealed and delivered in presence of us Warham Parks — Julia Parks — Lucy French. Signed sealed and delivered in presence of Submit French   Polly French
>
> SAMSON FRENCH
> LUSANNAH FRENCH

During all the years of his married life Samson French Jr. kept an account book, mentioned in the history of his father, Sampson French, as being the property of Mrs. Nellie Pendell of Binghamton, New York. This account book is of much value historically, as it contains the "Portion" given to each of his children at the time of their mar-

---
[1] From census report of 1790.

riage. the records of births and deaths, as well as many items of interest to the succeeding generations

From the "Account Book" kept by Samson French Jr is copied the "Portion" given to Josiah, at the time of his marriage to Lucinda Parker:

			£
1791 November		By one cow	4-00-00
1792		By one horse	8-00-00
1799 November		By one yoke of Steers	3-00-00
		To seed wheat & Genl Parkis Order	2-10-00
		By one horse that he let his Uncle Aaron French have	10-00-00
		By a 2 yr old heifer at Mr Waitdells Strongs with calf	2- 8-00
			29-18-00
			12- 8-00
			£42- 6-00
1805 February 26		cash	6- 0-00
		By paying Mr Smith and others to the amount of five pounds thirteen shillings	4-13-04
		By paying his note at Mr Hastings dated January 24-1801	7- 2-07
1799 March 6		Then sold the mill pond & Josiah received ten pounds at Mr Hastings	
		By a watch one pound ten shillings	11-10-00
		By paying Doctor Ashley	18-08
			12-08-08
1794		By 71 pounds of Beef at 2 pence half penny pr pound	14-10
		By cash Lent two Dolers	0-12-00
1795 April		By one bushel & half ry	0- 9-00
May		By cash paid for fish 9/0 shillings & Salt 2 shillings paid for us both	0-11-00

	Josiah swapped his steers the first week in March with Allen	
1796	by one peck salt	1–00
	By cash 3 shillings to get Shad	0– 3–00
	By five days work to get his hay at the mill pond the beginning of august	15–00
	By time to get a load of hay in my stable from for	2–00
	By two days to get coopers shop with Perkins	6–00
	By paying Sam Fowler	2– 3–00
	By two days with the team to sow his rye at the mill pond	0– 6–00
	By one pair of shoes of Capt Ives	7–00
1797	and one day to go with Tom	3–00
May	By other two Dollars to get fish	0–12–00
1798	By cash to pay on Execution in favor Thomas Eten 15 dollars	4–10–00
October	By cash lent — 3 shillings	0– 3–00
November	Turnips 3/2 and Staves one	
1803	hundred and 20	0– 6–00
		———
April 2	Then took his mare to keep	12– 6–04

By the first date given in this record it would seem that the marriage of Josiah occurred about 1791 and that his father continued to contribute to his support, is shown by the items under later dates.

The exact date of Sarah's marriage to Nathaniel Lee is not of record, but from this same "Account Book" is gleaned the following, as the portion given to her at the time of her marriage:

1792		
Sept. 19	SARAH	
	Sundry goods	£1–13–00
	Some Tin & earthen ware	0– 4–00
	Slise & tongs & tramel	0–18–00
	Sundry small things	0– 3–08
	One set tea cups & pepper castor	0– 3–00
	Iron hollow ware 1 pot & dish Kittle & 1 tea kittle & 1 spider	0–18– 2
	1 brass kittle which Nathaniel	

		L	s	d
1794	My son Thomas Dr towards his portion			
Novemb[e]r	by cash to go to the commencemt	0	18	0
1795 march 3	by cash for expences to move to Cambridg	4	12	2
	by cash paid Capt Gittel for going to Cambridge with his Hay Eight Doll[ar]s	2 9	0	
in May 1795	by a yoke of oxen twenty pounds	20	0	0
	sending cattle at the same time five pounds £5 0 0			
	by part of one Summer's Work after he was married 5—			
1797	by part of a crop of grain that he come from Cambridg	5	0	0
Feb[r]y 13	by cash — one doll[a]r			
1 may 1797	by one barel of cider to pay Turner	0	18	0
	by one bushel & half of oats	0	6	0
1798 January	in moving him from Cambridg by cash lent to pay Jared Hickok Eleven dollars	3	6	0
1799	by one cow & calf	4	15	0
January 1800	by one two year old steer past	4	0	0
	by my horse mare at twelve pounds	12	0	0
	one by a chist of drawes at five dolers			
	towards the mare	£ 47	3	0
1804 Septem[ber]	by a hors at 45 dollars	13	10	0
		60	13	

PORTION GIVEN TO THOMAS, BY HIS FATHER — SAMSON FRENCH

	paid 2 dollars toward it & I paid the remainder that was	0-12-00
	By bailing the said kittle (Above)	0- 7-00
	6 chairs at 3 shillings per chair	0-18-00
	1 old chest of drawers	0-15-00
	1 Table	1- 0-00
	24 yds linen for sheets & piler bers	2- 8-00
	1 Bed bolsters and tickens	1-14-00
	1 Bed stead & rope	0- 6-00
	9 yards Table linen	0-18-00
	2 Rugs	1-16-00
	1 — 1 cow	4- 0-00
	1 Pair and irons	0- 6-00
	1 Great wheel	0- 7-00
1803		
July 20	1 colt 2 years old	5- 0-00
		25- 3-10

The first record of any gift to "my son Thomas" is under date of November, 1794.

	By cash to go to the Neversink	£ 0-18-00
1795		
Mar 3	By cash for expenses to move to Cambridge	4-12-02
	By cash paid Capt Gillet for going to Cambridge with his sleigh eight dollars	2- 8- 0
In May 1795	By a yoke of oxen twenty pounds contrary credit at the same time five pounds £5-0-0	20- 0-0
	6 By part of one summers work after he was married £5	
1797	By a part of a crop of grain when he came from Cambridge	5- 0- 0
Feb 13 —	By cash one dollar	
1-May-1797	By one barrel of cider to pay Turner	0-18- 0
	& one bushel & half of oats	0- 6- 0
	for moving him from cambridge	
1798		
January	By cash lent to pay Jared Hiscock eleven dollars	3- 6- 0

1799	By one cow & calf	4-15- 0
	By one two year old Steer past	4- 0- 0
	By my roan mare at twelve pounds	12- 0- 0
	Credit by a chest of drawers at	
	five dollars toward the mare	£47- 3- 0
1804		
September	By a horse at 45 Dollars	13-10- 0
		60-13- 0

LUCY

Oct 1799		
	Sundries	£2-18-11
	1 pot 6/1 Kettle 4/6 1 tea kettle 6/	1- 0- 3
	1 spider	3- 9
	1/2 gross furniture	2- 0- 3
	1 whele	0- 1- 5
	1 shalloon quilt [1]	3- 4- 1
	39 yds old linen at 1 shilling per yard	1-19- 0
	1 bed	3- 8- 0
	1 poor bed	1-15- 0
	1 pair dog irons	0- 3- 0
	3 green dining chairs	1- 1- 0
	1 looking glass	0- 6- 0
	1 new Rug	1-18- 0
	Table linen	0-11- 6
	Slise & tongs	0- 9- 0
	1 pillion ("pilon")	0-15- 0
	1 pr flats	0- 3- 0
		21-19- 3

SUBMIT

1800		
Jany 29	1 chest of Drawers	£1-10- 0
	1 fall leaf table	1- 4- 0
	3 Green chairs	1- 1- 0
	1/2 gross furniture	2- 0- 3
	2 half Tubs	4- 0
	1 Stand table	0- 6- 0
	1 Looking glass — 12 earthen plates	0-12- 0

---

[1] A shalloon quilt was one pieced from woolen cloth.

	1 Bed and bedding	6- 9- 0
	Another bed not so good	4-14- 0
	Some things taken out of the house	0- 5- 5
	Hollow ware & sundries	3- 8- 5
	Table linen	0-12- 0
Apr-1804-	One iron kettle 11/4	0-11- 4
	Trimming to chest of drawers	0- 6- 9
	Set of knives & forks & 2 glasses	0- 6- 4
	1 Slise & tongs — The slise good and the tongs poor	0-13- 0
	3 chairs at 5 shillings per chair	0-15- 0
	1 small brass kettle	0- 9- 0
		25- 6- 6

On page 183 of the old "Account Book" we find the account of "My son Clement".

1804	By cash to go to Sandy Creek	£1- 4- 0
	By cash paid for a gun at Hastings	0-18- 0
1805	By cash	0-15- 6
	By pork	0-14- 0
	By ten dollars worth of goods at Smith's store	3- 0- 0
Febry 26	The day he set out for Sandy Creek — then let him have in cash fifty dollars and one shilling	15- 1- 0
	By a pair of steers	3- 0- 0
Febry 1808	By cash delivered to his Father Hawks seventeen dollars	5-12- 0
	Paid Mr Butler for pasturing his steers 3 dollars & quarter	0-19- 6
	By paying his note to Nathan Smith Dated Feb 21-1805 of	1- 1- 0
1806		
April	By a horse	13-10- 0
	by ten dollars in cash	3- 0- 0
		37-13- 0
		Dec
	FOR DAUGHTER CLARY	1805
	1 Shalloon bed quilt	£3- 1- 1

17 pounds "gees" feathers & bed tick bolsters & pillars	5- 0- 3
Slise & tongs new & good	16- 0
48 yards of linen for sheets	3- 6
India cotton for Table cloth 6/9 pint glasses	16- 4
2 bed quilts — not so good	2- 5- 0
2 yards table linen	4- 0
Goods at Ely & Stevens	4-12- 0
One poor bed	1- 0- 0
1 Dish Kittle & pot & tea kettle	0-15- 0
Dog irons 6/ — spider 5/6	0-11- 6
Chest of drawers	0-18- 0
3 chairs	0-15- 0
1 Table	1-04- 0
1 Little wheel	0-18- 0
1 great wheel	0- 5- 0

In addition to the amounts given his children at the time of their marriage, there were various items of interest in this "Account Book," some of which follow and will serve as illustrations:

1797 November 9th day	21 pounds of gees fethers at his hous but by my Stilards they waid but only 20 pounds.
1801 October	3 bushels winter apples at one peck of ryer per bushel.
1802 25 October Deerfield	David Graves Dr by dying blue yarn 2 pounds & 10 ounces 0-6-2
Feb. 9, 1805	Then reconed and found due to me six days work in dressing flax to be done in 30 days. Joseph Wise Jr. Account balanced Apr. 24, 1805.
Jan. 14. 1813.	Let Joshua Hawks have one hog drest to carry to Boston weighed 336 pounds.
1816 June 15—	Winchel & Chapen by one bushel ry bye a mistake we got wiske and they charged the wisk & we did not charge the rye 0-1-00

1817		
Feb – 15th –	Set out from Northampton for Decatur — arrived there the 19th	
1817		
Sept –	by one horse to Sheffield in the Bay State charged to Jonathan French	
	15 pounds venison	36
	5 quarts whiskey	47
	1 pint whiskey ½ pt rum	14
	Set out from Thomas at Decatur Mar 9th and arrived at chenango 12th of March 1819	
1823		
Feb –	Dr Brainerd Dr	
	To a part of a bottle of Harlem oil and my mare to ride 8 or 10 miles	
June 12 –	To mare to ride one day I know not where	
Aug 21st –	Paid him six pounds of sheeps wool 3 dollars and made a lumpen reckoning I took his receipt in full	
1823 –	Mr Bishop dr by my wagon to the pint mill & back to his hous at 3 sence pr mild 25 sence by my wagon to the twice to the pint 42 sence	
1824		
Feb 3rd	To 3 pounds of cheese at 8 cents per pound	
1824		
September 20	paid to Mr Abraham Bever for carding of wool by the hand of phines Marchant one shiling in ful for the cardine of about two pounds of wool	
1825	by my black mare & wagon Somwhere beyond the pint twice & cared his wife & staid over Saberdy gon 2 or 3 days 1 25 sence	
1828		
Dec 25 –	To a brass kitel two dollars	
	Began to board with Thomas Nov 17 – 1832 –	
	Left Thomas June 1st 1833 and went to live with Submit & Phineas and that day left him & paid him $10 & 3 crockery milk bowles	

The year before his death, the following was recorded

1833	
January 22 –	that day I went to Parley Lee & found him at his fathers lees hous & I held a smal noat against him &

> I told him I was in great Want of it & if he wod not settel it soon I would cal for it in a nothe way & he flue in a grat pashen & said he would pay the 1 dollar & 37 senc if I would produs it & that should be the last money he should pay for he could or he wold put the morged horses where I col not find them. I mit git my money if I could for he declar never woul pay me."

The story is told of Samson French being asked for the loan of some money, security for the same to be given on a span of horses. The old gentleman insisted on being shown the animals, and after a somewhat lengthy tramp through the woods to the place where they were supposed to be found, nothing but a pair of wooden saw horses was to be seen. It is needless to add that the money was not forthcoming.

From the old "Account Book" the following record is taken:

> Samson French removed his family from Massachusetts to Decatur, Otsego county, New York, reaching the last mentioned place February 19, 1817.

The deed to the property he sold on leaving the Bay state follows:

SAMPSON FRENCH. — DEED. — TO CLEMMON FRENCH

To all people to whom these presents shall come: Greeting. Know ye, that I Sampson French of a place called Zoar, in the county of Berkshire and Commonwealth of Massachusetts, Yeomen,— For and in consideration of the sum of one Hundred dollars in part payment to me in hand paid before the ensealing hereof by my son Clemon French of Zoar afore said, Yeomen, and in consideration of the love and good will I bear to my son Clemns as aforesaid do give him one Hundred Dollars of my free will as full payment for the Residue of the premises hereafter mentioned in this deed the receipt whereof I do hereby acknowledge and am fully satisfied, contented, and paid, *have* given, granted, bargained, sold, aliend, released conveyed and confirmed, and by these presents do freely, clearly and absolutely give, grant, bargain, sell, alien, release, convey and confirm unto him the said Clemon French, his heirs and assigns forever a certain piece of land on the northerly part of the farm conveyed to me by Elder Francis Wheeler, and is bounded as follows: beginning at the northwesterly corner of said farm at the foot of Hoosack mountain thence north, sixty seven Degrees East thirty six Rods to the bank of Deerfield river; thece south thirty one degrees east forty two rods; thence south twenty one degrees East Eighteen Rods to a birch tree, thence south Eighty two degrees west Eighty Eight rods, thence northerly on the west line of my Land to the first mentioned bounds, containing Twenty acres *To have and to hold*, the before granted premises, with the appur-tenances and privileges thereto belonging to him the said Clemon his heirs and assigns; to his and their own proper use and benefit and behoof forever, and I the said Samson French and my heirs and administrators, do covenant promise and grant unto and with the said Clemon his heirs and assignes forever.

That before and until the ensealing hereof I am the true, sole, proper and lawful owner and possessor of the before granted premises, with the appurtenances. And have in myself good right, full power and lawful authority to give, grant, bargain, sell, alien, release, convey and confirm the aforesaid, and that free and clear, and freely and clearly executed, acquitted and discharged of and from all former and other gifts, grants, bargains, sales, mortgages, wills, intails, jointures, dowries, thirds, executions, and incumbrances whatsoever *And furthermore*, I the said Samson for myself, my heirs, executors, administrators, do hereby covenant promise and engage the before granted premises, with the appurtenances, unto him the said Clemon his heirs and assigns forever, to warrant, secure and defend, against the lawful claims and demands of any person or persons whatsoever

In witness whereof I have hereunto set my hand and seal this twenty fourth day of April in the year of our Lord one thousand eight hundred and twelve

Signed, sealed and delivered
in presence of
Samuel Pettibone   SAMSON FRENCH
David Tuttle.

From Decatur the family removed to Broome county in 1819 and settled on a farm in Chenango, now known as Glen Castle, situated about six miles north of Binghamton, which farm was a part of the tract known as the "Boston Purchase of Ten Townships." Binghamton was incorporated as a village April 2, 1813, and it was here that Samson French and his family got their mail and went to "meeting"

The first saw-mill in Broome county was built in 1788 on Castle Creek by one Henry French, and the first grist-mill was built on Fitch's Creek, in Kirkwood, in 1790

In the office of the clerk of Broome county may be found the following, under date of April 14, 1819:

Deed from Clement French and Clara, his wife   Roland Lee and Polly his wife to Samson French — consideration $250. Lot No. 43 Town of Chenango — Boston Purchase containing 50 acres.

Samson French purchased the farm owned by his son Clement, on which he erected a comfortable dwelling house and out-buildings, but beginning to feel the weight of years, he gave to his daughters — Mrs. Lee and Mrs. Merchant — all of his land lying west of the highway and retired from business. The health of his wife was gradually failing, and she died September 11, 1829, being seventy-seven years of age. After her death, he spent most of his time visiting among his children, having two sons and two daughters living within a radius of two miles.

On page 36, Vol. 13, Broome county, New York, Records, an indenture made December 18, 1824, between Samson French of Chenango, Broome county, New York, and Sarah Lee, wife of Nathaniel Lee of the same town, for the sum of $70, a piece of land properly described, containing eight acres more or less — signed by Samson French. Witness — Clement French.

In the same volume, on page 416, an indenture made May 24, 1813, between Samson French of the town of Chenango, Broome county, and Parley Lee of the same place — consideration $400.

A parcel of land lying in this county, containing 30 acres more or less, which was subject to a mortgage executed by him to Martin Hawley & Julius Page. Signed SAMSON FRENCH.

Some idea of the conditions surrounding these people may be gained, when it is recalled that at this time there were no steam engines, locomotives, gas, or electric lights; no talking machines, steamships, power cranes, blast furnaces, rolling mills, or dynamos. Neither were they harassed by the fear of any Indian foe who might be lurking near, as were the people of the former generation. Their lives in most respects were quiet and uneventful — just the plain simple record of honest everyday people.

Soon after his ninety-second birthday, Samson French suffered a severe stroke of paralysis which destroyed his ability to walk or carry on conversation. In January, 1834, five years after the death of his wife, he died at the home of his son Clement. Although in comfort-

179

A Record of my Sons & Daughters Births

First Josiah was Born December the 22 day the 1768

Sarah was Born November the 15 the 1770

Thomas was Born Febewary the 13 the 1773

Rebeker was Born December the 23 the 1774

Ira was Born Febewary the 24 the 1777

Submit was Born December the 14 the 1778

the Child Born the 3 day of June the 1780

FAMILY RECORD KEPT BY SAMSON FRENCH

Lucy was born June 2 the 1781

Clement was born September the [?] of the month & the first day of the week & the first our of day in the yer 1783

Clary was Born the Septr 7 the 1785

Remembrance Clary was Born in February the 22 in the 1788

Iula was Born August the 25 the 1792

Charloty was Born January 10 day 1795 on Saturday

Ezra Williams was born May 31st 1790 —

A record of my age & my wife

I Squire was borne September 15 day 1[?]

& Lurenah my wife was Born in September 20 day 1752

FAMILY RECORD — CONTINUED

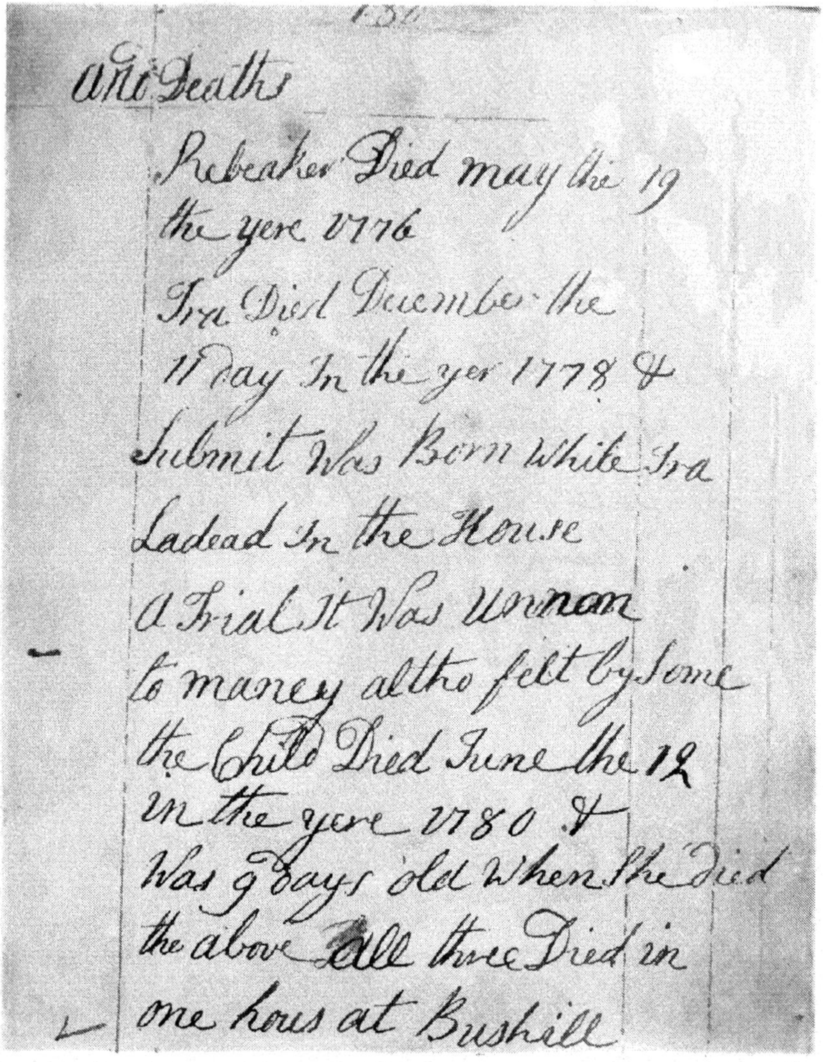

131

And Deaths

Rebeaker Died may the 19
the yere 1776
Ira Died December the
11 day In the yer 1778 &
Submit Was Born While Ira
Ladead In the House
A Trial It Was Unknown
to maney altho felt by some
the Child Died June the 12
in the yere 1780 &
Was 9 days old When she died
the above all three Died in
one hous at Bushill

Family Record — continued

Feather French Died the 19 of July
on Tusday in the yere 1785
Clary Died March the 6 the 1786 & was
Six month old wanting one day when she died
Pula Died on our Lextion day on may
29 the yer 1793 & was Eight mons.
old and 4 days old when She died
my doufter Lucy Frillet died February
28 day the yer 1821 was 39 years old and
8 months wanting 2 days

Holona Lee Bern march 21 1792

FAMILY RECORD — CONTINUED

Festus Moraien died September 23 day 1800
& was maried 3 mons wonting 3 day

Festus was born the 1 day of october 1800 at
my hous the eight day after his Father died

Mikel Tuttle Died august 21th 1816
on Winsday

Lusunah my most Efenate Companien
& wife Died Setember the 11 day 1829 and
was 77 yers old wanting 9 day & died in my hous
in Chenango in the County of broom in the
State of nue york & we lived as husband & wife
twogether over Sixty yers & altho death came
on Sloley oder it cam two Soon & I felt the
frat los & I my self was at that time 87
eighty seven wanting four days but I think
we shant be but a litel whil parted

FAMILY RECORD — CONCLUDED

able circumstances through life, he gave of his property to those of his children who were most in need, so that when all the funeral expenses were paid, only fourteen dollars of his estate remained

Samson and Lusannah French were buried on the farm where they had lived, but when it was sold their bodies were removed to the Wilcox burying ground near Castle Creek, Broome county, New York, where they now rest

Ninth Generation

THOMAS[9] FRENCH (Samson Jr,[8] Sampson,[7] Joseph,[6] Samuel,[5] William,[4] Thomas,[3] Thomas,[2] Thomas[1]) second son of Samson Jr and Lusannah French, was born in Southwick, Massachusetts, February 3, 1773 He married Polly Hiscock (born in Southwick 1774) in 1793 To them were born eight children:

I   Marietta, born in Southwick 1794; married David Stever at Chenango, Broome county, New York, in 1830 To them were born seven children.
   1 Marietta, born in Chenango 1832; married —— Van Alstine, and resided at Pike Creek, Broome county.
   2. William, born in 1834 or 1835 In 1861 he was living at Norwich, New York.
   3 Jane, born in 1834, married Samuel Bishop
   4 Dolly, born in 1840; married —— Johnson
   Three more children were born of this union, but their names are not of record

II   Samson, born January 19, 1796, in Cambridge, Massachusetts, married at Decatur, Otsego county, New York, March 3, 1818, Elizabeth Seaward (born February 7, 1798) To them were born thirteen children

III.   Nancy, born in Southwick 1798; married Philo Ferris To them were born nine children
   1 Wesley
   2 Lucy Jane
   3 Hannah Eliza
   4 George

5. Polly Lodema.
6. Mariah.
7. Watson.
8. Philo.
9. Phoebe.

The four last named children were minors at the time of the death of their grandfather, Thomas French.

IV. Polly, born in Southwick about 1801; married Marcena McIntyre. Have record of only four children born to them:
1. Ebenezer.
2. Franklin.
3. Chauncey.
4. Thomas.

V. Hiram, born in Southwick, Massachusetts, about 1804; married Amanda Waterman, at Chenango, Broome county, New York, about 1826. To them were born five children:
1. Thelismar, born 1828; married Anna Wright.
2. Jared A., born 1831; never married; died about thirty-one years of age.
3. Julia, born 1833; married Levi Phillips.
4. Alta, born 1835; died when about nine years of age.
5. Amanda, born 1837; married J. G. Sanders.

The children of Hiram and Amanda French were all born in Chenango, with the exception of Amanda, who was born in Michigan, where the family had removed about 1836 or 1837.

Amanda (Waterman) French died when her daughter Amanda was a babe; later, Hiram French married Rhoda ———. They had no children and were not living together at the time of his death.

VI. Thomas, born in Southwick, Massachusetts, about 1806 or 1807; married in 1830, Polly Temple of Chenango, Broome county, New York, daughter of James and Alenda Temple, who moved from Buckland, Massachusetts, to Chenango. To them were born eight children:

POLLY TEMPLE, WIFE OF THOMAS FRENCH JR.

THOMAS FRENCH AND THREE OF HIS CHILDREN

FRENCH AND ALLIED FAMILIES

1. Nancy M, born January 20, 1833; died December 29, 1836.
2. Mary A, born November 7, 1833; died May 18, 1853, Burlington, Michigan
3. Rebecca J., born in Chenango December 2, 1835; married J S. Hudson, died at Ganges, Allgum county, June, 1877.
4. James Marshall, born in Chenango December 29, 1837; married Catherine C Osborne
5. Sydney J, born in Chenango July 30, 1840, died in Burlington, Calhoun county, Michigan, June 5, 1849
6. Martin V, born in Chenango, July 17, 1842; married Bell Cole
7. Dallas A., born in Burlington, Michigan, January 5, 1845, married Ida Loomis
8. Nancy Alenda, born in Burlington, Michigan, October 20, 1847, married William Cowles

The five oldest children were born in the old mill house, at Glen Castle, New York

VII Chauncey, born at Tyringham, Massachusetts, September 20, 1812; married September 11, 1833, Catherine Bishop (born April 6, 1811) of Castle Creek, Broome county, New York To them were born four children, two dying in infancy

1. Marcena, born October 29, 1834, Decatur, New York; now living in Denver, Colorado.
2. Helen Melissa, born Glen Castle, April 5, 1837; married Judson Alderman (born August 2, 1836, Castle Creek) at Castle Creek, Broome county, New York; both now living in Anamosa, Iowa They have two children, Newell and Etta

VIII. Harriett, born in Decatur, Ostego county, New York, in 1816; married Edwin Lee, at Glen Castle, New York, about 1839; she died June 22, 1861 To them were born three children

1. Alamanson, born Glen Castle, New York, about 1842

2. Polly Jane, born Glen Castle, New York, June 11, 1844; died at Glen Castle, September 20, 1864.
3. Morris, born about 1847.

After the marriage of Thomas French and Polly Hiscock, they moved to Cambridge, Massachusetts, as an item taken from his "Portion" in the "Account Book" of Samson French shows:

Mar. 1795   By cash for expenses to move to Cambridge 4–12–2

That his residence in this place was but a brief one, is shown from another entry made in the same account book, under date of January, 1798, where he enters a charge for moving Thomas from Cambridge back to Southwick. From this place he removed to Tyringham, as there is record of his buying on the 13th day of March, 1812, from Stephen Seaward of Decatur, Otsego county, New York, a piece of land for which he paid fifty dollars, his residence in the transaction being given as Tyringham. About that time (1812) he removed with his family from Tyringham to Decatur, the deed for the land not being recorded until 1827. Although Thomas French was by occupation a farmer he had learned the business of cloth dressing, which he pursued many years in this place, removing in 1826 to Glen Castle, Broome county, where he purchased a farm of nearly two hundred acres quite well covered with timber. Here he reconstructed a grist and saw-mill, situated on Castle Creek, which ran through the farm, and added cloth dressing and dyeing to the establishment.

When Thomas first moved to Glen Castle he lived in what is known as the "old mill house," which was built in 1810 and is still standing, being now occupied by Mr. George Johnson. In 1830 he built south of the mill house, and when completed moved to this new home which faced the west. This structure has suffered some changes during the passing years, but the general outline still remains the same.

Thomas French was successful in business and acquired quite a fortune for those days. He possessed one tract of land which was covered with a fine growth of timber, and the story is told of some parties who wished to gain his consent to hold a camp meeting in this grove, but feared his refusal, for it was well known that he did not believe in these meetings. Upon gaining courage to ask, they were

Rear View of Old Mill House (built in 1810)
Home of Thomas French   The Old Grist Mill on Castle Creek

surprised to receive from him a ready assent, providing the living trees should not be harmed He afterwards gave the site on which was built the Methodist church in Glen Castle, and attended its services

Polly, wife of Thomas French, died in 1839 after an illness of six years, and in 1843 he married (second) Elizabeth, widow of Reed Brockway of Lisle, New York, with whom he lived until his death, which occurred August 21, 1861 He was buried by the side of Polly, his first wife, in Glen Castle cemetery, where many of the French family have been laid to rest.

WILL OF THOMAS FRENCH, ON FILE IN THE COUNTY CLERK'S OFFICE, IN BINGHAMTON, BROOME COUNTY, NEW YORK

In the name of God — Amen, I Thomas French of the town of Chenango, co of Broome and state of N Y aged 87 years, and being of sound mind and memory do make, publish and declare, this my last will and testament in manner following — that is to say —

First — I give and bequeath unto my wife to whom I have been married about seventeen years, a good and comfortable maintenance and support during her natural life, or until she shall again marry, which I hereby make chargable upon my real estate And I give and bequeath to her, one cow which she is at liberty to select from my cows — and my one horse wagon I also give and bequeath all the household furniture, bed, bedding and clothing which belonged to her when I married her and which she brought with her to me, and also one half of the bedding and linen made and belonging to me since said marriage, also all comfortables that have been made by my said wife and her daughter All of which provision for her I intend to be in lieu of dower

Second. I give and bequeath unto my son Samson French now residing in the state of Ohio, the sum of Three hundred dollars to be paid out of my real and personal estate

Third I give and bequeath unto the heirs of my deceased son Hiram French the sum of Four Hundred dollars to be paid as aforesaid

Fourth I give and bequeath unto the heirs of my deceased son Thomas French the sum of Four hundred dollars to be paid as aforesaid

Fifth I give and bequeath to my son Chauncey French the sum of Three hundred dollars to be paid as aforesaid

Sixth. I give and bequeath unto the heirs of my deceased daughter Nancy Ferris the sum of One hundred and twenty five dollars to be paid as aforesaid.

Seventh. I give and bequeath unto my daughter Harriet Lee the sum of thirty dollars.

Eighth. I give and bequeath unto my children living and to the heirs of those deceased all the remaining and residue of my estate not herein otherwise disposed of, to be divided equally among the living and an equal share to the heirs of each deceased child.

Ninth. I give and bequeath unto my daughter Harriet Lee and to the daughter of my deceased daughter Marietta Stever, all the remaining and residue of my household furniture beds and bedding and clothing and linen not hereinbefore disposed of to be divided the one half to Harriet Lee and the other half to my said granddaughter.

Tenth. I give to my sons living at my decease my wearing apparel, and it is my will and I direct that the aforesaid legacies be paid within three years after my decease, and that the distribution of my estate as above specified be made within the same time.

Lastly. I hereby appoint my son Chauncey French and B. N. Loomis of Binghamton N. Y. executors of this my last Will and Testatment with full power and authority to sell and convey my real estate, to carry out the provisions of this will, hereby revoking all former wills by me made. In witness whereof I have hereunto set my hand and seal this 24th day of April 1860.   Signed   THOMAS FRENCH. (L. S.)

The above instrument, consisting of one sheet, was at the date thereof signed, sealed, published, and declared by the said Thomas French as and for his last Will and Testament in presence of us who at his request and in his presence and in the presence of each other have subscribed our names as witnesses thereunto.

    Signed   FRANK LOOMIS of Binghamton, Broome Co., New York.
                 E. G. CRAFTS "   "   "   "   "   "

INVENTORY OF PROPERTY OF THOMAS FRENCH DECEASED

Property set off to the widow under the Revised Statutes:

1 cooking stove and furniture.
1 Parlor stove.
2 Spinning wheels — 1 swifts.
1 family bible — family library consisting of 20 Vols.
1 cow — 2 swine.
    Wearing apparel of widow.
1 bedstead — 1 bed.
2 cotton sheets — 1 coverlid — 1 pillow & case.
1 table — six Windsor chairs — 6 knives and forks.

FRENCH AND ALLIED FAMILIES

6 tea cups & saucers
6 plates, one sugar bowl
1 tea pot — 1 milk cup
    Property set off to widow under the law of 1842

1 Bay mare	$85
1 church $1 1 clock $1 50 1 top buggy $50 1 chain 8 00	60 50
6 flag bottom chairs $3 1 looking glass $1 75	4 75

    Property inventoried as assets —

1 note against Henry Siver, dated July 13, 1859, for $80 Endorsed 18 Sept / 60, $50 Mch 16/61 $5 00	
1 note agt Silvester Booth date 29 – April / 59	5 05
1 note agt P & P Brooks date 4 april 56 for $80 Endorsed $70	
1 note agt T Lorm & H. Shear date 4 Feby – 1860	15 87
1 note against Ezra Johnson date April 1861	55 00
	226 17
Money in hand	3 00
1 yoke of oxen $100 1 brindle cow $15 pied cow 18	133 00
1 old cow brace on horns $12	
lopped horn cow $12	24.00
1 old red cow $15 1 young red cow $16	31.00
1 hog $6 28 bush corn in ear 5 60	11.60
358¾ lbs butter	60.99
Twin calves $5 00 1 heifer calf $3	
1 bush turnips $2 38	10 38
40 bush potatoes $8 1 – 2 horse wagon $5 cart & rigging $7	20 00
A one horse wagon $15 1 plough $1 50	16.50
2 ploughs 50 cts Harrow $2 75 — 1 harrow $1	4.25
1 cutter $6 1 log chain $1 1 do 50 cts — 2 chains 38	8 13
1 dung fork .75c — 3 pitch forks 75c	
59 milk pans $7 38	8 88
89 bush oats $24 92 — 48 bush buckwheat $18 50	43 42
2 crow bars $/ 13 1 sett whiffle trees 75	88
1 lot of old ham $2 1 buffalo robe 75	2 75
Small lot of lumber	2 75
1 neckyoke 25c 3 ox yokes $2 50	2 75
a quantity of old iron $6 1 horse fetters .13	6.13
1 ox sled $1 50 — 1 bob sled .25c — fanning mill $2 50	4 25
2 rakes 13c — 2 flasks .13c — 1 cutting box 50c	76
barril and dry casks $1 25	

1 tar sack .25c	1.50
	638.34
½ bbl vinegar $1 — cask & boiled cider .13c	1.13
pork in barrel $2 1 rose coverlid 1.50	3.50
1 plad coverlid .75c 1 bed & bedding $14.00	14.75
1 black cow $18 1 table .75c	18.75
1 quilt $1 2 pillows .37c 1 cotton sheet .25c	1.62
1 quilt .25c 1 candle stand $1	1.25
1 bed & bedding in kitchen $12	
1 server .50c	$12.50
5 cotton sheets $1 1 linen sheet .75c	1.75
4 pair pillow cases .50c 2 table cloths .50c	1.00
1 tureen .25c 6 german silver teaspoons .38c	.63
1 desk & drawers	3.50
1 work stand	.25
2 looking glasses	.50
1 chest of drawers & 3 chests $1	
3 milk pails .63c	1.63
1 basket .25c — 1 wood saw .25c	
1 hand saw .25c	.75
4¾ augurs .75c 1 chisel .25c 1 square .13c	1.13
1 plane & mallet 1 adze 1 axe 6cts	.25
1 drawing knife 13c — 1 cattle leader 3c	.16
3 bush hooks .25c 2 pr stillyards $1	
1 wedge .25c	1.50
1 steel trap .13 cts 1 pr sheep shears 6 cts 1 strainer pail 6c	.25
1 market basket 6c 1 iron kettle $1 1 potash kettle .50c	1.56
Trunk .38c 1 brass kettle .50c	.88
	707.58
1 rock chair .75c 1 bedstead 75	1.50
16 yds carpet 1.25 1 table spread .38	1.63
12 milk pans 1.50 — 1 strainer pail 50c — 1 wooden pail 6c	2.06
5 table spoons .13c 1 cullender 6c quart cup 6c	.25
wash bowl 13 mortar & pestle 25c	.38
1 pr brass candle sticks 13c 1 fluid lamp 18c	.31
1 iron cricket 6c wire strainer 13 50 pieces crockery $1.25	1.44
1 pan 13c 1 jar .25 2 jugs .25 1 oil can .18	.81
1 sugar box 13 2 wash tubs 50c	1.25

FRENCH AND ALLIED FAMILIES

14 tons hay	77.00
1 bedstead 1 25	1.25

794 84

Dated this 11th day of November A D 1861

WALTER CARY } Appraisers
DANIEL D LEE }

This list of names is a copy of the original record in the court house, Binghamton, New York:

The heirs of Thomas French were

Chauncey French, a son, at Binghamton, N. Y.

Marietta Van Alstine, residing at Pike Creek,

Wm Stever, residing at Norwich, Chenango Co , N. Y.

Jane Bishop and Dolly Johnson residing at Chenango, Broome Co , N Y heirs of Marietta Stever, a daughter deceased,

Thomas French, residing at Westford, Otsego Co., N. Y.,

Lucy Queal, at Whetstone P O , Morrow Co , Ohio,

John French, Polly Smith (whose place of residence after diligent search cannot be located),

Oscar French, Martin French, Alva French, severally residing at Whetstone, Morrow Co., Ohio, heirs of Samson French deceased,

Thelismar French, Amanda Sanders and Julia Phillips, severally residing at Burlington, Calhoun Co Mich. heirs of Hiram French — a son — deceased,

Ebenezer McIntyre, Franklin McIntyre and Chauncey McIntyre, severally residing at Maine, Broome Co , N. Y. and

Thomas McIntyre, whose place of residence after diligent inquiry cannot be ascertained, heirs of Polly McIntyre, deceased

Rebecca Hudson and Martin French, severally residing at Burlington, Calhoun Co , Mich ,

Marshall French, whose place of residence cannot be ascertained,

Aaron D. French and Nancy Alenda French, severally residing at Burlington, Mich , heirs of Thomas French — a son — deceased,

Polly Jane Lee, Charles Lee, and Morris Lee, severally residing at Binghamton, Broome Co , N Y , heirs of Harriet Lee, a daughter of Thomas French, deceased,

Wesley Ferris, whose place of residence after diligent inquiry cannot be ascertained, Lucy Jane Ferris, whose place of residence after diligent inquiry cannot be ascertained, Hannah Eliza Ferris, Enoch George

Ferris, Polly Lodema Ferris, Maria Ferris, Watson Ferris, whose places of residence after diligent search cannot be ascertained — heirs of Nancy Ferris, daughter deceased,

The above named Aaron D. French, Nancy Alenda French, Polly Jane Lee, Morris Lee, Philo Ferris, Phebe Ferris, Maria Ferris and Watson Ferris are minors.

That the said deceased left him a widow surviving named Elizabeth French, residing in the town of Chenango, Broome Co., N. Y. Petition therefore prays that the said last will and testament may be proved — Aug 29-1861

The following deed is on file in the court house at Binghamton, New York:

This Indenture made the twenty-ninth day of June in the year of our Lord one thousand eight hundred & twenty nine Between Joseph C. Yates of the city & county of Schenectady of the first part & Thomas French of the town of Chenango in the county of Broome of the second part

Witnesseth that the said party of the first part for & in consideration of the sum of seven hundred dollars Lawful money of the United States to him in hand paid by the said party of the second part the receipt whereof is hereby confessed & acknowledged hath granted bargained sold remised released aliened & confirmed & by these presents doth grant bargain sell remise release alien and confirm unto the said party of the second part & to his heirs assigns forever all that certain piece or parcel of land situate lying & being in the town of Decatur in the county of Otsego in the fifth allotment of Skinners Patent being the northern one hundred acres of lot number thirty six in the subdivision of said allotment —

In witness whereof the said party of the first part hath hereunto set his hand and seal the day and year first above written —

Sealed and delivered in presence of
EDWARD YATES   JOSEPH C. YATES "L S"

The following transactions in real estate are given to show the fluctuations in land values during a period of forty years, in the region in New York where the French family resided:

In 1829 Joseph C. Yates of Scheneectady deeded to Thomas French of Glen Castle, New York, for seven hundred dollars, a farm in the town of Decatur, Otsego county, New York. In 1836 Thomas French deeded this farm to Samson French, his son, for the sum of nine hundred dollars. Samson French sold this property in 1847 to

John Shelland of Westford, New York, for nineteen hundred dollars, and Shelland sold it to Edwin C Cheseboro May 20, 1847, for the same amount as he paid for it On March 1, 1851, the latter deeded this land to Charles Devanpeck for twenty-five hundred dollars Ten years later, Devanpeck sold to Samuel Russ for thirty-six hundred fifty dollars, who in turn transferred to Giles Goodenough in 1868 for five thousand dollars April 1, 1873, Giles Goodenough sold the farm to Ichabod Bulson for fifty-five hundred dollars, who transferred it to David Cipperly for forty-five hundred dollars, and he in turn to Mrs Hallock for four thousand dollars; Mrs Hallock to Fred Winnie — the present owner — for twenty-seven hundred dollars, which last named party has refused an offer of four thousand dollars, considering its value to be at least five thousand dollars in the year 1912 Mrs Hallock had taken the farm to satisfy a mortgage of four thousand dollars which she held against it What a history is interwoven with these transfers!

Tenth Generation

SAMSON[10] FRENCH (Thomas,[9] Samson Jr.,[8] Sampson,[7] Joseph,[6] Samuel,[5] William,[4] Thomas,[3] Thomas,[2] Thomas[1]) second child of Thomas and Polly (Hiscock) French, was born in Cambridge, Massachusetts, January 19, 1796; married Elizabeth Seaward (born February 7, 1798) at Decatur, New York, March 3, 1818 To them were born thirteen children·

    I   James Thomas, born January 29, 1819, at Cherry Valley, married Calphurnia Treat, in Decatur, Otsego county, New York, in 1844; died April 19, 1867, at Warnerville, New York

    II.   Lucy Oletha, born February 16, 1821, at Decatur, New York; married Rev. Atchison Queal, of Worcester, New York, April 9, 1845; died March 15, 1885, at Des Moines, Iowa A complete history of Lucy French will be found with that of her husband, Atchison Queal

    III. Stephen Henry, born December 30, 1822, in Chenango, New York; died April 18, 1823

GENEALOGICAL HISTORY OF THE

- IV. A son, born March 5, 1824, in Chenango, New York; died April 13, 1824.
- V. Dewitt Clinton, born April 21, 1825, in Chenango, New York; died October 18, 1825.
- VI. John Seward, born October 29, 1826, in Chenango, New York; married Susan Barfoot (born October 15, 1837) at Kickapoo, Illinois, November 28, 1857. John Seward French died December 24, 1904, at Wayne, Nebraska.
- VII. Mary, born December 6, 1829, at Decatur, New York; married Dr. Nathan M. Smith. Mary died June 28, 1908, at Kingston, Missouri.
- VIII. Orestus, born May 7, 1832; died March 10, 1837.
- IX. Oscar L. R., born October 18, 1834, in Decatur, New York; married Mary Clevenger of Morrow county, Ohio, November 15, 1855, who died February 17, 1856. Oscar married (second) December 24, 1857, Cidney Ellen Keech of Westchester, Pennnsylvania. Oscar French died in Johnsville, Ohio, March 26, 1896.
- X.
- XI. } Martin and Marvin, born January 29, 1837; Marvin died August 16, 1839. Martin married Belle Chamberlain of Ames, Iowa, in 1877. One child was born of this union — Clare Vernon, who died in infancy. Martin French died in Ames, Iowa, August 1, 1900.
- XII. Alva C., born April 15, 1839, at Decatur, New York; married Lydia Elder.
- XIII. Calvin D., born May 4, 1842, at Decatur, New York; married Libbie Jones of Clarksville, New York.

When fourteen years of age, Samson French removed with his parents from Tyringham, Massachusetts, to Decatur, Otsego county, New York, where he worked on the farm with his father and also learned the business of dyeing and fulling cloth. After his marriage to Elizabeth Seaward, they began housekeeping in Cherry Valley, New York (where the Indian massacre occurred in April, 1780), and lived there for two years. They then moved to Decatur, at which place they remained for three years, at the expiration of which time

MARY FRENCH SMITH
Taken in 1857

SAMSON FRENCH'S HOUSE AT DECATUR, WHERE LUCY
FRENCH WAS MARRIED TO ATCHISON QUEAL

FRENCH AND ALLIED FAMILIES

they took up their residence in Glen Castle, Broome county, where they lived until 1827, when they returned to Decatur, purchasing the farm owned by Samson's father, Thomas French, who moved to Glen Castle The house is still standing where Samson French lived, and where a number of his children were born. No changes have been made in this building, but new siding and a slate roof have replaced those originally used In this house Lucy French, mother of the author, was married April 9, 1845.

As the sons of Samson and Elizabeth (Seaward) French grew to manhood they acquired habits of industry and frugality, working on the farm during the summer and in the winter attending school in the "French" school house, which is still used for that purpose and is of much historic interest Their son, James Thomas French went to Ohio in the spring of 1842, where he spent the summer, returning to Decatur in August of the same year, and it was not long until the Ohio "bee was buzzing" in his father's bonnet

Some years before, Daniel Flint, who married Mehitable Seaward, sister of the wife of Samson French, had moved to Marietta, Ohio In 1846 they returned to Decatur, New York, for a visit, and while at the home of Samson French, told such wonderful stories about the "Ohio country" that he returned home with them. Daniel Flint owned forty acres of land near Iberia, Morrow county, Ohio, and together they looked that part of the country over, seeking a suitable home for the French family They found what is now known as the Flint farm, it then being owned by a Mr Dana, who had bought a large amount of land in Morrow (then Marion) county Flint was to buy the land and make the first payment in the name of Samson French, as the latter had not sold his farm in the east at that time Returning to his home in New York, Samson sold his farm the following January, and in March they removed with all their children except Thomas and Lucy (they having married previous to this time) to Ohio, going to Fort Plain, New York, where they took a canal boat for Sandusky, Ohio, from which place they went in covered wagons (which had carried grain to that city from the southern part of the state) to the farm which Samson French supposed he had bought on the state road near Iberia. Imagine his surprise on arriving, to find that Flint had bought the place for himself, and was living in a log cabin near the south line of the farm. There being another log cabin about one-half mile distant, Samson moved his family into this house and began search for a home. He finally located in Washington township, about one mile north of Smith's Mills, buying eighty acres of land from Joseph R. Baldwin, who lived in Pennsylvania. Here he built a log cabin with one room and a "lean-to" across the back, which was used for a kitchen in the summer and woodshed in the winter. The cabin also contained a "loft" with a window in each end, which was reached by very steep stairs. The following extract is taken from a book kept by Samson French: "Moved on to my farm Oct 19 – 1847 and commenced anew to clear my land."

This land was heavily timbered with maple, beech, oak, and hickory — forty acres of which had been "deadened" and was ready to be cleared when he purchased it. In addition to this, he hired a man to "slash" ten acres, who felled the trees in windrows, picked up and burned the brush and smaller logs, for which he received five dollars per acre. The logs that could not be burned were "logged" by Samson and his sons. When done with the help of the neighbors, they called it a "logging." The remainder of the land was cleared without hiring help. The ashes from the burning of the logs was scraped up in piles and sold to a man who lived in Iberia for one or two cents a bushel, to be used in making potash.

This eighty acres of land had a road running along its north and east side, and in addition to this was fenced into seven fields. Some idea of the number of rails that Samson and his sons were obliged to split in order to make the necessary amount of fencing for the farm may be gained when it is known that the fence was seven rails in height and required fourteen rails to each rod.

A year or so later he purchased forty acres across the road north of his farm from Mr. Dana. This land contained what was known as the "little meadow," which consisted of about three acres surrounded by timber. In this little opening, "Johnny Appleseed" had some time before planted an orchard, but the seeds had been placed so close together that the orchard was just a big clump of trees, the fruit it bore being of a very inferior quality This man — known as "Johnny Appleseed" — whose real name was Jonathan Chapman, was born in Boston in 1775 Being somewhat eccentric in his nature, he conceived the idea of traveling over the country planting apple seeds, which he gathered from the cider mills in Pennsylvania. These seeds he carried in leather bags, and whenever he came to an open place on the loamy lands that bordered the creeks, or rich secluded spots hemmed in by giant trees, he would plant some of these seeds, so that at the time of his death his labors had borne fruit over a hundred thousand square miles of territory. He also believed that the offensively odored weed known as dog fennel, possessed valuable anti-malarial virtues; so he procured some of these seeds and sowed them in the vicinity of every house in the region of his travels In consequence, the weed spread over the whole county and caused almost as much trouble as it was intended to avert, and to this day the dog fennel introduced by Johnny Appleseed is one of the worst grievances of the Ohio farmer.

In 1849 an orchard was set out on the south side of the home of Samson French, the trees for which were bought at Cardington from a Quaker named Morris. The hens used to "steal" their nests in the grass in this orchard, and the quails would lay their eggs in the hens' nests The diary kept by Elizabeth, wife of Samson French, records under date of October 25, 1860 "Our folks have gone for the first time to make cider from our trees "

In 1854 Samson French planned to build a frame house, but after getting the logs to the mill and having the lumber ready, he found that forty acres of land adjoining the forty he had bought two years previous, could be purchased, so he sold his lumber and secured the land for about six hundred dollars; two years later selling the same to his son-in-law, Atchison Queal, for one thousand dollars The house which he planned was not built until 1857 and the following is the article of agreement made with the "carpenter and joiner".

An Article of Agreement between Samson French of Morrow Co,

State of Ohio, and Adam Sell of Morrow Co., State of Ohio, for the building of a house by said Sell for said French, made this 27th day of Feb. 1857. Samson French agrees to furnish all the building material, shingles, a foundation ready to lay the timbers upon, to board the workmen while laboring in construction of said house, also furnish all panel doors and the window sash. Adam Sell agrees to do the carpenter and joiner work of the house, to be 34 feet long and 24 feet wide double sealed, partitioned below as follows: A sitting room in the northeast corner, a bedroom in the southwest corner, a recess for a bed at the southwest side of the sitting room, a clothes press directly south of bed recess accessible from the southwest corner bedroom. A kitchen in the northwest corner and south of the kitchen a bedroom, buttery and stairway. The cellar accessible from the buttery also by a door near the southwest corner of the house from the outside, the cellar doors to be batten doors. The upper part or chamber to be partitioned unto four rooms. The doors above are to be batten doors. There is to be one east, one west, and one north outside door. There is to be four north, four east, (two above and two below) two or three south and three west (two above and one below) windows. Said Sell is to hang all the doors, fit all the window sash, make all the batten doors inside stairways, case the bed recess, fire place, put on the mop boards, chair railings, etc. In short to finish the carpenter and joiner work of the house in a substantial workmanlike manner by the tenth day of Oct., 1857. For which Samson French agrees to pay Adam Sell $135.00, one-half to be paid when the work is done, the other half in two months from that time. We hereby bind ourselves to fulfill our parts of the above agreement respectively by the signature of our names.

SAMSON FRENCH

Dated Feb. 27, 1857.   ADAM S. SELL [1]

The interior arrangement of the house was somewhat changed in the construction, but the general plan of the building remained the same.

In the fall of 1857 the family moved from the log cabin into their new home. One side of the sitting room contained a large fireplace, which would hold a log four feet in length. In the winter a "backlog" about two and one-half feet in circumference was first put in the fireplace; then two smaller ones of graduated size, were placed on the larger log; then with the "andirons" in front and a "forestick" upon them, the wood was piled on this foundation, and in a few moments a roaring fire would cause the circle about the hearth to widen.

---

[1] Adam S. Sell enlisted in the Civil War and died in Libby Prison.

SAMSON FRENCH HOUSE, BUILT IN 1857
Morrow County, Ohio

Demit from Masonic Lodge at Worcester, New York, given Samson French in 1833

There was always plenty of apples and nuts with which to while away the evening hours, and after the "chores" were done, Samson would pull off his boots with the old fashioned "boot-jack," put on his "slips" and sitting in his old arm chair (now the property of the author), would read his paper, eat his scraped apple, and doze by the fire. He never used tobacco in any form and was a great advocate of temperance, drinking nothing stronger than sweet cider

Samson French was a lover of good horses, and has been known to say, "The grass never grows under my horses' feet, for I drive fast in winter to get out of the cold, and in the summer to make a breeze." He was for a number of years justice of the peace, being known throughout the country as "Squire French"; in politics, a stanch Republican, his last vote being cast November 6, 1860, for Abraham Lincoln When quite a young man, very much against his wife's wishes, he joined the Ancient Free and Accepted Masons, and became a member of Charity Lodge, in Worcester, New York, which later surrendered its charter, probably in the year 1833, as the demit which was given to Samson French bears date "seventeenth day of September in the year of Masonry A L 5833," meaning the year of Light, and is fixed by adding four thousand years to the Christian era, which would make the date correspond with that given

After the removal of Samson French to Ohio he affiliated with the lodge at Mt Gilead, where he continued a faithful member during the remainder of his life Much as his wife disliked Masonry, she consented to have him buried with Masonic honors His sons all belonged to the Masonic fraternity, as do most of his grandsons, as well as some of the next generation

In the spring of 1825, Samson French was induced to buy a ticket in the Union Canal Lottery of the Commonwealth of Pennsylvania He may have had visions of vast wealth when he made this purchase, but if so they faded, as no record is made of their realization. All there is to show that he was ever interested in this scheme is the ticket itself, which was preserved by his wife and may have been kept to remind him of his folly The French family, so far as is known, have never made a living except by hard work

In June, 1860, all of the children of this family were at home together, with the exception of the daughter Mary. Their son John had been out in the world for seven years, and Thomas had never visited his parents' home since their removal to Ohio, thirteen years previous. In view of these facts and the advancing age of their parents, it was decided to have their "likeness" taken together, which was accordingly done. On that visit they presented their father with a gold headed cane which at his death was to go to the eldest son and so on down the generations, it now being in the possession of Leslie R. French, of Schenevus, New York.

Samson and Elizabeth French performed a similar service for posterity the same summer, as the diary of the latter bears the following entry: "Friday Sept – 14 – Not well this morning. Went to Mt. Gilead today — had our likeness taken to leave for the children — we have performed a good office."

Samson French was a member of the Methodist church, he having been brought into the faith during a series of meetings held in the "French" school house at Decatur, New York. That he was a faithful consistent Christian may be known from the following resolution written by himself, under date of January 4, 1842:

> Samson French   Resolve made with the assistance of God to Serve him with all my might mind and strength   January 4th, 1842
> February 22 still continue of the same mind and have been Blessed to a wonderfull rate when faithfull.
> December 17–1852 still striving to pursue the christian course

On April 11, 1861, occurred the death of Samson French, and on August 24th following, that of his wife Elizabeth. Of their immediate family but two remain — Alva C. French, living at Galion, Ohio, and Calvin D. French of Binghamton, New York.

At a special meeting of Mt. Gilead Lodge No. 206 of Free and Accepted Masons called by the worshipful master on the account of the death of Samson French, the following resolutions were adopted unanimously:

> Whereas, in the dispensations of an all wise Providence, our worthy Brother, Samson French, has been removed from this Terrestrial Lodge to

Lottery Ticket held by Samson French

THOMAS FRENCH JOHN FRENCH OSCAR FRENCH

MARTIN FRENCH ALVA FRENCH CALVIN FRENCH

the Celestial on high, "that spiritual building not made with hands, that house eternal in the heavens" where the Supreme Architect of the universe presides, therefore

Resolved — that we have heard with deep regret of the death of our esteemed Brother, who was one of the true and tried Masons during the Morgan excitement that withstood firmly the storms of persecution which swept over the land and for a time covered with obloquy the known and recognized Members of our Fraternity whenever found, and who clung with an enlightened zeal to the tenets of our order, "Brotherly Love Relief and Truth";

That in his death this Lodge has sustained the loss of a valuable and cherished Member, the craft a devoted and consistent workman, his family a kind husband and affectionate father, and the community an upright and exemplary citizen;

That we sincerely and heartily sympathize with his afflicted family in their irreparable berevement, and tender them the consolations found in the promise of Him who "tempers the wind to the shorn lamb" that He will be a husband to the widow and a father to the fatherless;

That at the request of our deceased Brother, and in token of our high regard for him as a Mason, this Lodge will attend his funeral and give him a Masonic burial, and wear the usual badge of mourning for thirty days,

That the Secretary present a copy of these resolutions, under the seal of the Lodge, to the family of the deceased

Wm S Clements	
Wm H Burns	Committee
Jno C. Baxter	

SEAL   In testimony whereof I have hereunto set my name and affixed the seal of said Lodge this 18th day of April A D. 1861

Silas Holt, Sec'y of
Mt Gilead Lodge No 206 of F A M.

Elizabeth, second daughter of Stephen and Lucy (Ingalls) Seaward, was born February 7, 1798; she married Samson French (born January 29, 1776) at Decatur, New York, March 3, 1818 To them were born thirteen children In those days the name Elizabeth was nicknamed Betsey, and by this latter name she was always spoken of in her family She was a sensitive, retiring child, thinking no evil of any, and wronging no one by word, act, or thought Elizabeth early took upon herself a large share of the burdens of the family, assisting her mother in the duties and responsibilities of the home.

Before her marriage she spun the flax for her linen, and the wool which made her blankets and "coverlids." Such accomplishments as these all girls were expected to acquire before they were deemed competent to marry. At the early age of ten she made a "sampler," thus learning the cross-stitch, later making a "needle book" in the same stitch. In after years, the family records of her grandfather Seaward and of her father's family were kept in this book; also a record of her own birth and marriage, as well as the births of her children.

Elizabeth was given a common school education and gained much additional information by the reading of books and in study at home. She taught school for two summer terms in an adjoining district, living with her parents. She early united with the Methodist Episcopal church and was a faithful conscientious Christian during her entire life.

Elizabeth was small in stature, but endowed with ability and energy; she met life's problems bravely on all occasions, finding time from her manifold household duties to teach her older children the catechism, they in turn helping to teach the younger members of the family. She was a careful, prudent mother, with puritanical ideas as to the raising of her family, ever being loved, respected, and obeyed by her children.

The Seaward family were closely bound together by the ties of affection and took great pleasure in visiting and keeping in touch with each other. In 1860 — the year before Elizabeth's death — she kept a diary. Her health was much impaired and she was gradually failing, but each day found something for which to be thankful. On Saturday the 24th of March, she wrote in her diary: "My dear cousin, Eliza Garfield, has come to visit us; how glad I am to see her, as we have not seen each other in forty-five years. Sister Mary Flint came too."

In September of the same year, Elizabeth, in company with her sister, Mrs. Flint, went to visit her cousins, Eliza Garfield and Alpha Boynton, living near Cleveland, Ohio. On Sunday, the 24th, her diary reads: "Went to Solon; heard cousin James Garfield preach."

On the 31st of December she wrote: "I am now about to close my

Sampler made by Elizabeth Seaward

Needle Book made by Elizabeth Seaward and later used by Her for the Family Record

diary Little did I think at the commencement of the year I should live to see its close Omnipotent power has ruled I am thankful to Him for all mercies"

In the following February (1861), seventh day, she wrote· "My birthday has again arrived. I wonder and am astonished that my Heavenly Father has seen fit to still keep me alive No doubt it is for the best Oh that I may have patience and wisdom to direct me aright, that I may not murmur or complain against His chastening rod, but in the hours of grief and pain may lean upon my God"

The last entry in this diary follows· "My beloved companion, Samson French, departed this life after four weeks painful suffering with fever, the eleventh day of April, 1861 I was sixty-three years old the 7th of February; my companion was sixty-five the 19th of January."

Elizabeth (Seaward) French died August 24, 1861, and was buried by the side of her husband in the Ebenezer church-yard, about five miles northeast of their home The stones which marked their graves having been broken, were replaced by their grandchildren with one granite stone in the summer of 1911, a matter of regret to the family being an error in the spelling of the name, which was cut in the stone as Seward, the original and true spelling being Seaward

The following very curious and ancient prediction, entitled, by popular tradition, "Mother Shipton's Prophecy," was published about 1576, and was found among the papers belonging to Elizabeth French:

>   Carriages without horses shall go
>   And accidents fill the world with woe.
>   Around the earth thought shall fly
>   In the twinkling of an eye
>   The world upside down shall be
>   And gold be found at the root of a tree
>   Through hills men shall ride
>   And no horses be at their side
>   Under water men shall walk,
>   Shall ride, shall sleep, shall talk
>   In the air men shall be seen

In black, in white, in green.
Iron in the water shall float
As easy as a wooden boat.
Gold shall be found, and shall be shown
In a land that's not now known,
And no man living under the sun
Shall know when the end of the world will come.

Eleventh Generation

JAMES THOMAS FRENCH was born in Cherry Valley, Ostego county, New York, January 29, 1819; married Calphurna Treat in Decatur, New York, January 2, 1843. To them was born one child:
I. Leslie Russell, born September 18, 1847; married Ann Groff February 2, 1868. To them were born two children:
    1. Mary F., born July 14, 1869; married Theodore Knapp; live at Elk Creek, Otsego county, New York; two children.
    2. Harry G., born November 24, 1873; married Grace Witt in October, 1895. To them have been born two children. Reside at Schenevus, New York.

Soon after the birth of James Thomas French, his parents moved to Decatur, where he grew to manhood. He obtained a common school education in the "old French school house," attending school in winter and working on the farm during the summer months. In addition to the work on the farm, he assisted in the dyeing and fulling of cloth in the mill and continued in this work for his father for a year after attaining his majority. His health becoming somewhat impaired and hoping a change might prove beneficial, he went in the spring of 1841 to Franklinville, Cattaraugus county, New York, where he attended school. The following winter he taught near Franklinville, receiving fourteen dollars per month for his services. In the spring of 1842, his health being much improved, he started for the west, trusting to find lucrative employment. He went to Buffalo, New York, from there to Cleveland, Ohio, by boat, and down the Ohio Canal, visiting Cincinnati and many other points on the Ohio River; but finding no employment to his taste, he turned his face homeward, reaching Decatur August 11, 1842. The following January he was married and later moved to Westford, Otsego county, New York, where he took up the study of medicine and was given a diploma by the "Thompsonian Botanic Medical Society," of Otsego county, New York. After practicing his profession for a few years, his failing health required him to give up his country patients and confine his attention to office practice alone.

In politics James Thomas French was a Democrat and held the office of postmaster from June 16, 1853, until the year 1861, when his successor was appointed by President Lincoln. He was made a Mason April 11, 1865. In November, 1862, he purchased what was known as the "Spafford farm," where he lived until April, 1866, moving to Warnerville, Schoharie county, New York, where he died April 19, 1867. After his death, his wife Calphurna lived with her son, who moved to Elk Creek, where he owned a saw-mill and was engaged in the lumber business for a number of years. She died in 1900. Leslie R., son of James Thomas and Calphurna French, is now living (1912) at Schenevus, Otsego county, New York.

JOHN SEWARD FRENCH, born in Chenango, Broome county, New York, October 19, 1826; married Susan, daughter of Adam and Elizabeth Barfoot (born at Kickapoo, Illinois, October 15, 1837) at Kickapoo, Illinois, November 28, 1857. To them were born:

    I. Harry Seward, born April 30, 1858; married Anna Thomas. They live at St. Louis, Missouri. No children.

    II. Flora, died in infancy.

    III. Nellie, born September 5, 1861; married William A. Ivory February 22, 1888; died at Wayne, Nebraska, October 1, 1891. One child was born of this union; mother and babe resting in cemetery at Peoria, Illinois. Nellie was a member of the Methodist church in Wayne at the time of her death. The husband remarried and resides in Philadelphia, Pennsylvania.

    IV. Gilbert Edward, born April 30, 1873; unmarried; lives at

Winside, Nebraska, where he is engaged in the banking business.

V J Fred, born September 12, 1875; married Ina M Orcutt, daughter of Seldon D and Mary Orcutt, born October 17, 1875, at Independence, Iowa; married at Atkinson, Nebraska, August 11, 1904 To them have been born:
1 Gilbert Orcutt, born August 23, 1906; died January 28, 1907.
2 Seldon Orcutt, born December 28, 1907; died Septemtember 25, 1908
3 Mary Suzanne, born at Olathe, Colorado, May 30, 1909
4 Harriet Gilberta, born at Olathe, Colorado, August 1, 1911.

J. Fred French lives in Olathe, Colorado He is engaged in the business of real estate, loans, and insurance

The children of John and Susan French were born in Peoria, Illinois John French went with his parents from Otsego county, New York, to Morrow county, Ohio, in 1847 In October of that year he attained his majority and the following winter he taught school in what was afterwards known as the "Flint school house " During this term of school five of his cousins — Stephen Flint and his sister Sharille, Stephen Tripp and two sisters, Lucy and Mary — were among his pupils In the spring of 1851 Henry Tripp, a cousin of John French, began work for Henry Miller of Columbus, Ohio, as a book solicitor, his territory embracing the state of Illinois Two years later he returned to Ohio, where he formed a partnership with John French for the sale of books, they afterward joining forces with G and S H Burnett, of Peoria, Illinois, but he continued to travel until the Burnetts sold out to Henry Nolte. Henry Tripp remained in the employ of Nolte as head clerk, and John French engaged in business with a Mr. Mawhyrter, making clothing for men, and keeping a general supply of men's furnishings

That John French had loaned money to his father, is shown by the following extract taken from a letter written by his mother to his sister, in 1854· "Received a letter from John, dated February 25th;

was doing well; thinks $100 laid out in land in that country would in a year or two, be worth $500. He would be glad to have us get the land with the money he loaned us, says he will not push us, for he owes us a great deal for his bringing up and the little education he has, and a great deal *more* for a good character."

From 1882 to 1886, after having gone out of the merchant tailoring business, he was in the employ of the government as storekeeper in the revenue service connected with the distilleries at Peoria, Illinois In 1886 he removed with his family to Wayne, Nebraska, where he engaged in the real estate and banking business, being actively interested in this work until a short time previous to his death In politics he was a Republican, and was for years a member of the Ancient Free and Accepted Masons. For several years prior to his death he spent the winters in San Diego, California, where his widow, Susan French, now resides. His death occurred at Wayne, Nebraska, December 24, 1904, and his body rests beside that of his daughter at Peoria, Illinois John French was successful in business, honest and upright in all his dealings, and he made it a strong point with his sons to keep their promises and to treat others as they themselves would wish to be treated

MARY FRENCH, sixth child of Samson and Elizabeth French, was born in Decatur, Otsego county, New York, December 6, 1829 The early years of her life were spent with her parents on the farm, where as a child she developed a great love for nature, which dominated her whole life An incident of her early childhood shows that what she undertook to do she accomplished.

When about eight years of age, a heavy rainfall caused the streams to overflow After the sky cleared and the spring sunshine had come out in all its glory, Mary, with a sunbonnet tied under her chin, and an injunction from her mother not to take it off, started for the woods to gather wild flowers Decatur Creek — a small stream which ran through her father's farm — was out of its banks, and as she came near she saw a great number of fish which had found their way into the stream from the river near by, which had backed its waters over the low lands. One of these fish — a large one — was so near the shore that Mary thought she could easily reach it Being barefooted and not realizing the depth of the stream, she waded in and caught the fish but went under the water. Still clinging to her prize, she laid the slippery creature on the grass long enough to get her breath, then bearing it home, entered the kitchen exclaiming· "Oh mother, I caught it but lost my bonnet!"

When about sixteen years of age, she became dissatisfied at home, and much against her mother's wishes, went to Troy, New York, where she was employed in a cotton factory, "clearing nineteen shillings a week " Six weeks sufficed to satisfy all aspirations in this direction and Mary returned to her home, happy to again be a member of the family circle. Her education was gained in the country school maintained near her father's home and later on, in a seminary in Worcester, New York.

She went with her parents to Morrow county, Ohio, in 1847, and a short time after, the following incident occurred·

Two and one-half miles from their home was a store and one or two houses, which comprised the little village of Westpoint Mary was sent to this place with a basket of eggs which she was to exchange for sugar. She went on horseback, her father giving her explicit directions to follow, as this was a heavily timbered country through which she must pass on this — her first visit to the store After riding a long distance and not seeing the town, she overtook a man walking, and asked him if he could tell her how much farther she must go to reach Westpoint Imagine her surprise when she found she had passed through the village and had not recognized it as the "town "

While engaged in teaching school during the summer of 1848, she met Dr Nathan M. Smith, a young physician located at Kirkersville, Ohio, and they were married at Mt Gilead February 22, 1849 Seven children were born of this union, six of whom grew to maturity.

I. Viola, born at Mt Gilead October 22, 1850, died at Sibley, Missouri, August 2, 1854
  II Lafayette F., born October 6, 1853; died January 26, 1854
 III William Shakespeare, born July 5, 1855; married Emma Baker, Quincy, Illinois, 1883 To them were born: Junius, Louis, George, Jessie, Helen, Pet.
  IV Ada S., born March 14, 1858, married T. Jefferson Davis (deceased) in 1877 To them were born four sons and one daughter
   V Stella, born November 22, 1861; married John E. Johnson Stella died in 1895 Her husband and three children living.
  VI Louis N., born October 12, 1868; is married, resides in Kansas City, Missouri.
 VII Mary, born May 28, 1872; married J. Mason Price in 1895. To them have been born three sons and two daughters, reside in Kansas City, Missouri.

Dr Nathan M Smith (husband of Mary French) was born near Wheeling, West Virginia, April 17, 1825; was of Scotch descent, and a man of brilliant mind He received the degree of doctor of medicine at Newport, and first practiced his profession at Wheeling

In 1852 Dr. Smith and his brother William started for the gold fields of California, leaving Mary and her baby with her parents. The difficulties of travel, Indian skirmishes, and the possibility of never again seeing the loved ones left behind, caused them to conclude their journey at what is now known as Kansas City; and at Sibley, a town forty miles north of this place, situated on a high bluff overlooking the Missouri River, Dr Smith finally decided to locate Here he built the first brick house in that part of the country, and a flourishing little city grew up around him He sent for his wife and baby daughter, and as passengers on the "Isabella" they left Cincinnati November 2, 1852, changed boats at St Louis, coming via the Missouri River to Kansas City, finally arriving at Sibley after a somewhat eventful journey

The residents of Sibley and vicinity were people of refinement and culture, and the kindness and courtesy shown to Dr Smith and his wife won their hearts and made them feel at home among their newfound friends This was a slave owning community, distinctly southern in its sympathies, and they — like their neighbors — soon became owners of slaves

In the spring or early summer of 1861 Mary paid a visit to her Ohio home, for her father had died in April, and her mother, who had been in delicate health for a number of years, was failing rapidly. Her convictions as to the right of the southern cause were as intense and radical as were the northern principles of her brothers in Ohio A bitter quarrel followed their many heated discussions and a family breach ensued which was never healed. She returned to her husband and southern friends, and her sojourn among these people she declared to be the happiest of her entire life

The Civil War, beginning in 1861, bearing havoc and sorrow in its train, brought about a condition of extreme bitterness in this part of the country and the people of the community became widely scattered Dr. Smith was pursued by the bushwhackers numberless times during the days of their activity, there being a price upon his head At one time he hid behind a clump of bushes and listened while some of these guerrillas laid plans to take his life The last experience which drove him from Jackson county, was a thrilling episode. A week or so previous a raid had been made upon his property and his live stock stolen, he being obliged to borrow a horse for his daily calls, as his riding horse had been taken with the others One day he went to Independence, about fifteen miles distant, to draw some money from the bank with which to purchase a horse It grew late before he started on the return journey, and when a short distance from home, a man on horseback suddenly emerged from the side of the road and ordered him to halt It was dark and instead of doing as commanded, he put spurs to his horse, a bullet grazing his cheek as he sped onward in the darkness His pursuer followed only a short distance, and then returned to his companions — members of Quantrill's band

The doctor reached home in safety, and having five hundred dollars in his belt, handed it to his wife Hearing the tramp of horses' feet, Mary blew out the light, flung all the money (with the exception of eighty dollars in greenbacks which she secreted in her sleeve) under the bed, and helped her husband out of the back window, for she knew it was death if they found him. He escaped to the woods just beyond his home. By this time the door was forced from its hinges and six men entered the house She lighted the lamp and with perfect calmness, asked what they wanted, to which they replied: "We want Doc Smith and we'll fix him, we know he has money; where is he?" Mary told them he was not at home, but that they were at perfect liberty to search the house. They demanded her money, threatening to shoot the baby sleeping in the cradle if she did not accede to their demands She drew the bills from her sleeve, giving them fifty dollars, but they were not satisfied until all of the eighty dollars she had secreted there, was in their possession Not seeing the doctor's horse, which had wandered away into the timber, they thought he had not yet reached home, so guarded the house all night awaiting his return.

For three weeks Mary heard nothing from her husband, and when she finally despaired of ever seeing him again, a message came telling her to come to Kingston, and with it, directions for the journey Her husband met her before she reached her destination, and when she saw him, she fainted; his hair — black when they parted — was now white as snow.

After this terrible experience, Dr Smith and his family moved to Kingston, county seat of Caldwell county. He enlisted in the Thirty-third Missouri regiment as surgeon, and at the close of the war bought one hundred acres of land near that city, and there made a home where he and his wife spent the remainder of their days Meantime he had returned to the spot where the great tragedy of their life was so narrowly averted, and secured the silver and other valuables which Mary had buried in anticipation of the visit described

Dr. Smith took great pleasure in beautifying his home, planted fruit trees of every variety that would grow in that climate, and cultivated flowers, all of which combined in making what for many years was known as one of the "show places" of Caldwell county Mary was a great botanist, and had collected flowers from all over the country; she embroidered in colored silks, using the living flowers as studies. She was a woman of strong character and indomitable will, possessed of tact, wit, and a personal charm all her own.

Dr. Smith was an active member of the Grand Army of the Republic, and when his death occurred, June 21, 1893, this organization took charge of the funeral services. Mary French Smith died June 28, 1908, and their bodies now rest in the cemetery at Kingston, Missouri.

OSCAR LUMAS RUSSELL FRENCH, ninth child of Samson and Elizabeth French, was born in Decatur, Otsego county, New York, October 18, 1834; married Mary Clevenger, of Morrow county, Ohio, November 15, 1855. She died February 17, 1856. He married (second) Cidney Ellen Keech (born April 5, 1836, West Bradford township, Chester county, Pennsylvania) December 24, 1857, Rev. Atchison Queal performing the ceremony. To them were born eight children:

 I. Mary Clevenger }
 II. Laura Alfaretta } born April 25, 1859, Edison, Ohio.

  Mary Clevenger married George Hellinger in January, 1882. To them was born one child:

  1. Bessie, born November 7, 1882; died 1884.

  Laura Alfaretta married Dr. Frank Rule March 6, 1886, in Johnsville, Ohio. To them was born one child:

   1. Harry Hamilton, born March 6, 1886, in Johnsville, Ohio; unmarried; linotype operator at Bucyrus, Ohio.

  Dr. Rule died March 11, 1891, at Huron, Kansas.

  Laura married (second) Carmi Kelly in 1893. To them was born:

  2. Lucy May, May 29, 1898, in Caledonia, Ohio.

 III. Bayard Taylor, born Pulaskiville, Morrow county, Ohio, August 2, 1860; married Lue Lincoln Walters January 30, 1884, at Johnsville, Ohio. Bayard Taylor French came to Iowa in the spring of 1880 and began work for the firm of J. H. Queal & Co., lumber dealers; he later became a mem-

Lucy French Stoner

FRENCH AND ALLIED FAMILIES 187

ber of the firm, and is now vice president of the corporation; lives at Hawarden, Iowa. Lue Lincoln Walters was born November 3, 1862, in Morrow county, Ohio. To them were born:
1. Leslie Ray, born in Hawarden, Sioux county, Iowa, December 20, 1885; married Carrie Watters April 16, 1911. To them has been born one child:
    a. Elizabeth.
2. Clarence Walters, born December 7, 1887, Hawarden, Iowa.
3. Helen Beatrice, born April 12, 1890; died June 1, 1891.
4. Sherman Queal, born April 28, 1892, Hawarden, Iowa.

IV. Garfield, born April 28, 1866, Westpoint, Ohio; was drowned May 29, 1869.

V. Samson Babb, born April 28, 1866, Westpoint, Ohio; married Georgianna Almy at Yankton, South Dakota, February 15, 1893. To them have been born:
1. Howard Almy, born September 10, 1894.
2. Cidney Evelyn, born October 31, 1895.
3. Wendell Phillips, born August 28, 1898.
4. Gordon Russell, born November 26, 1900.
5. Netha, born September 19, 1902.
6. Harriett,
7. Herbert George, } born June 30, 1907.

VI. Malinda Keech, born March 9, 1868, Johnsville, Ohio; married Edward Snyder June 1, 1889, Johnsville, Ohio. To them have been born:
1. Edna, born September 19, 1890; married Elroy Smith March 8, 1911; one child.
2. Helen, born February 21, 1892.
Edward Snyder died April 9, 1904.

VII. Lucy May, born May 2, 1870, Johnsville, Ohio; married August 16, 1900, Clarence Birch Stoner. To them have been born.
1. Lowell French, born August 1, 1901.

2. Helen Constance, born September 27, 1902.

Clarence Birch Stoner's work the past year (1911) has been: Statistician for the bureau of business research of the Harvard Graduate School of Business Administration; also assistant in the course in economics, "Principles of Accounting." He received the degree of master of business administration from Harvard College June, 1911. His special line of work is accounting; has been auditor for a firm in Boston for about two years and has spent considerable time in establishing a system of accounts in various hospitals. Removed in 1912 to Pittsburg, Pennsylvania, where he is connected with the Carnegie Institute of that city.

VIII. Belle, born March 6, 1876; married Albert C. Rummel July 31, 1902. To them has been born one child:
1. Robert French, born July 12, 1907.

Albert C. Rummel is superintendent of schools at St. Clairsville, Ohio.

Oscar Lumas Russell French was but thirteen years of age when he went with his parents to Ohio, where he worked on the farm with his father and brothers. In the spring of 1848 he helped his father plant an orchard, the growth of which was watched by the members of the family with great interest until the first fruits were gathered some years later. Being of a studious mind he improved every opportunity within his reach to gain an education; was a student for one year at Delaware, Ohio, but with this exception, his mental training was obtained in the common school of the community where he resided. His first term of school was taught on the state road near the Flint home; the second, at Hell's Half Acre, northeast of Westpoint. The winter of 1857 was spent teaching in what was known as the "eight square" school house, which is still standing, being used at the present time for a tool house and work shop.

In 1858 he went west and on his return in September moved to Edison, where he taught three terms of school and where the twins were born. One year later he engaged to teach in Pulaskiville, Morrow county, and his parents persuaded him to bring his wife and babies to their home, where they remained during the winter, joining him in the spring of 1860

These were warm political times and the shadow of war hung heavily over the country Oscar French had early taken an interest in political affairs, being a staunch Republican for some time before he was old enough to vote The New York *Tribune*, to which his father had been a subscriber before leaving the state of New York, was carefully read, and helped in a great measure to form his political beliefs His vote, cast November 6, 1860, was one of the 1,866,352 which elected Abraham Lincoln president of the United States When the War of the Rebellion broke out, he was ready to answer his country's call, so moved his family to Westpoint where his wife's parents resided, and joined the Twenty-sixth regiment, Ohio Volunteer Infantry, June 6, 1861, serving under Rosecrans in Kanawha Valley He was taken ill with typhoid fever on October 10, 1861, at Mt Cove, West Virginia, and was moved about three weeks later to the Third Street Military Hospital, Cincinnati, Ohio This illness rendered him unfit for military duty, and he was discharged in the spring of 1862 In September of the same year, when Governor Tod called for minute men to go to the "Southern border" to repel Morgan's band of invaders, Oscar French organized a company for this service These men are known in history as "Squirrel Hunters." He also assisted in organizing the National Guards of Morrow County in 1863, and this body enlisted in the spring of 1864, in response to a call for volunteers for one hundred days of service, Smith Irwin being colonel of the regiment Later he helped to organize a company for one year's service, being assigned to Company C, One Hundred Eightieth Ohio Volunteer Infantry, which was sent to Tennessee to do garrison duty. Early in 1865 they were ordered to join their corps at Washington From this place they were sent to Charlotte, North Carolina, where they again did garrison duty, and were at Raleigh, North Carolina, when Johnston surrendered his army

Oscar was fond of good living, and the following extract from a letter written to his wife while at Deckard Station, Tennessee, November 13, 1864, illustrates the fact that sauer kraut and pickles were favorite articles of food: "Cidney, I will have to excuse you on the kraut, but if you can send me the pickles, without too much trouble, you may do so, but it is not very particular, as it will cost five or six dollars to get them here, which will make them pretty dear for us." In this same letter he says: "Please send me the *Tribunes* along as you read them; I would give more for the *Tribune* than any paper I ever read."

The following letter received by his wife while he was still in the service contains much of interest:

Raleigh, Sunday April 16th, 1865.

. . . . I thought I would write you today, although it may be some days before I can send it as the railroad is not finished, but will probably be done in a day or two. As I sit in the office of the provost marshal, there are two officers (Confederate) who have come through from Grant. They are Lee's officers, and are on their way to their homes with passes from General Grant to pass through our lines and on government railroads and on board transports, &c, &c. One brigadier general came in this morning who lived in this town. He reported here first, and then said he must go home and see his wife. I expect it was a joyful meeting. The report was rife in town yesterday that Joe Johnston was surrendering. I suppose they are making the terms. General Hardee (rebel) was in town yesterday. Johnston wanted an armistice to send word to Grant, but Sherman sent word to him that he would take him in on the same terms that Grant did Lee — that is — all men to be paroled, officers to retain their side arms, private property and horses. General Sherman came into the office and is talking to these two Confederate officers. There is a great crowd of soldiers outside trying to get a glimpse of him. He is a very sensible old man; is not quite as good looking as John Sherman. I think he is older, perhaps. Major General and Brigadier General Moore are both in here; they are brothers-in-law of Colonel Warner. . . . We have just learned that General Sheridan is in Johnston's rear, so he is soon bound to surrender. . . . . . . Mondaay afternoon . . . but my dear wife, I am sad, oh so sad. We have received official news (as we suppose) that President Lincoln has been assassinated. My God, is it possible that the best man this nation ever knew has been taken away from us! *God forbid*! I do hope it may prove false. It seems as though it cannot be possible that the man who has carried us so safely through a civil war of four years, and now on the eve of peace, should be ruthlessly murdered in cold blood. The army was to have moved this morning, but it did not. General Sher-

CERTIFICATE OF SERVICE GIVEN O. L. R. FRENCH

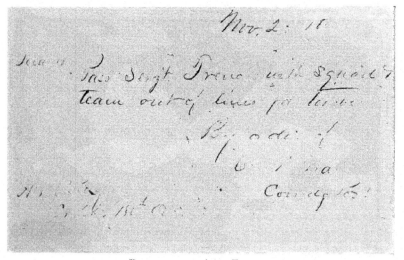

PASS GIVEN TO ALVA FRENCH

man started out to see Johnston to have him surrender or to take him in I have not heard what the result has been General Stiles asked me yesterday how soon I thought I would see the twins. I told him I thought by the 4th of July "Well," says he, "I think so too " I begin to feel more anxious than ever now to get home, as I think the war is over The paroled rebels are passing through here today, en route for their homes. They have been, since Lee surrendered a week ago, coming through General Sherman told Colonel Warner yesterday to give them any papers and transportation that they might want to carry them through to their homes   .   .

(Signed)   O L R FRENCH[1]
Lt & A P M 1st Brig 1st Div 23 A C

Oscar French returned home from the war July 25, 1865, and shortly after moved with his family to Johnsville, Morrow county, Ohio, where for some years he was principal of the school He was elected county surveyor October 18, 1869, in which capacity he served one term; afterwards engaging in the lumber business at Lexington, Ohio, which occupation he diligently pursued until November 17, 1890, when he was again elected county surveyor, serving his third term at the time of his death, which occurred March 25, 1896.

The friends of Oscar French were numbered by his acquaintances, for he was a genial man, and no one more enjoyed a good joke, even though it were on himself. He was upright in character, honest in all his dealings — a good citizen He was a member of the Masonic fraternity in Mt Gilead, of the Independent Order of Odd Fellows at Johnsville, of Justus Paxton Post of the Grand Army of the Republic, the Rebekahs, and the Grange

Few men leave a more interesting history or a better record than Oscar French, who, in war as well as in peace, served his country and his fellow-men faithfully and well He was a resident of Johnsville about thirty years, where he was known as a kind, affectionate husband and father, and a faithful friend His widow still lives in the old home at Johnsville, Ohio

---

[1] Oscar French Lieutenant and assistant paymaster, First brigade, First division, Twenty-third Army Corps.

MARTIN AND MARVIN FRENCH, born in Decatur, Otsego county, New York, January 29, 1837. Martin French married Belle Chamberlain of Ames, Iowa, May 16, 1879. One son, Clare Vernon, was born of this union, who died when about one year of age.

Marvin died August 16, 1839.

Martin French was reared on the farm and obtained a common school education. He moved in 1847 with his parents to Ohio, where he helped his father and brothers to clear the land and put in the crops, attending school during the winter months. After reaching his majority he continued to work for his father, receiving wages for his labor. In August, 1860, he went to New York state, thinking he might like to locate there, but after a visit with the friends and relatives returned to his father's home in Ohio, having been gone but twenty-three days. On September 18th of the same year he started for the West, going from Mt. Gilead to Columbus, Ohio, where he remained but a short time, journeying on to Peoria, Illinois, and from that place to Sibley, Missouri, where he resided until the following May, when with his sister, Mary Smith, and her two children he returned to Ohio. In September, 1861, after the death of his parents, at a public sale of their personal property, Martin and his sister Lucy bought in partnership a team of horses, some cows, and part of the farm implements, rented the farm for one hundred fifty dollars per year, and for two years continued to work together. In the spring of 1863, having disposed of his interests to his sister, he again started westward, with the hope of working his way to fame and fortune in the gold mining districts of California and Nevada. For six years his business ability brought him a measure of success, but the reverses consequent upon the years of depression that followed the Civil War were experienced by him, and in 1872 he returned to Missouri, where for four years he engaged in the drug business in Ray county, going from that state to Deadwood, South Dakota, in 1876. In 1878 he went to Salida, Colorado, the distributing point for Gunnison county, at which place he again engaged in business as a druggist, which occupation proved quite remunerative.

While visiting his sister at Ames, Iowa, in 1876, he met Miss Belle

Discharge given Alva French from Squirrel Hunters

FRENCH AND ALLIED FAMILIES

Chamberlain, who in the spring of 1879 went to Salida, where they were united in marriage May 16th. In 1898 he sold his business in this place and moved to Ames, Iowa, where he was employed in a drug store when able to work. He was a member of the Masonic fraternity, having received the degree of Knight Templar in that order. His first presidential vote was cast for a Democrat and he never changed his politics. His early political and religious views were dominated by those of an uncle, Daniel Flint (in whose family he often visited during his boyhood years), who believed in universal salvation, and that the slave question was one with which people should not interfere.

Martin French died of Bright's disease at Ames, Iowa, August 1, 1900, leaving a widow, who still resides in that place.

ALVA C. FRENCH, twelfth child of Samson and Elizabeth French, was born in Decatur, Otsego county, New York, April 15, 1839; married Lydia A. Elder (born March 19, 1847, Morrow county, Ohio) in Galion, Ohio, August 9, 1862. To them were born six children:
  I.   Kirby C., born July 12, 1863; died September 8, 1864.
  II. Abbie, born June 2, 1865; married Ferd Nichols May 10, 1880. To them were born six children, four of whom are living.
  III. Ellsworth, born September 9, 1869, at Kingston, Caldwell county, Missouri; died September 28, 1877.
  IV. Charles, born February 12, 1873; died December 22, 1894.
  V.   Chauncey, born October 9, 1876; married Ada Sipes September 25, 1901. To them have been born three children.
  VI. Carrie, born October 18, 1874; married Karah Mountz October 22, 1903. To them have been born two children.

Alva C. French was but six years of age when his parents moved to Ohio. He grew to manhood on the farm of his father, and industry was one of the lessons learned early in life. About 1850 the Cleveland, Columbus & Cincinnati Railroad was built, the track running within two miles of his parents' home. He listened with delight to the whistle of the engines and determined to engage in the railroad business when he grew to manhood. In accord with this resolution, after reaching his majority he went into the railroad shops at Galion, Ohio, to learn the business, but two years later, owing to impaired health, was obliged to give up this particular occupation, taking instead a position as conductor on a through freight, running from Galion, Ohio, to Union City, Indiana.

In September, 1864, when an urgent call came for troops, Alva enlisted with his brother Oscar in Company C, One Hundred Eightieth Ohio Volunteer Infantry, of which company he was color bearer, and went to Tennessee, where the troops did garrison duty until 1865. As winter approached, they were busily engaged in the woods about a mile from camp, cutting and loading logs for their new winter quarters. The order pictured on page 191 shows that Alva French was detailed to assist in this work.

In the early spring of 1865 the regiment was ordered to Charlotte, North Carolina, where they again did garrison duty, and later on to Raleigh, at which place they were located when Johnston surrendered to General Sherman.

After the close of the war he returned home and again entered the employ of the railroad company as conductor. While on his regular run from Galion to Union City he met with a serious accident at a point named Quincy Curve, which place has since been called "Dead Man's Curve," owing to the number of accidents which have occurred there. This injury so impaired his health that he left the employ of the railroad company, and in 1868 removed with his family to Kingston, Caldwell county, Missouri, near which place they resided for five years, returning at the expiration of that time to Galion, Ohio, where he entered the employ of the Atlantic & Great Western Railroad, continuing in the service of this company until he removed to his farm in Morrow county. Here he lived for thirty-five years, leaving in 1912 to again take up his residence in Galion, where with his wife he expects to spend the remainder of his days.

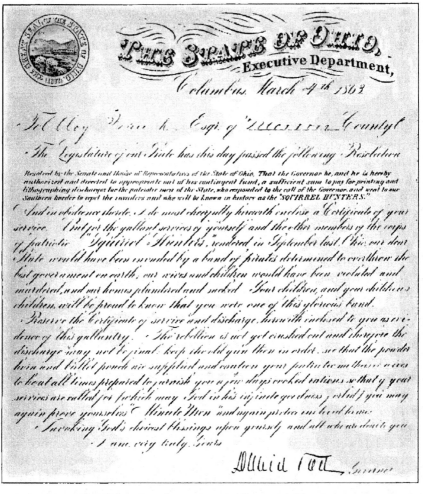

CERTIFICATE OF SERVICE GIVEN SQUIRREL HUNTERS

SEWARD H. FRENCH

Alva C French joined the Masonic fraternity when a young man, and is a member of the order in Galion, Ohio

The original demit from Charity Lodge of Worcester, New York, granted to his father, Samson French, in 1833; also the resolutions of respect from the Masonic lodge in Mt Gilead, Ohio, passed at the time of his father's death in 1861, are valued possessions of Alva C French and will be found in another part of this volume

CALVIN DAY FRENCH, born at Decatur, Otsego county, New York, May 8, 1842; married Elizabeth Jane Jones (born June 1, 1850, at Clarksville, Albany county, New York) November 21, 1869, at Delmar, Albany county, New York To them were born four children:

I Orva Martin, born at Albany, New York, November 17, 1871; married in 1898 Jessie Carmer of Athens, Pennsylvania Now living at Chandler, Arizona. No children

II Chauncey, born Delmar, New York, September 25, 1876; married June 1, 1898, Grace Miller (born North Fenton, Broome county, New York, 1877) at Binghamton, New York Is a member of the firm of Woodward, Wight & Co, general supply house, New Orleans, Louisiana, in which city he and his family now reside Two children have been born of this union
   1. Lewis M, born Binghamton, New York, August 8, 1900
   2. Richard Calvin, born New Orleans, Louisiana, January 30, 1909

III. Seward Haight, born Delmar, New York, December 27, 1877; married Lena Pearle Woodruff (born October 13, 1877, Binghamton, New York) December 25, 1900, who died September 10, 1901; married (second) at St Louis, Missouri, November 26, 1906, Mary Littell Halley (born April 11, 1885, Cincinnati, Ohio) Is cashier Binghamton, New York, postoffice, and local secretary United States Civil Service Commission. Two children have been born of the second marriage:

1. Seward H. Jr., born November 5, 1907, Binghamton, New York.
2. Alice Gertrude, born June 4, 1911.

IV. Katherine May, born Binghamton, New York, May 4, 1881; married Frank Kresinger (born Des Moines, Iowa, January 1, 1875) August 25, 1908, at Binghamton, New York. Live at Des Moines, Iowa, where Frank Kresinger is employed with the J. H. Queal Lumber Co. No children.

Calvin Day French, the youngest of thirteen children, was but five years of age when his parents moved to Morrow county, Ohio, from Otsego county, New York, journeying by Erie Canal to Buffalo, thence by the lake to Sandusky, and by covered wagon the balance of the journey. He was at that time and for some years after, his mother's constant companion, helping her with the work and learning many useful lessons in the art of housekeeping, which required some skill, with only a living room and "loft" in the log cabin, especially when it is remembered that there were seven members of the family who lived there at that time. From a letter written by Calvin's mother to his sister Lucy in March, 1854, is copied the following:

> You would be pleased to see how good a boy Calvin is to help me; he has done the three last washings, only I suds and rinse the clothes. He makes me think of his oldest sister, he is so willing to favour me. I often think that promise is being verified to me that I received the first night after his birth — "This same shall comfort you." I firmly believe it. In how many ways he may sooth and comfort my declining days, I know not, but I have no fears.

Calvin was a generous boy, always kind and gentle, but was in no way effeminate; loving out of door sports and always ready to join in them, he grew up a favorite with both the boys and girls of the neighborhood. As he grew older he worked with his father and brothers on the farm, attending school during the winter months. It was not always easy to get help in the house in those days and he always gave of his time and strength cheerfully to aid his mother. Being religiously inclined he at an early age united with the church and is at present a member of the Chenango Street Methodist Episcopal church at Binghamton, New York.

After the death of his father, in the spring of 1861, Calvin hired out to work on a farm, and after his mother's death, which occurred in August of the same year, he enlisted at Mt Vernon, Ohio, in Company B, Forty-third regiment, Ohio Volunteers, September 14, 1861, for service in the Civil War From Mt Vernon the company went into camp at Camp Chase, Columbus, Ohio From this place the troops went down the Ohio and up the Mississippi River to New Madrid and under General Pope's command participated in the Missouri campaign He was present at the capture of Island No 10 This fort had been in the possession of the rebel forces and was the key to the upper Mississippi and Missouri Rivers His brigade was later assigned to the Army of the Tennessee, the most important battles of that campaign being Iuka and Corinth. He was taken prisoner before Atlanta, Georgia, and sent to Andersonville prison, where he was confined for several weeks While being transferred to a prison further south, he and a comrade jumped from the train and escaped, returning after much hardship to the Union lines in time to go with Sherman to the sea A story of his capture and escape, as written by him, will follow this sketch He served throughout the war and at its close returned to Ohio and lived with his brothers, Alva and Oscar, and was employed as a trainman on the Bellefontaine & Indianapolis Railroad, now a part of the New York Central lines He soon after decided to go west and take a position with the Union Pacific Railroad, then building to the Pacific Coast, and was about to leave when he received a letter from his brother Thomas, asking him to come to Warnerville, Schoharie county, New York, to take care of him, as he was feeble in health So Calvin went east instead of west and nursed his brother Thomas through the illness which proved to be his last, as in a few weeks he died Calvin then went to Cobleskill to see about a position on the Delaware & Hudson Railroad, and was referred to the superintendent at Albany, who gave him a position This was in 1867 His run took him from Albany to Sidney, about one hundred and three miles, the latter place then being the terminus of the road. One day as the train was running through a little country village called Adamsville (now Delmar), New York, his attention was attracted to a rosy cheeked country lass who lived near the tracks. A flirtation began. He threw off a note from his train; the answer was favorable, and he called on the young lady. Two years later they were married and spent a few years beside the tracks where the romance began. Calvin was employed as trainman, then conductor for a term of seven years. He was in charge of the first train that ran to Sharon Springs, Schoharie county, New York. In 1874 he began working for the National Express Company and remained in their employ for thirty-three years, principally as messenger. On November 10, 1907, he was retired by the express company on a pension. He moved in 1880 to Binghamton, New York, where he and his wife still reside.

CAPTURE, IMPRISONMENT IN ANDERSONVILLE, AND ESCAPE OF CALVIN D. FRENCH
COMPANY B, FORTY-THIRD OHIO VETERAN VOLUNTEER INFANTRY
AUGUST 4 TO SEPTEMBER 21, 1864
AUTOBIOGRAPHY

On the morning of the 4th of August, 1864, our regiment with others was ordered to advance the Union lines in front of Atlanta, Georgia. We had come here a few days before, driving the rebels all the way from Chattanooga. Our regiment was put on the skirmish line, after piling all of our knapsacks together, each company's by itself.

We started from a deployed line about nine in the morning, and went over fences and ditches into a dense underbrush. The rebel infantry was firing into this brush, and the batteries in the rebel forts were covering them with the big guns as fast as they could be loaded and discharged. The bullets were coming thick and fast, and I stepped behind a tree, which was so small I had to stand sidewise to get under cover. I continued to fire my gun as rapidly as possible in the direction of the enemy, who were concealed in the thick underbrush directly ahead. Suddenly a rebel appeared at my left, closely followed by others. I had become separated from the rest of the company in the rush which followed our advance, and only Barney Keyes and one other member of my company were in sight. They turned and ran, but Keyes stubbed his toe and fell. I thought he had been shot. Realizing that I was surrounded, my first impulse was to break my gun against the tree, and as I raised it to do so, a reb ordered me to halt at the point of his gun, and I was compelled to hand my Enfield over to him. "Come on, you Yank," he said, and I was marched back through the rebel

FRENCH AND ALLIED FAMILIES

forts to Atlanta, which was just east of their lines As I remember it, Atlanta was a very small place, not much over a thousand population

The guard took me with a few others they had captured, into an old barn, where we were kept under guard for the night The next morning we were marched about six miles south, to a station called Eastport, and in the evening were put on a train and started for Andersonville, where we arrived about ten o'clock the following morning As we got off the train we could see the prison, which was not far from the station It was a stockade, built of pine logs set on end in the ground, each log touching the other. It was about fifteen feet high This ran all the way on four sides, enclosing about thirty acres of ground The rebel guards were stationed on top of this stockade, at intervals of about fifty feet, where a small guardhouse was built, reached by stairs from the outside.

It did not take us long to reach the pen, into which we were driven like cattle There were three from my company — John H Rogers, James B Bowen, and myself — all of us young, stout and healthy The first night we went to the north side of the prison and with my blouse for a blanket and my shoes for a pillow, began my service in Andersonville, the stars for consolation and the rebel guards for protection When I shook my blouse in the morning, a multitude of maggots dropped to the ground, which awakened me to the real conditions under which we were placed

The site of Andersonville was a solid pine forest before the war, and when the first prisoners were brought there they had built some small shanties or huts with some of the trees which were left after the stockade and other rebel buildings had been constructed These shanties were all occupied by prisoners, and some others had dug-outs in the ground covered with split timbers, but those who came in the summer of 1864 had the sky only for their covering.

There was a low piece of ground toward the south end of the enclosure where the water from the rebel soldiers' camp came down through the prison This stream was bridged with a plank covering at one place, to convey prisoners from one side of the prison to the other This stream was filled with filth which came from the rebel camp above, but it was the only source of water supply for the new recruits The older prisoners had dug wells, but they were insufficient to supply more than their own needs, and the spirit of the prison was "every man for himself in the desperate struggle for existence" There was a market street where Union soldiers had dried roots to sell, also biscuits, which they had made from flour purchased from the rebels. They got the roots by rolling up their breeches and sleeves and digging in the swale filled with the refuse of the prison Once a day the rebs would send a wagon through the prison with corn bread or baked beans which was distributed to the prisoners. When we got bread we got no beans, and when we got beans we got no bread. Food! food! was the great cry of the prison, and the only thing talked about was something to eat. I have seen stout, robust men look over the situation when they arrived as prisoners of war, lie down in the hot sand and in a day or two were so weak they could not stand up. They would simply root their heads in the sand and in a short period of time, die. It was such a common occurrence that no one paid any attention to such a thing. To live through such an ordeal required steel courage and not a thought of despair. While it looked hopeless, some of us had a ray of hope that Sherman would make it so warm for the rebels that they would be compelled to transfer us to a safer place.

While I was there, the Providence spring broke out. During the night a very heavy thunder storm came down on the camp, and it rained torrents. Some of the stockade was washed down. In the morning there was a spring with running water — nice and cool — between the dead line and the stockade. They run this water over the dead line so we could get it. Each man took his turn to drink or take a canteen of water away with him, and there was a continuous line of men from daybreak in the morning until dark. This was the best water I ever drank, and the spring was rightly named "Providence."

The dead line was constructed of a narrow piece of board nailed on stakes about fifteen feet from the stockade all around the prison. If a prisoner touched or fell on the line — even though from weakness — the guards killed him. Commencing at dark and lasting until daylight, on the hour the guards would pass along the call, "Eight o'clock and all's well," "Nine o'clock and all's well," and so on through the dismal night.

Well time passed on, even though it did seem to stop sometimes, and we learned that Sherman had captured Atlanta. Rumors came that we were to be moved to Charleston, South Carolina, and at last the tidings came true and the start was made. September 11th it came my turn to march to the depot, and about eight o'clock in the morning we were put in box cars and started for Charleston. At Macon we changed engines and were allowed to be around some, under guard. After leaving Macon one prisoner said to me that he would have gotten away there if someone had gone with him. I told him that I would have done so, and then told him of a plan which had come to me during our journey to Macon. We agreed that we would work over near the door of the car, and when the train was running slowly I would get off, and he would follow as soon as possible. We were then to walk toward each other, and make for the Union lines together. Soon the train began to slacken its speed, and he took hold of my hand and let me down until my feet touched the ground, and let go I rolled over and over to a ditch beside the track, and lay quiet until the train had passed. The guards in the cars and on top failed to see me, and I was a free man again for the moment at least. In getting me down from the car my left leg struck against a tie, and when I got up after a few minutes found that I was quite badly hurt, although I could walk I then started in the direction the train was moving to meet my comrade I went some little way and saw a cabin by the side of the track A negro was living there and he got me some cold water with which to bathe my leg, and I also bartered my blouse for his gray coat He gave me some corn bread and I went on down the track.

After going a little further I heard some one whistle, which was our prearranged signal, and my comrade in the escape, who I later learned was George H Wagerley of Chillicothe, Ohio, came up the bank and we shook hands I tell you we were glad to see each other We went back the way we had come and stopped at the negro shanty. The darky told us to go back the railroad track about three miles, until we came to a road crossing, then to turn to the right and follow the road We were now in the enemy's territory and had to use every precaution in our movements When we reached the road crossing we saw a fire and found it was a rebel picket with three men around the fire. We went back a hundred paces or more and removed our shoes and then slowly and quietly got by them.

We deemed it wise not to go in the road but to keep in the woods and open fields. We turned into a path in the underbrush and followed it until daylight, when we camped near an open field in some low bushes. We slept some during the day Some negroes passed close by, but we lay low waiting for night to come Then we went to the nearest plantation and made friends with a negro, who got some johnny-cake for us which we relished very much. We then struck out, taking the moon and stars for a guide, traveling through corn fields, swamps, wet grass, sometimes eating sweet corn, and now and then some raw sweet potatoes We kept clear of the road although progress was very slow otherwise We got wet through and before morning were hardly able to walk, but our only thought was of escape and return to the Union lines At the break of day we would find some low bushes and camp for the day This we kept up for seven or eight days and nights, depending upon the negroes at the plantations for most of our food

The eighth night, when we got our corn bread from the darkey at a plantation, he said "Massa, there is no rebs in these parts; why doan you all take the road" So that night we took the road and went as directed, but about nine o'clock here came a man on horseback at full gallop right toward us, before we could get out of sight. We were pretty well scared thinking he was a reb, but he asked where some doctor lived, and we quickly told him there was one three miles straight ahead. He whipped up his horse and away he went while we drew a long breath of relief.

Toward morning we came to an outpost of rebels. We went around them and soon came to a railroad that had been torn up by Sherman's army before he took Atlanta. A burned bridge impeded our progress, and we had considerable difficulty getting over the river. That day was Sunday and we camped in the woods. We did not think anyone would be walking there, but about three o'clock saw some women and children coming toward us. We went over the hill on a jump and into a big swamp, where we remained until darkness came. We could hear the bark of bloodhounds in the far distance and thought they might be on our trail, but the sounds gradually died out. It would have meant the end of our hopes had the hounds been on our trail, for we had no means of defense and our strength was on the wane.

Progress in the swamp was very difficult. Every step we would go down in the mud and water, then get up again only to fall headlong the next step. When we finally did get to dry ground again we were a dilapidated looking sight. We moved at a slow pace but were not disheartened. In a little while we began to smell the camp fires, and soon after midnight we could see our pickets a short distance ahead. It was necessary at this point to use great precaution in advancing for fear we would be mistaken for rebels. At four in the morning we were halted by our guards and we told them we were escaped prisoners. We were escorted to the picket post and every one greeted us with open arms. It was the happiest time of my life. Once more back to real freedom! When our thoughts reverted to the prison pen, where thirty-two thousand were huddled together in about thirty acres, and where they died at the rate of ninety a day during our confinement there, it made us thankful beyond expression for our deliverance.

After being fed and given some clothing, we were taken by wagon to Atlanta, Georgia, four miles south. Brother Oscar came to see me before we started. For him, it was almost like the dead coming to life, for they had all believed that I was killed instead of being captured. At Atlanta we were taken to the Soldiers' Home, where we had plenty to eat. It was at this place that my comrade in the escape, George H. Wagerley of Chillicothe, Ohio, and I became separated, and I have never seen him since. It has only been recently that I have been able to get into communication with him, as the correspondence in the following pages indicates.

I found some of the boys from my company, and went with them to

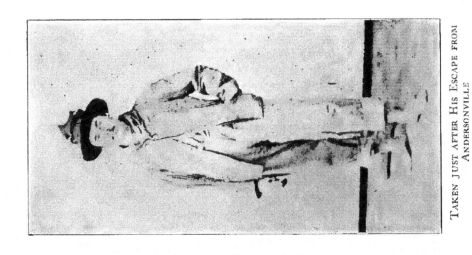

Taken just after His Escape from Andersonville

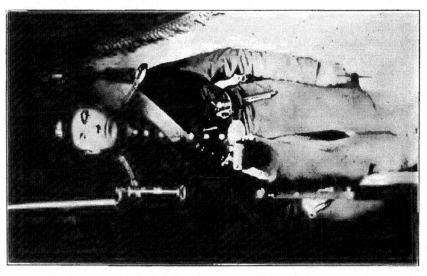

Calvin D. French at Time of Enlistment in 1862

where our regiment was camped. They gave me a great reception. Barney Keyes was one of the first boys I met. In a few days I was granted a furlough and went home. When my furlough of thirty days had expired I went back to Atlanta and arrived just in time to go with Sherman on his march to the sea.

REMINISCENCES

One night during the escape we lay by a picket garden fence waiting to see some negro, when a lady in the house began playing on the piano some beautiful melodies. It was the first piano music I had heard in years and it brought the tears to my eyes. After a while we found a negro in a shed feeding mules. We went up to him and touched him on the shoulder. He was so scared he jumped at least fifteen feet away and it was some time before we could get him to come near us. After telling him who we were and assuring him of our friendliness, he said he would send us something to eat. Soon an old negro came out with a pail on his arm filled with food. He directed us to a spring near by and there we ate our lunch. There was plenty of the inevitable hoe cake, but we were very thankful for even that. On the march with Sherman to the sea, we passed by this same plantation, but this time we did not hear any Southern melodies. The occupants had deserted the place and gone within the Confederate lines.

. . . .

I have often seen General Wirz ride around the prison between the stockade and dead line, with his orderly behind him, and it was difficult to realize that a man of the same blood as we were could look at such a terrible condition and let it pass without an effort to improve it. He was hung after the war, but that was sweet punishment compared with what he caused the thousands of prisoners placed in his charge at Andersonville, to endure.

. . . .

We never lived so well as during the march to the sea. We were dependent upon the country for all of our provisions and we necessarily cut a wide swath. Waste and ruin were left behind us, but it was one of the emergencies and necessities of war. From Savannah we took transports to Beaufort, South Carolina, and there disembarked and marched to Charleston, South Carolina. Then we marched to Raleigh. Just beyond Raleigh we learned that Richmond had been taken, and soon after, peace was declared.

. . . .

After peace was declared we slackened pace and strode leisurely north, for we were a very tired and tattered army. We passed through Richmond and by the famous Libby Prison. On the march we walked two abreast. We arrived in Washington and joined with the Army of the Potomac in the Grand Review. At this time we marched four abreast. The Army of the Potomac, which had a direct line of communication with the North during the siege of Richmond, presented a handsome appearance at the Review, but Sherman's army, in direct contrast, showed the stains of months of hardship and lack of commissary replenishment as a result of the detachment from the lines of supply. The march of Sherman to the sea has gone down in history as one of the greatest military accomplishments ever known, and it will undoubtedly be recognized with greater renown as time passes on.

Copy

Binghamton, N. Y., June 30, 1909.

War Department,
    Washington, D. C.

Sir: I have been endeavoring for several years to locate a Union soldier by the name of George H. Wagerley, who joined me in a successful escape while being transferred from Andersonville to another rebel prison. He belonged to an Ohio regiment, but further than that fact and his name I have no knowledge, as we were separated when we reached the Union lines and I have never been able to locate him since.

Any information your department can furnish me will be greatly appreciated.

                      Very respectfully,
                          (Signed)   CALVIN D. FRENCH.

Copy

                          DEPARTMENT OF WAR,
                      Washington, D. C., July 2, 1909.

Mr. C. D. French,
    13 Robinson St., Binghamton, N. Y.

Sir: Replying to your inquiry of the 30th ultimo, the records show that one George H. Wagerley was a Sergeant in Company I, 26th Ohio Infantry, and that he escaped from Confederate prison September 20, 1864. If he is living, his address can probably be obtained from the Commissioner of Pensions, Washington, D. C.

                      Very respectfully,
                          (Signed)   J. M. DICKINSON
                                      Secretary of War

Copy

DEPARTMENT OF THE INTERIOR, BUREAU OF PENSIONS
Washington, D C., July 24, 1909

Western Division,
Cert No 938,319,
George H Wagerley,
Co I, 26 Ohio Inf.
Mr. C D French,
  Binghamton, N Y
Sir   In response to your request, received the 19th instant, you are informed that the last known postoffice address of the above named soldier is Bucyrus, Crawford County, Ohio
Very respectfully,
(Signed)   J L DAVENPORT,
Acting Commissioner

Copy

G H. WAGERLEY
BOARD SOLDIERS' RELIEF COMMISSION
CRAWFORD COUNTY
Bucyrus, Ohio, July 30, '09

Mr C D French,
  Binghamton, N Y
Dear Comrade. I received your welcome letter a few days ago, and am glad that you are still among the living   I see by your letter that you think that I was with you on the night of September 10, '64, which I think was Saturday, and about fifteen miles east of Macon, Georgia   I think it was between eight and nine o'clock that night   I think I jumped off first. I thought that one of the guards shot at you   Then we took the back track. We went about a mile and we came to some negro shanties, and we made a noise and one negro came to us and we told the negro who we were — that we were Yankees and that we wanted him to tell us the direction to Atlanta from there. He gave us the direction, and then we asked if he could give us some corn bread, and he said he would go and get it   He came back with four loaves of corn bread and four large onions   I think it was the best corn bread I ever ate   He told us to go up the track about a mile, then cross the railroad crossing and take to the right, and that would take us to Atlanta   We got to the road and went along about a hundred yards when we came to a house, and as we were going by the man in the house hollered to us that we needn't try to slip by, as he heard us   I then thought we were caught, but we made fast time till we came to a river and bridge   We saw a light on the other side and some persons at the fire, and so we took a sneak

in the brush till they left, and then we crossed the bridge and went on our march. The next day I think was Sunday, and as we lay in the brush trembling, we could hear the bloodhounds bellow. I thought that the longest Sunday of my life. How does this correspond with your recollections? If you told me your name I had forgotten it.

I will close for this time, hoping to hear from you by return mail.

Yours truly,

(Signed) G. H. WAGERLEY.[1]

P. S. My company was Company I, 26th O. V. I.

From the Morrow County *Sentinel*, published at Mt. Gilead, Ohio, under date of May 18, 1911, is taken the following:

Calvin D. French, of Binghamton, N. Y., and George H. Wagerley, of Bucyrus, met on Saturday for the first time in forty-five years. Mr. French is a former Morrow County man, and served as a member of Company B, Forty-third Ohio Volunteer Infantry, enlisting when nineteen years of age and serving until the close of the war. He is a brother of Alva C. French, of near Iberia, and of former County Surveyor Oscar L. R. French, deceased. Mr. French and Mr. Wagerley were prisoners in Andersonville during the war, and made their escape together.

Extracts from diary of Calvin French kept during the Civil War:

Forty-third Regiment Ohio Volunteer Infantry,
Camped at Bethel, Tenn.
Monday, May 11, 1863.

We were ordered to report at 6 a. m. at the station, ready to move. 5 p. m. We have not gone yet, but expect to leave in the morning at 7 o'clock. The cars are here ready to load the rest of our baggage, and I am detailed to help load them. We bid good bye to the noble Seventh of Iowa, which came here when we did. May 13th, we arrived at Memphis, Tenn., where we are camped.

Tuesday, May 26, 1863.

Good news from Vicksburg, if true. P. M. News from Vicksburg still good tonight.

Friday, May 29.

We are just ordered to go with Company A, of our regiment, to the river, with three days' rations to guard prisoners. We get to the landing about 4 p. m.; get aboard a boat and go out, and change guards with the boys that came from Vicksburg. There are about five thousand rebs. We are soon detailed for guard.

---

[1] George H. Wagerley died in May, 1912.

Saturday, May 30th

We are still anchored at Memphis   3 p. m , we have just started up the river   The lines run smooth   We are on the packet Omaha.

Sunday, May 31st.

We are still moving up the river   We passed Ft Pillow last night   Passed Point Pleasant a little before dark, and New Madrid at 7 p m   Got to Island No 10 about 10 o'clock

Monday, June 1st.

We pass Columbus, Ky , at daylight; arrive at Cairo 9 a m , and anchor about the middle of the river

Tuesday, June 2d

Got off the boat this morning and get aboard the cars, and at 7 a. m. we start, over the Illinois Central   When we reach Indianapolis are relieved of the prisoners, and march to the Soldiers' Home, stack arms, and are furnished a good dinner.

Friday, June 5th

The Thirty-ninth regiment go with the prisoners to Sandusky tonight, and will meet us at Crestline tomorrow night   We leave at 4 p m   When we got to Union City, I met my brothers, Alva and Oscar.

Monday, June 8th

We get to Pittsburg at 4 p. m , and have to change cars here   We pass through the tunnel of the Alleghany Mountains   I am to be on guard tonight. Get to Harrisburg at 10 a m , run our train on wharf, and commenced unloading   I ate supper at the Soldiers' Home   Everything is nice

Wednesday, June 11th

We are at Fort Delaware; the prisoners are getting off the boat now   We get off the boat, and march up to the fort, and at 12 m get dinner   Got tents for our company, and I have one to sleep in.

Friday, June 12th

We leave the Island at 7 a m , get to Philadelphia, take the train for Pittsburg   Go to Columbus, get a furlough from there and go to Galion, visit my brother Oscar and family, and sister Lucy, and Alva's family

Saturday, June 20th.

Leave on the night express from Galion, go to Columbus, visit friends here.

Monday, June 22d

Leave for Cincinnati   The next day I leave for Memphis, and again take up my work as a soldier

They camped at Memphis, Tennessee, from Tuesday, May 12, 1863, until October 18, 1863, this being the longest time they remained in one place during the war. Again we quote from the diary:

October 13, 1863.

We are not relieved until afternoon, on account of the election. The sixty-third was to vote before coming out. We got to camp about 2 p. m.; find the election is going off very quietly. All of our Company go for Brough, and the regiment give but fifty votes for Vallandingham, and three hundred thirty-five votes for Brough.

Wednesday, Oct. 14th.

We learn that Vallandingham got but ninety-two votes in our brigade, consisting of the Forty-third, Sixty-third, Thirty-ninth and Twenty-seventh regiments.

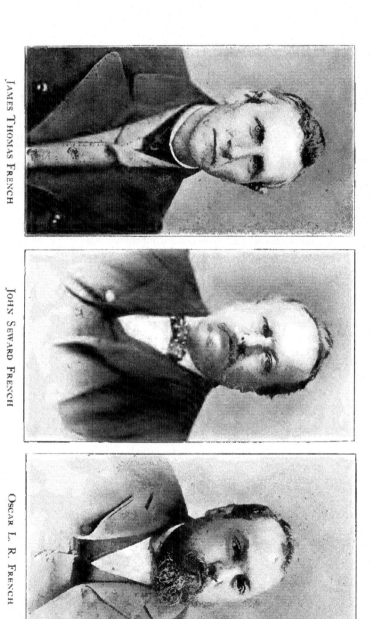

James Thomas French

John Seward French

Oscar L. R. French

Martin M. French   Alva C. French   Calvin D. French

THE INGALLS FAMILY

THE Ingalls family [1] was one of the earliest in this country, coming only eight years after the landing of the Pilgrims at Plymouth, and have as a whole maintained an honorable place in history, the majority of them being tillers of the soil.

The name is supposed to be Scandinavian, and derived from Ingialld. During the ninth century the Scandinavian pirates often descended upon the east coast of Great Britain, and in after years many of this nationality made settlements in Lincolnshire. These people were a hardy seafaring race, owing to the nature of their country, but under changed conditions of environment settled down to tilling the soil. The name of Ingalls is still common in England, its etymology being "By the power of Thor."

The earliest document on record, is the will of Henry Ingalls, made in 1555, he probably having been born about 1480.

First Generation

Will of HENRY INGALLS of Skirbeck found in the Probate Court attached to Lincoln Cathedral, June 1, 1555: Gives to his wife Johan: He wills that his youngest children shall have every one £10 which was left to them. If any should die before coming of lawful age that share to be divided amongst the rest; gives to the maintenance of the high alter 12d; the balance of his effects to be divided amongst his six children, Johan, wife, executrix; names a sonne James and broinlaw Thos. Wytton.

Second Generation

The next record is that of ROBERT, descendant of Henry Ingalls, the will which follows, being the only document on file:

---

[1] Up to the seventh generation taken largely from the *Genealogy and History of the Ingalls Family in America*, by Charles Burleigh, M. D., of Malden, Massachusetts.

WILL OF ROBERT INGALLS OF SKIRBECK, JULY 12, 1617

In ye name of God Amen. Robert Ingalls of Skirbeck quarter of Skirbeck in the Co. of Lincoln, yeomen, being sick in body but of good & perfect memorie &c I give Elizabeth my wife during her natural life. After her decease to Edmund my eldest Sonne who was lawfully begotten and for want of issue after Edmunds death to ffrancis my youngest Sonne and failing issue to the natural heirs of me Robert Ingalls forever; Gives Robert Ingalls £20 Gives ffrancis £30 both one year after his decease. Gives his maid servant Anne Cleasbie £5 & to all of Henry Cleasbies children one ewe lamb, Gives his brother Henry a black fleeced cow, Gives to the poor of Skirbeck 10s ½ at once, Wife and Edmund Executors, Wm Shinfold & Robert Harrison supervisors of the will, Gives them 2s 6d for their pains.

The will is signed with his mark.

Third Generation

EDMUND^3 INGALLS (Robert,^{2} Henry ^{1}) was born in Skirbeck, Lincolnshire, England, about 1598; came to Salem, Massachusetts, in Governor Endicott's company in 1628. With his brother Francis and four others he commenced the settlement of Lynn in 1629. He was a man of good character, even though the following court record is found, in 1646: "Edmund Ingalls was fined for bringing home sticks in both his arms on the Sabbath day from Mr. Holyoke's rails — Witnesses Joseph fflood, Obadya fflood, Jane fflood." These were probably jealous neighbors, and it shows the strict observance of the Sabbath in those days. His name is often found in the town records, showing him to have been one of the prominent citizens. In March, 1648, while traveling to Boston on horseback, owing to a defective bridge he was drowned in the Saugus River. His heirs recovered damages from the town. His will was probated September 16, 1648.

WILL OF EDMUND INGALLS

I, Edmund Ingalls of Lynn, being of perfect memory commit my soul unto God, my body to the grave and dispose of my earthly goods in this wise.

Firstly, I make my wife Ann Ingalls, sole executor, leaving my house and houselot, togather with my stock of cattle and corn, to her. Likewise I leave Katherine Shipper with my wife.

Item, I bequeath to Robert my sonne & heir four pound to be payd in two years time by my wife, either in cattle or corn. Likewise I bequeath to him or to his heirs, my house & houselot after the decease of my wife

Likewise I bequeath to Elizabeth my daughter, twenty shillings to be payd by my wife in a Heifer calf in two years time after my decease.

Likewise to my daughter Faith, wife to Andrew Allen, I bequeath two yearling calves, and inform my wife to pay him forty shillings debt in a years time after my decease

Likewise to my sonne John, I bequeath the house & ground that was Jeremy fitts, lying by the meeting house, only out of it the sd John is to pay within four years, four pounds to my sonne Samuel, and the ground to be his security, further I leave with said John, that three Acres of land he had in England fully to possess and enjoy.

Likewise, I give to Sarah my daughter, wife of William Bitnar my two ewes

Likewise, to Henry my sonne, I give the House that I bought of Goodman West, and six Acres of ground, lying by it, and three Acres of Marsh ground lying at Rumley March, and this the sd Henry shall possess in two years after my decease Only out of this the sd Henry shall pay to my sonne Samuel, four pounds within two years after he enters upon it

Likewise I bequeath to Samuel my sonne, eight pounds to be discharged as above, in the premises

Lastly, I leave with Mary the Heifer calf that she enjoyed and leave her to my wife for future dowry

Finally, I appoint Francis Ingalls, my brother & Francis Dane, my sonne in law, overseers of my will, and order that those things that have no particular exemption in the will mentioned, to be taken away after my decease and entreat my overseers to be helpful to my wife in ordering her matters

His
EDMUND X INGALLS
Mark

Children:

Robert, born about 1621; married Sarah Harker

Elizabeth, born 1622; married Rev Francis Dane; died June 9, 1676

Faith, born 1623; married Andrew Allen.

John, born 1625; married Elizabeth Barrett

Sarah, born 1626; married William Bitnar.

Henry, born 1627; married Mary Osgood; married (second) Sarah Farnum.

Samuel, born 1634; married Ruth Eaton.
Mary, born ——; married John Eaton.
Joseph; died young.

Fourth Generation

JOHN⁴ INGALLS (Edmund,³ Robert,² Henry¹) son of Edmund and Ann Ingalls, was born in Skirbeck, England, in 1625; married Elizabeth Barrett of Salem May 26, 1667. He settled at Rehoboth, Massachusetts, and it is recorded: "Old John Ingalls died Dec. 31, 1721."

JOHN INGALLS — HIS WILL

In the name of God Amen, the sixteenth day of Aprill on thousand seven hundred and eighteen, I, John Ingols of the town of Rehoboth in the County of Bristoll in the Province of the Masachusets Bay in New England, yeoman, being weak of body but of sound and perfect memory praised be the Almighty God for the same; I calling to mind the onsertaine and transitory estate of this life, that all flesh must dy and yeild to death when it shall please God to call, doe make and ordaine, constitute and declare this to be my last will and testament in manor and forme following (that is to say) revoaking and annulling and by these presents, all and every testament and testaments and will and wills heartofore by me made and declared either by word or writing; and this is to be taken for my last will & testament and non other. And first of all I give and recomend my soule in to the hands of God that gave it, and as for my body I commend it to the earth to be buried in a Christian like and decent maner at the discretion of my executor; nothing doubting but at the general resurrection I shall receive the same againe by the mighty power of God, and as touching such worldly estate as the Lord hath lent me, my will and meaning is in maner and forme following:

Impr. I will that all my just and lawfull debts which I justly owe to any person or persons whomesoever be well and truly paid in convenient time after my decease.

Itim. I give to my son John Ingols twenty shillings and the reason why I give him no more is because he hath bene a disobedent and ondutyfull son to me.

Itum. I give to my two daughters Elizabeth Crabtre the wife of Benjamin Crabtre and Sarah Hayward wife of William Hayward all my movable estate within dores that is to say, my uttensels, household stuff in what maner or kind they may be found and that my two daughters shall devide between them theire mothers cloathes, and if my two daughters cannot agree in the devidmg of the movables that then they chuse two indifferent men to mak an equall devition between them.

Itim I doe make, constitute and ordaine my well beloved son Edmund Ingols to be my only and sole executor of this my last will and testament, ratifying and confirming this and no other to be my last will and testament.

In witness whearof I have hereunto sett to my hand and seale the day and yeare first above written &c. &c. &c.

Signum
JOHN X INGOLS { Seal }

Signed, sealed, published and pronounced by the sd John Ingols to be his last will and testament, in presence of us the subscribers

Approved Feb 5, 1721/22

JOHN WEST
HENRY WEST

Fifth Generation

EDMUND [5] INGALLS (John,[4] Edmund,[3] Robert,[2] Henry [1]) son of John and Elizabeth Ingalls, was probably born at Bristol or Cumberland, Rhode Island; married Eunice Luddin of Braintree November 29, 1705. He moved to Rehoboth, Massachusetts, where he died

Sixth Generation

EBENEZER [6] INGALLS (Edmund,[5] John,[4] Edmund,[3] Robert,[2] Henry [1]) son of Edmund and Eunice (Luddin) Ingalls, was born July 14, 1711; married Elizabeth Wheeler June 5, 1735 To them were born ten children:

I. Elizabeth, born May 5, 1736.
II. Henry, born October 12, 1738; married Sybil Carpenter.
III Frederick, born December 7, 1740
IV Alithea, born November 18, 1741; married Samuel Fuller Jr. December 3, 1762
V Ebenezer, born June 30, 1744; married Rachel Wheeler
VI Mehitable, born January 3, 1746 or 1747.
VII Lois, born February 16, 1750; married James Kelton (born February 16, 1750) June 13, 1773 To them were born seven children.

VIII. Hannah, born ——; married John Turner December 23, 1773.
IX. Benjamin, born ——.
X. Sabia (or Sabina), born ——; married James Campbell November 25, 1778.

Seventh Generation

HENRY[7] INGALLS (Ebenezer,[6] Edmund,[5] John,[4] Edmund,[3] Robert,[2] Henry[1]) son of Ebenezer and Elizabeth Ingalls, was born at Cumberland, Rhode Island, October 12, 1739; married Sybil Carpenter (born February 26, 1739) at Rehoboth, Massachusetts, November 21, 1761. To them were born ten children:

I. Elizabeth, born 1762; married James Cook.
II. Mehitable, second child of Henry and Sybil (Carpenter) Ingalls, was born ——, 1764; married James Ballou Jr. at Richmond, New Hampshire, the ceremony being performed by the bride's father, who was justice of the peace. For a complete history of Mehitable Ingalls Ballou and her descendants see close of the Ingalls genealogy.
III. Ruth, third child of Henry and Sybil Ingalls, was born in 1767; married Benjamin Ellis.
IV. Rufus, fourth child of Henry and Sibyl Ingalls, was born in 1769; married Mary Cole.
V. Ebenezer, fifth child of Henry and Sybil Ingalls, was born in 1771; married Mary Mann. To them were born:
  1. Abram; married Mehitable Ballou (born March 15, 1799) in Perry, Muskingum county, Ohio, in 1815.
  2. Rufus.
  3. Hiram.
  4. Isaac; married Portia Howard March 21, 1851.
  5. Ebenezer.
  6. Candace.
  7. Olive.
  8. Roxie.
  9. Mary.

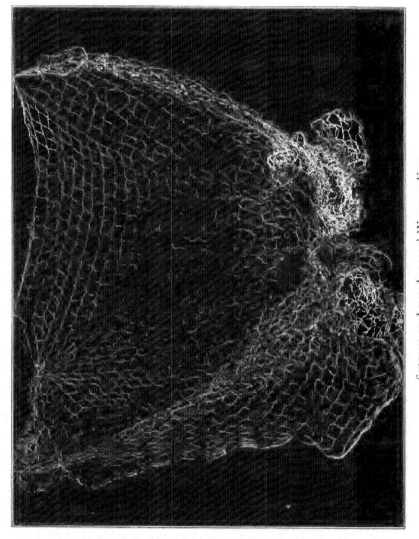

Section of Lucy Ingalls' Wedding Veil

10   Eliza
VI   Sybil, sixth child of Henry and Sybil Ingalls, was born in 1774; married —— Skinner.
VII Lucy, seventh child of Henry and Sybil Ingalls, was born June 24, 1777; married Stephen Seaward (born June 13, 1772) February 19, 1795, at Decatur, Otsego county, New York To them were born nine children (See Seaward genealogy)

Lucy lived with her parents on "Ingalls Hill" until her marriage, and was early taught the art of housewifery, especially as pertaining to the needlework done in that day, and before her marriage she netted her wedding veil out of white silk thread, a portion of which is in possession of the author

VIII. Alpha Ingalls, eighth child of Henry and Sybil Ingalls, was born in 1780; married James Stone
IX   Henry, ninth child of Henry and Sybil Ingalls, was born in 1783; died at the age of fourteen years
X   Sebra, tenth child of Henry and Sybil Ingalls, was born in 1785; married Alva Clark. To them were born·
   1. Eunice; married —— Bliss. To them were born
      a. Luna; married —— Lucas
      b Jesse Chandler
      c. Edwin Ruthwin.
      d. Eliza Prudence; married —— Holcomb.
      e Sarah Louisa; married Thomas Needles, who was auditor of state (Illinois) for two terms; afterwards state senator.
   2 Stephen, son of Sebra and Alva Clark. His children were:
      a James Stone; last known address, Yarn Hill, Oregon
      b Alva; married Caroline Gregory; lived at one time at Osage Mission, Neosha county, Kansas
      c Harvey Cunning
      d. Eliza Cram

e. Angeline.
f. Elizabeth.
3. Eliza, daughter of Sebra and Alva Clark, was born in Otsego county, New York, December 28, 1806; married Joseph Crane (born January 12, 1802, White Creek, Pennsylvania) March 9, 1826. To them was born.
   a. Evan Joseph Crane, born April 26, 1827; married Casander Gier, in Muskingum county, Ohio. In April, 1864, they moved to Iberia, Morrow county, where Evan kept a general store, and was for many years postmaster. To them were born:
      aa. Marion.
      bb. Rosetta.
      cc. Florence.
      dd. George.
      ee. Della.
   Evan Joseph Crane and his wife died at Iberia, Ohio.
   Eliza, wife of Joseph Crane, died January 1, 1830.
4. Alva.
5. James Stone.

Henry Ingalls moved from Rehoboth, Massachusetts, to Richmond, New Hampshire, and his record as a soldier is found in the *Revolutionary Rolls of Massachusetts and New Hampshire*, from which the following is taken:

> Henry Ingalls — Richmond — Captain Oliver Capron's Co. Col. Ephraim Doolittle's (24th) Regiment — Receipt for advanced pay signed by said Ingalls and others. Detail camp at Cambridge June 24th 1775. Also Sergeant in same Co. and Reg. Muster roll dated Aug. 11, 1775. Enlisted May 5, 1775, service three months four days. Also company returned (probably Oct. 1775).
>
> Also order for bounty coat or its equivalent in money.
>
> Henry Ingalls Sergeant — Richmond — Capt Oliver Caprons Company Col. Ephraim Doolittle's Regiment at Winter Hill Oct. 6, 1775. Lieutenant, Capt. Oliver Capron's Co. Col. Samuel Ashley's Regiment; marched to relief of Ticonderoga, June 18th to Sep 27th 1777.

In Vol 13, p 315, of the *State Papers of New Hampshire*, is found the following record

A Return of A Leagal Town meeting Held in Richmond in the Colony of New Hampshire on the 15th Day of July Last — firstly Chose A moderator to govern said meeting then Voted and made Choice of Lieut Henry Ingalls for a justice of the peace

Attest HENRY INGALLS Town Clerk
August ye 2nd A D 1776

DANIEL READ } Selectmen
JOHN DAULY

State of New Hampshire
To the Honnarable Councel and house of Representatives Convened at Exeter in said state the prayer of your Humble petitioners sheweth that at our Last annual march meeting the town of Richmond voted pettion your Honors would take it unto your wise Consideration and grant us the priviledge to Hold our anual meeting on the first munday of march annually as the Last wednesday in march is the season of the year that wee make shuger as your Humble petitioners in Duty Bound shall Ever pray in Behalf of the town

Richmond October ye 20th 1779

HENRY INGALLS Town Clerk

On page 318:

(Petition for Henry Ingalls 1785)

The Petition of the Inhabitants of Richmond in the County of Cheshire, Humbly Sheweth, that when the Late Constitution took Place Henrey Ingalls Esqr was not Reappointed we your Petitioners humbly Pray that the Said Henrey Ingalls may be Reappointed and duely ortherrised to act as A Justice of the Peace for the County aforSaid, for that wee your Petitioners Humbly conseive that he is a man agreably Qualified for that Important Service and Lives near the Senter of Publick Bisness for the town, and also Sutes the maners and Costumes of the People, and your Petitioners Humbly Submits this Petition to your Excelancies Grace Beleving your Excelancey in your Grate wisdom will do the thing that is Right as wee in duty Bound will ever Pray —

Richmond October 10th A D 1785:

Daniel Read	John Bools	
Abraham Man	Levi Morey	Cadis Boyce
Moses Read	Darius Taft	Allen Grant
David Barney	Silas Taft	Jonathan Sweet

| William Barney | Edmund Ingalls | John Boyce |
| John Garnsey | Paul Boyce | Nathan Boyce |

Henry Ingalls moved with his family and a company of neighbors to Otsego county, New York, in an early day, and settled on what was called "Ingalls Hill," near Worcester. He lived highly respected by all who knew him, and died in June, 1813, at the age of seventy-five years.

The date of the death of Sybil (Carpenter) Ingalls, wife of Henry Ingalls, is not known, but she died on Ingalls Hill, at Decatur, New York.

James Ballou Jr., husband of Mehitable Ingalls, when a young man was a teacher and for years was successful in that vocation. Astrology being a favorite study, he became noted the country around as a diviner of future events. One of his descendants relates the following story in the Ballou genealogy.

> "One day," said he, "a queer looking maiden rode into our open dooryard on a little dapple mare. On dismounting, she delivered her pony for stable care. She told me she had come forty miles to consult the great fortune teller on an important matter, but that her story must be short, and she must return as soon as possible. She therefore wished an immediate private consultation. I inferred from the urgency of her manner that some murder, robbery, or theft had been committed at her home, or that some valuable articles of property had been lost. On seating her in my reception room, she looked furtively around, and inquired if that was my most private apartment. I took her into one more retired and less exposed to intrusion or overhearing, and now came out, in an anxious, half suppressed tone, her momentous errand — 'Shall I ever be married?' I concealed my astonishment, glanced inoffensively at her uncouth physiognomy, and felt that it was a hard case, for nature had knocked her forehead one way, her chin the other, set her blear eyes askew, twisted her sharp nose badly, and given her lank face a skin as brown as a dried shad. Well, what was to be done? I went through my customary formula and ciphered out her destiny as quickly as possible. I gave her as hopeful a forecast as the nature of the case permitted, and sent her off with the most comfortable assurance my ingenuity could deduce. I never heard of the fair maiden again." This was told with such sarcastic gravity, such lurking twinkles of fun, and such ineffable airs of drollery, that all present were convulsed with laughter.

James Ballou Jr. later formed a mercantile partnership with his cousin, under the firm name of Cook & Ballou, near Richmond Center, New Hampshire. Trade was not in the line of his mission, for they failed in business about the year 1804 He did his utmost to settle honorably with his creditors, but could not overcome the entail of embarrassments He died April 30, 1808, and his widow, who settled his estate, was able to pay only about twenty per cent of the indebtedness against the same. No one breathed a word of reproach, however, or had aught but respect for his memory and sympathy for his family.

In 1810 Stephen Seaward, the brother-in-law of Mehitable Ballou, went from Decatur, New York, to Richmond, New Hampshire, and moved the Ballou family (mother and five children) to a farm owned by him in Decatur, where she lived until after the death of her father, when she removed to "Ingalls Hill" In the autumn of 1814 she loaded her family and household effects into heavy carts and with others in the party started to find a new home in the west After a journey of six weeks, they finally located at Perry, Muskingum county, Ohio Only seven years of life were her portion in this new home, for she died December 4, 1821 Mehitable (Ingalls) Ballou was a woman of strong personality, bearing without a murmur the cares and responsibilities incident to the life of one left to fight its battles single-handed and alone.

To James Ballou Jr. and Mehitable (Ingalls) Ballou were born six children.

1. James, son of James and Mehitable Ballou, was born October 15, 1794 After his father's death he moved to New York state with his mother and when the War of 1812 broke out, enlisted, serving until its close Shortly after his return he moved with his mother to Ohio, where he married Rebecca Ellis in October, 1815

2 Henry, second son of James and Mehitable Ballou, was born September 6, 1796; married Phebe Tanner of Perry, Muskingum county, Ohio, March 20, 1823 She was the daughter of Jacob and Lydia (Passmore) Tanner, formerly of Chester county, Pennsylvania, and was born November 25, 1803 They

settled on a farm one mile west of Muskingum and fourteen miles below Zanesville. Henry Ballou was a man of ability, and filled to public satisfaction, several township and county offices. He died in 1857. His wife, Phebe (Tanner) Ballou, lived for many years, and was beloved by every one who knew her. She was gifted as a letter writer, which is evidenced by the many interesting epistles received by the author, some of them written after her eightieth birthday. To Henry and Phebe Ballou were born three children:

a. Jacob T., born March 4, 1824; married Emily Evans December 25, 1845.
b. Ellis, born July 9, 1828; married Laura Clark.
c. Orrin, born September 21, 1831; married Matilda J. Price. Orrin died April, 1895.

The above mentioned children were born and married near Zanesville, Muskingum county, Ohio. The mother, Phebe (Tanner) Ballou, survived her son Orrin but a few months, dying in September, 1895, at the home of her granddaughter, Mrs. Rufus Dutro, at Canalsville, Ohio, aged ninety-two years. She was laid to rest beside her husband, in Virginia Ridge cemetery, Muskingum county, Ohio.

3. Mehitable, daughter of James and Mehitable Ballou, was born April 15, 1798; married Abram Ingalls in 1815. To them were born four children. After the death of Mehitable, which occurred near Cincinnati, Ohio (date not obtained), Abram Ingalls married (second) —— ——. To them were born two children — a son and daughter.

4. Rufus, born in 1799; died at the age of one month.

5. Eliza, daughter of James and Mehitable Ballou, was born September 21, 1801, at Richmond, New Hampshire; married Abram Garfield (born in Worcester, Otsego county, New York, 1799) February 3, 1820. To them were born:

a. Mehitable, born January 28, 1821; married Stephen Trowbridge.
b. Thomas, born October 16, 1822; married Jane Harper.

Eliza Ballou Garfield

FRENCH AND ALLIED FAMILIES

 c. Mary, born October 19, 1824; married Marenas G Larabee

 d James Ballou, born ——, 1827; died 1829.

 e James Abram, born November 19, 1831, married Lucretia Rudolph

The above named children were born in Newburg, Cuyahoga county, with the exception of James Abram, born in Orange (same county), Ohio

When two years of age, Abram Garfield lost his father, who died with small-pox, and the boy was left in charge of his uncle, James Stone. When Eliza Ballou went west with her mother, she carried with her the heart of young Garfield, and it was not long until he followed where his heart prompted, for in the autumn of 1819 he journeyed westward to claim his bride They were married in Perry township, Muskingum county, Ohio, February 3, 1820 Before the birth of their son James Abram, they moved to Orange, Cuyahoga county, Ohio, buying fifty acres of land in what was practically a wilderness, there being but one house within seven miles of their log cabin He managed the farm, clearing an acre or two each year, while his wife attended to the affairs of the home. In the summer of 1833, while fighting a forest fire which threatened his fields of wheat ripening for the harvest, Abram Garfield caught a severe cold from the effects of which he died after a two days' illness, leaving his wife, four children, and many friends to mourn his loss.

6 Alpha, sixth child of James and Mehitable Ballou, was born May 19, 1806, at Richmond, New Hampshire; married Amos Boynton, near Cleveland, Ohio, in 1826 To them were born·

 a William, born ——; died, aged twenty-nine years

 b. Henry Ballou; married Susanna Smith

 c Harriet; married Daniel Clark

 d Phebe; married John Clapp

 e Silas; married Ann Thorne He was a doctor of considerable note; they lived in Cleveland, Ohio

Alpha Ballou Boynton died at Hiram, Ohio, April 22, 1882.

There is so much of historic interest connected with the later years of Eliza (daughter of James and Mehitable Ballou), wife of Abram Garfield and mother of the martyred president, James Abram Garfield, that a more extended mention of her life seems fitting in this place. The sorrows, trials, and hardships she endured, the brave struggle that she made to properly care for and rear her little family, can only be fully understood by those who have had the experience incident to such a life; but that the results were commensurate with the effort made, can be realized from a study of the life of the youngest of the four children left to her care — James Abram Garfield. The mother was spared for many years to enjoy the fruits of her labor, being the honored member of the family circle during their residence in the capital city, and later on, in the executive mansion. She survived her illustrious son for seven years, dying January 21, 1888, at the age of eighty-seven.

The following is a copy of a letter written by Eliza Garfield to her cousin, Mary Flint, at Peoria, Illinois:

Mentor, Ohio, Sep. 17th, 1880.

My dear Cousin: With much pleasure I received your very welcome letter; having got your letter I resolved to answer it without delay. In the first place we are all well, for which I am truly thankful. I hardly know where to begin. It will be seventeen years in December since James first went to Congress. He has been there ever since, winters, I mean. I have been in Washington thirteen winters. We always come to Ohio summers. Four years ago James bought a farm near Mentor, in Lake county, of one hundred and fifty-six acres. It is a splendid farm. We have horses and cows and sheep and hogs and turkeys and hens. We enjoy living on the farm very much; it is only sixteen miles from Orange, where James was born. My children are living near me, all but my oldest son; he lives in Michigan, is a farmer, has two children, a son and a daughter, both married. The girls both live where they did when you were here. James has five children, four sons and one daughter. The two oldest boys are in school at Concord, New Hampshire. They have been there one year and are going another year. Henry will be seventeen next month and James will be fifteen. How I wish I could see you, and what a good time we would have, but my sands of life are nearly run out; I shall be seventy-nine next Tuesday, but my health has been good for four or five years. The last few

weeks I have not felt well, we have had such a rush of company since the nomination that I get real tired. I expect to be, till after the election. If James is elected, as I hope he will be, I pray he may have judgment and wisdom and strength to steer the ship of State to safe moorings If I do say it, he is a very smart man Our friends are dropping to the right and to the left, it will soon be our turn. Let us be prepared for the change that when we are done with earth we may meet in heaven Give my kind regards to all your children, and with much love I remain, Your Cousin,
ELIZA GARFIELD.

Another letter, written just after the inauguration of President Garfield, follows·

White House, March 7th, 1881
My dear Cousin — I received your good letter and your picture also, and would have answered sooner, but waited to get my picture I have some and will send you one, though they are not good I am happy to tell you that we are all pretty well, but a good deal tired out We have passed through the greatest rush of people for the last six months that I ever saw Since the inauguration it is one steady stream of old friends calling It takes pretty much all the time to entertain them, they want to see the President's mother I am the first mother that occupied the White House and her son President, but I feel very thankful for such a son I don't like the word proud, but if I must use it, I think in this case it is quite appropriate How many times my mind goes back to our girlhood school days, but changes take place I have seen sorrowful days and have seen happy days. "I was once young but now am old but I have never seen the righteous forsaken or his seed begging his bread." I have a very pleasant room, nicely furnished, and am waited on in the very best manner possible Now I want you to write to me. Our folks all send love to you With very much love I remain your aged Cousin,   ELIZA GARFIELD — to Mary Flint

The following is copied from a Washington special to the Cincinnati *Commercial*, under date of March 5, 1881:

The aged mother of the President was taken directly to the White House by Mr Webb Hayes, and installed at once in the apartment previously arranged for her It is a large square room on the south side of the mansion, about midway in the wide hall that serves as a sort of sitting and reception room for the President's family The room is a sunny one, made more cheerful by a bright axminster carpet and window drapings to correspond, and a wood fire in a wide old fashioned grate with glittering brass andirons and fenders. To have her home in the White House, the most honored figure within its walls is certainly a great change from other days within her remembrance when, left a widow in straightened circumstances, she washed, and cooked, and toiled, and saved, that her children might be educated Her stalwart son who, over thirty years ago, grew so tall that she could walk under his outstretched arm without stooping, still defers to her slightest wish with the same obedience that he rendered when a boy. Hers has always been a post of honor at the General's table, and no matter what distinguished guests are present, she is invariably served first

A sweeter picture has seldom been seen than this little white haired matron made, whose head barely reaches her son's elbow, when she came proudly forward with tears in her eyes, to be the first to receive him as he entered the Executive Mansion, President of the United States, escorted thither by the grandest civil and military display that Washington has ever witnessed

President Garfield died as Washington died, mourned by a nation of freemen, loved by his countrymen for all the qualities that constitute a great man, even among the great men of the earth He died as Lincoln died, the grief of his countrymen intensified by the horrible circumstances of his murder His whole public record was a succession of intellectual convictions of right and a courage to assert them At the very moment he was stricken to the earth, he was conspicuous as the most acceptable of all the rulers of nations He died September 19, 1881, at Long Branch, surrounded by his loved ones.

SEAWARD GENEALOGY

THE Seawards are of Scotch-English descent, a tradition in the family giving the name originally as Ward Some of the family living near the sea were designated as Sea Wards, and thus they finally came to be known as Seaward or Seward

First Generation

WILLIAM[1] SEAWARD, born in England, 1627; married Grace Norton of Guilford, Connecticut, April 2, 1651   To them were born

- I. Mary, born February 28, 1651 or 1652, at New Haven; married March 12, 1673, John Scranton Jr. of Guilford He died September 2, 1703 She died in 1688.
- II. John, born February 14, 1653 or 1654; died December 6, 1748
- III. Joseph, born ——; died February 14, 1731-2.
- IV. Samuel, born August 20, 1659; died young.
- V. Caleb, born March 14, 1662 or 1663; died August 2, 1728.
- VI. Stephen, born August 6, 1664; never married
- VII. Samuel, born February 8, 1666 or 1667; died April 8, 1689.
- VIII. Hannah, born February 8, 1669 or 1670; married Joseph Hand; married (second) John Tustin, by whom she had one son — John Jr
- IX. Ebenezer, born December 13, 1672; died October 19, 1701.

William Seaward was born in England in 1627 He came from Bristol to New England and is said to have been in Taunton, Massachusetts, in 1643 He settled in New Haven shortly after arriving in America, and while residing there married Grace Norton of Guilford, to which place he removed shortly after. He took the oath of fidelity there, May 4, 1654

He was a tanner, a man of considerable property and eminence in the town, and was for a long time commander of the train band He frequently represented the town in the General Assembly He died March 29, 1689. His will was dated the day of his death, and was proved June 7, 1689 He left his wife the use of one-half the dwelling house for her life, and an annuity of forty shillings per annum from each of her six sons One-half of the moveable estate, except the stock of the tan house, was left to her absolutely His son Stephen seems not to have been capable of caring for himself and a life estate in the dwelling and thirty acres were given him under the trusteeship of John, who was to inherit the property absolutely after Stephen's death Samuel, Caleb, and Ebenezer are confirmed in the possession of lands already given to them. Each of the children of his daughter Mary was given a cow, and the other half of the moveable estate was given to his daughter Hannah The tan-yard and meadow land were directed to be equally divided among the sons

Second Generation

CALEB[2] SEAWARD (William[1]) born March 14, 1662 or 1663; married July 14, 1686, Lydia Bushnell of Saybrook, Massachusetts She died August 24, 1753 To them were born:

    I   Daniel, born in Guilford, Connecticut, October 16, 1687; died April 28, 1688
    II   Lydia, born in Guilford, May 22, 1689; married John Howe April 5, 1714.
    III   Caleb, born in Guilford, January 12, 1692
    IV   Thomas, born in Guilford, December 19, 1694
    V.   Noadiah, born in Guilford, August 22, 1697; died in 1744
    VI   Ephraim, born in Durham August 6, 1700, first white child born in the town, died 1780
    VII   Ebenezer, born in Durham June 7, 1703, second white child born in the town

Caleb Seaward was a tanner, and the first settler of Durham, Connecticut, whither he removed May 4, 1699 He died August 2, 1728.

Third Generation [1]

EBENEZER [3] SEAWARD (Caleb,[2] William [1]), seventh child of Caleb and Lydia Bushnell Seaward, was born in Durham, June 7, 1703; married Sarah Wells October 19, 1730 To them was born one child, Chloe, born November 20, 1731 She married January 1, 1753, Joseph Talmage   Sarah Wells Seaward died December 22, 1731 Ebenezer Seaward married (second) Dorothy Rose November 22, 1732 To them were born

- II Joel, born November 25, 1733; married Laurana Seaward, a cousin
- III Sarah, born ——; married —— Coe
- IV Ebenezer, baptized March 18, 1738 or 1739; died young
- V. Damaris, baptized July 20, 1740
- VI Noadiah, born February 14, 1742
- VII Ebenezer, baptized September 23, 1744.

Dr Ebenezer Seaward removed from Durham to New Bedford, Massachusetts, in 1737

Fourth Generation

NOADIAH [4] SEWARD (Ebenezer,[3] Caleb,[2] William [1]), born February 14, 1742, married October 30, 1765, Sarah Swain (born October 13, 1746, Philadelphia, Pennsylvania), at Granville, Massachusetts To them were born twelve children:

- I Noadiah Jr, born October 11, 1766; married at Granville, Massachusetts (name of wife not known)   To them were born two children:
  1. ——; married —— Fenner
  2. ——; married —— Morey
- II John, born April 10, 1768; married Betsey Flint   To them was born·
  1. Porter; married Martha Barney
  2. John; died September 29, 1796.
- III. Eliphalet, born April 7, 1770; married —— ——   Two children:

---

[1] The first three generations are taken from *New England Historical and Genealogical Register*, Vol 52

GENEALOGICAL HISTORY OF THE

       1. ——; married Pomeroy Wright.
       2. Orpha; married Nathaniel Brown.
IV. Stephen, born June 13, 1772; married Lucy Ingalls.
V. Sarah, born September 9, 1774; died September 24, 1777.
VI. Swain, born March 9, 1777; married Sarah ——. To them were born seven children:
       1. Laura; married —— Fowler.
       2. Dolly; married Thomas W. Treat.
       3. Sarah; married Loren Benton.
       4. Sabina; married Hezekiah Bell.
       5. Rachel; married —— Tedman.
       6. John; married Rhoda Kelley.
       7. Seneca; married Caroline Parmalee.
Sarah, wife of Swain Seaward, died January 16, 1848.
VII. Dorothy, born October 9, 1779; married Jacob Flint. Dorothy died October 10, 1836.
VIII. William, born February 23, 1782.
IX. Jesse, born April 26, 1784; married Sophia Peake.
The aforenamed nine children of Noadiah and Sarah Seaward were born at Granville, Massachusetts.
To Jesse and Sophia Peake Seaward were born six children:
       1. Calvin; married —— Vanduzen.
       2. Olive; married —— Washburn.
       3. Stephen.
       4. Charles; married Julia Moon.
       5. Robert.
       6. Emmeline; married Cyrus Lewis.
Jesse Seaward moved to Kankakee, Illinois, where he died. His wife, Sophia Peake Seaward, died December 26, 1847.
X. Calvin, born October 5, 1786, at Chester, Maryland; died April 29, 1796.
XI. Catherine, born December 26, 1788, at Chester, Maryland; married Solomon Hoag. To them were born two children.
XII. Sarah, born February 12, 1793, at Cherry Valley, Otsego county, New York; married March 16, 1834, Calvin Day.

ALPHA SEAWARD ARNOLD   MARY SEAWARD FLINT
JAMES SEAWARD
SIBBEL SEAWARD McNALL   DELILAH SEAWARD PAUL
Children of Stephen and Lucy Ingalls Seaward

² Lucy French Queal   ³ Mary Queal Beyer
¹ Elizabeth Seaward French
⁴ Lucy Beyer Engelbeck   ⁵ Elizabeth Engelbeck
Direct Descendants of Henry and Sybil Ingalls

FRENCH AND ALLIED FAMILIES

Noadiah Seaward died March 29, 1825, at the home of his son, Stephen Seaward, in the eighty-fifth year of his age. Sarah Swain, wife of Noadiah Seaward, died July 29, 1820, at Decatur, New York, aged seventy-six years.

Fifth Generation

STEPHEN[5] SEAWARD (Noadiah,[4] Ebenezer,[3] Caleb,[2] William[1]), born June 13, 1772, at Durham, Massachusetts; married Lucy Ingalls (born June 24, 1777, at Rohoboth, Massachusetts) at Decatur, New York, February 19, 1795. To them were born:
  I. Alpha, born February 18, 1796; married David Arnold.
  II. Elizabeth, born February 7, 1798; married Samson French. See tenth generation of French family for history of Elizabeth.
  III. Mary, born December 26, 1799; married Nathan Tripp.
  IV. James, born January 19, 1802; married Clarissa Barnes.
  V. Stephen, born January 28, 1804; died November 7, 1824.
  VI. Lucy, born January 28, 1806; married Asa Palmerlee.
  VII. Mehitable, born July 27, 1808; married Daniel Flint.
  VIII. Sibbel,[1] born April 15, 1811; married William McNall.
  IX. Babe, born May 1, 1813; died when a few hours old.

Lucy Ingalls Seaward died May 1, 1813, at the birth of her ninth child. She was possessed of a sweet disposition, quick to see a need and ready to relieve distress whenever found. She was a faithful consistent member of the Methodist church, and died beloved by all who knew her. She was laid to rest in the cemetery at Decatur, Otsego county, New York. Her father, Henry Ingalls, attended the funeral services of his daughter, and died seven weeks later.

Stephen Seaward married (second) Sally Parker August 16, 1814, at Decatur, New York. To them were born:
  X. John, born August 8, 1818.
  XI. David, } born August 21, 1821.
  XII. Delilah, }
        David married Lucinda ——. To them were born seven

---
[1] Name is always spelled "Sibbel" in this family.

children — five girls and two boys   In 1861 this family removed from Cattaraugus county, New York, to Columbus, Ohio   On August 24, 1862, while riding on a load of lumber, an accident occurred in which David and his son Orlando were both killed, and two weeks later, his baby daughter died   Hettie, the oldest daughter of David Seaward, married Frank Gilmore of Iberia, and later moved to Columbus, Ohio, where they still reside

Delilah (twin sister of David) married David Paul at Franklinville, Cattaraugus county, New York   They lived later at Williamsville, a suburb of Buffalo, New York.

XIII.   Emily, born July 25, 1823
XIV.   Electa, born December 31, 1825

Stephen Seaward went when but a lad with his parents from Massachusetts to Decatur, Otsego county, New York, where he grew to manhood on the farm owned by his father   Before his marriage he bought a farm in Decatur, on one corner of which he built a small mill, where he carded wool, making it into rolls ready for spinning   The farmers' wives and daughters in the neighborhood spun the yarn, and it was woven into cloth   Home spun and home cut garments were in vogue in those days, and "linsey woolsey," a mixture of flax and wool, was used for dresses in winter   The family linen was made of flax raised on the farm, and each girl had her "stent"; that is, she must spin so much flax on a "little wheel" each day   The value of a girl's services was often rated by the number of knots of flax or wool she could spin in a given length of time   Stephen Seaward's older daughters assisted in the carding mill during the busy season, when they could be spared from household duties

In the spring of 1812 Stephen sold the piece of land upon which the mill stood, to Thomas French, by whom the mill was enlarged, and dyeing, fulling, and dressing of cloth were added to the establishment.   The sum paid for this piece of land was fifty dollars

Stephen Seaward lived on the direct road to Albany, and as there were no railroads in those days and travel was entirely by team or on horse-back, taverns were to be found every few miles along the main roads, one of which was kept by him and well patronized by the traveling public. Operating his mill until 1812, looking after his farm and this public house, were his occupations during the years he lived in Decatur.

The following incident has been handed down by the descendants of Stephen Seaward, who was at one time the owner of a valuable iron gray horse of which he was very proud. One night it was stolen from his stable, and while he made diligent search throughout that part of the country, no trace of the missing animal could be found. A year or so afterward, a neighbor who had been to Albany, told him of having seen in a stable in that city a horse which he believed to be the one he had lost. Stephen immediately went to that city, where he explained the situation to the man who had the horse in his possession, to which explanation the man replied: "If you can prove your statement, the horse is yours." "I will prove it by the horse himself," returned Stephen Seaward. He stepped into the barn and the horse neighed, as had been his habit upon the approach of his master. He then went up to the horse and patting him, said: "Prince, address yourself!" and he immediately stretched himself upon his hind legs, and then on his fore legs. Then his owner said: "Take my hat," which the horse immediately did; then he requested him to make a bow, which the animal proceeded to do. "The horse is yours," said the man, and Stephen returned home, happy to again be the possessor of this much prized animal.

In 1828 he moved with his son James and the younger members of his family, to what was then known as the far west — Cattaraugus county, New York. There his children who were in the home, married and settled around him. For a number of years before his death he and his wife occupied a part of the home of his daughter, Sibbel McNall, where he died January 22, 1852, aged eighty years. His wife, who survived him some years, spent her last days at the home of her daughter, Delilah Paul.

Sixth Generation

ALPHA[6] SEAWARD, daughter of Stephen and Lucy (Ingalls) Seaward, born February 18, 1776, Decatur, Otsego county, New York; married David Arnold of Herkimer county, New York, September 15, 1815 To them were born nine children, the names of only seven being known to the author

    I. Lucy, born 1816; married —— Parker, was living in Omaha, Nebraska, in 1909, aged ninety-three years
   II Lovina; married —— Comstock.
  III Samuel
  IV. Mary.
   V David
  VI. Edward.
 VII. Stephen, born April 25, 1830, New Concord, Muskingum county, Ohio; married August 24, 1854, Elizabeth Gill, at New Concord. To them were born four children:
    1 Mrs Alice Russell, Kalamazoo, Michigan
    2. Rose Shannon, Chicago, Illinois
    3 Minnie Crocker, Minneapolis, Minnesota.
    4 Harry Arnold, Pecos, New Mexico

Stephen finished his college education, and after his marriage, went with his bride to Galesburg, Illinois, where he engaged in the milling business Soon after, he heard the call of his country and in 1861 enlisted in Company G, Fortieth regiment, Iowa Volunteer Infantry, and served during the entire war In 1881 he moved to Chariton, Iowa, where he died January 27, 1909

Alpha Seaward was born in her father's tavern, and in her girlhood days was accustomed to meet people from different parts of the world, as her father's house was a favorite stopping place As she grew older, she was fearless and strong, which served her well in her undertakings in future life When quite a young girl, a peddler who was stopping for the night at her father's house, heard some of the other guests laughing at Alpha because of some feat she had performed, and asked her what she could do, to which she answered that she could do anything she undertook Lying out in the back yard was a good sized log, which he bantered her to chop in two Replying that she thought she could, he told her that if she completed the task before breakfast the next morning, he would present her with a pair of slippers. About sunrise the ring of an axe was heard, and before breakfast Alpha had finished her task. She received the slippers amid shouts of laughter, and that night she danced in them until their soles were worn off, feeling that she had not been overpaid for the work of the morning.

She and her husband moved to Ohio two years after their marriage, living there until 1855, when they removed to Lucas county, Iowa. At that time Ohio was a wilderness, while Iowa comprised part of that vast region known as the great Northwest.

Alpha (Seaward) Arnold was of that splendid Puritan ancestry who were pioneers, not only in the early settlement of the country, but the advance guard in that mighty column of civilization which has converted the then unknown West into a magnificent galaxy of free states. Her life embraced nearly the entire history of the republic. She witnessed the most wonderful and rapid development of wealth, science, art, and mechanical invention. She lived to see the greatest war of modern times, and sent her sons forth to battle in the mighty conflict for freedom. Through all the vicissitudes of the passing years, she lived a quiet, exemplary life. After the death of her husband in 1880 she made her home with her two sons — Edward, who lived on a farm, and Stephen, who resided in Chariton, Iowa, where she died October 5, 1891, being in the ninety-fifth year of her age. She retained her mental faculties until the end, and greatly enjoyed living over with her friends, the events of a long and useful life.

MARY [8] SEAWARD (commonly called Polly), third child of Stephen and Lucy (Ingalls) Seaward, was born at Decatur, New York, December 26, 1799; married Nathan Tripp (born May 22, 1776) January 26, 1826. To them were born five children:
    I. Robert Edwin, born January 27, 1827; married Almaretta Adams (born 1830). To them were born six children:

GENEALOGICAL HISTORY OF THE

1. Mary.
2. Emma
3. Ella.
4. Stephen.
5. Edwin
6. Minnie.

Almaretta Adams Tripp died March 6, 1869.

II David Henry, second child of Mary and Nathan Tripp, was born November 24, 1828; married Mary B. Tripp, September 29, 1853, at Peoria, Illinois. To them were born six children:

1. Stephen H, born September 19, 1854; married Callie Minor; two children Lives at Peoria, Illinois
2. Mary E., born May 12, 1857; died in childhood
3. Della C, born September 18, 1859; married Otis M. Easton; two children Resides at Peoria, Illinois
4. Jennie V, born April 28, 1862; married George H Gibbs; two children Living at Peoria, Illinois
5. Charles H, born March 17, 1865; married Jennie ——; one child Lives in Fresno, California
6. Sidney C., born January 12, 1869; married —— ——; no children.

David Henry Tripp removed from Ohio in 1857, and settled in Peoria, Illinois, where he opened a book store, which he owned at the time of his death, the store now being conducted by his son, Stephen H Tripp Mary B Tripp died August, 1912.

III Lucy Helen, third child of Mary and Nathan Tripp, was born February 11, 1832; married John Kirk, at Iberia, Ohio, in June, 1852 To them were born three children:

1. Stephen Efner, born at Iberia, Ohio At two years of age he removed with his parents to Fort Madison, Iowa, where they made their home until 1866, moving thence to Havana, Illinois In 1877 Stephen was married to Miss Ella Covington. He was then commercial agent

FRENCH AND ALLIED FAMILIES 251

for the Cincinnati Railroad Company, at Muskegon, Michigan. After some years he was transferred to Detroit, Michigan, where he died October 13, 1909
2. Mary Edna, second child of John and Lucy (Tripp) Kirk, was born at Fort Madison, Iowa, and married B F. Yates They are living (1912) in Beaumont, Texas
3. John, third child of John and Lucy (Tripp) Kirk, died in infancy.

IV. Stephen Seward, fourth child of Mary and Nathan Tripp, was born November 14, 1835, at Decatur, Otsego county, New York, married Amelia Snyder October 27, 1868, at Havana, Illinois To them were born seven children·
1 William Kirk, born July 14, 1869
2 Anna Pearl, born February 10, 1871; married October 21, 1891, Guy T Mowat To them were born twin daughters, June 28, 1894 They are living in New Orleans, Louisiana.
3. Ida.
4. Maud. Triplets — born January 19, 1874, died March
5. Minnie 24, 1874, of spinal meningitis, and were buried in one casket
6. Jennie May, born April 20, 1875; died August, 1875
7 Virginia Mabel, born December 25, 1876, married June 4, 1902, Dee Robinson. They reside (1912) at 422 Sixth avenue, Peoria, Illinois

Stephen Seward Tripp, father of these children, when seventeen years of age, went to Peoria, Illinois, where lived his brother, David Henry Tripp, and later became a partner in the firm of D H Tripp & Company, in the book and stationery business About 1900 he disposed of his interest in the store, and devoted his time to an experimental farm in Peoria county, Illinois, where he raised pure blooded Jersey stock In the early days of the Civil War Stephen enlisted in the Eleventh Illinois Cavalry and gained recognition for his bravery and skill as an officer A matter of pride to

Captain Tripp was the fact that his was the only company of cavalry for which a memorial was erected in the cemetery at Vicksburg. He also claimed the distinction of having led his company by the side of General Sherman on his march to the sea, and was personal escort to General Blair during that famous march. Stephen Seward Tripp died suddenly at his home, 422 Sixth street, Peoria, Illinois, May 4, 1912.

V Mary Elida, youngest child of Mary (Seaward) and Nathan Tripp, was born April 2, 1838; married at Peoria, Illinois, to William O. Hoover, of Fort Madison, Iowa, November 13, 1872. To them were born:

1. William Henry, born September 16, 1873.
2. Stephen Delbert, born September 25, 1875.

Mary and William Hoover reside in Fort Madison, Iowa; their sons are living at Prescott, Arizona.

Mary (Seaward) Tripp early imbibed habits of industry and cheerfully performed her part in the home duties, attending school in a building near where now stands the old "French" schoolhouse. Even with the limited advantages of those days she obtained a good education, which enabled her to teach, and this occupation she pursued for seven summers. She had been taught to sew and spin, and when a little girl assisted her father in the carding mill, as well as running errands, her bright, happy face carrying sunshine wherever she went. She was a delicate, refined girl, and a general favorite with all who knew her.

Mary was married to Nathan Tripp, son of David and Mary (Dickinson) Tripp, who was born and reared in Rhode Island, and who, in early manhood, moved to Otsego county, New York, being the first supervisor of Decatur township; also being twice sent to the New York Assembly. Nathan Tripp owned a small farm about three miles from the home of Mary's father. On this farm was a living spring, soft and cool, a short distance from the house, which supplied all the water for family needs. There was a fine orchard, also a "sugar bush" where they made their own sugar and syrup each spring for the year's supply. He was a turner by trade and with his lathe made wooden bowls and many other needful articles for home use Wool from the sheep which they raised was made into garments for the family, they selling what was not needed for their own supply In those days the wool was "picked" by hand; that is, pulled apart, and burrs or other foreign substance removed, after which it was sent to the mill, carded and made into rolls Mary spun the yarn and Nathan's sister Polly wove the cloth, which was then taken to French's fulling mill, where it was dyed, fulled and pressed, after which Hannah Tripp, another sister, came each fall and made up the goods into clothing for the family After the death of her husband in 1841, Mary Tripp carried on the work of the farm with the assistance of her children As showing the advantage taken at this time of untoward conditions, there was a ravine back of their home, and one winter the snow blew into this gully until it was filled level with the ground, and as many crusts had formed while it was filling, it became at length almost as solid as the earth itself. The son, Robert Edwin, dug out a room in this snow-filled ravine, about eight feet wide, ten feet long, and seven feet high; placed poles across, securing them in the drifts until they were solid, then fixed a door in front, and there they hung their supply of meat, making a smoke under it The meat is said to have had a fine flavor, after having been smoked in a snowbank

In the spring of 1847 Mary Tripp rented her farm and taking her children (with the exception of Robert Edwin, the oldest son, who was living with an uncle, in order that he might learn the blacksmith trade — which occupation he followed as long as he lived — and who preferred to remain where he was, because of the business), went with her brother-in-law, Samson French, and family to Ohio The year following, her farm in New York state was sold. Upon their arrival at the new location they moved into a log cabin with Daniel Flint, whose wife Mehitable was Mary Tripp's sister During the summer Daniel Flint built a frame house, into which he moved with his family in September, Mary Tripp and her children going with them, as her sister was ill and needed her care Soon after moving into the new home, Mrs Flint died, leaving four children, the youngest but two years of age, and thus the care of the two families fell upon Mary's shoulders. In November, 1848, she was married to Daniel Flint, who in the spring of 1850 went to California, where he spent three years seeking his fortune in the gold fields, leaving his wife to manage the farm and look after the family, which duties she bravely performed. In 1855 their home was burned, but was replaced the following year by a brick house, which is still standing on the "Flint farm" in Morrow county, Ohio.

The railroad was but a short distance from the Flint home, and during the early days of the Civil War trains loaded with soldiers were almost daily to be seen on their way to the South, and quite frequently carried the prisoners northward en route to Johnson's Island, where they were to be kept in confinement, all of which added interest to those stirring times of war.

In the spring of 1862 Mary Flint visited her children in Peoria, Illinois, also her daughter, Mrs. Kirk, whose home was in Fort Madison, Iowa. The following is taken from her diary, under date of Monday, June 16th: "Between sundown and dark a cry of fire was heard. The penitentiary was on fire. The shops on the north side were all burned down. Loss said to be $20,000." Her son-in-law, John Kirk, was a guard at the penitentiary. On Monday, the 23d, she writes: "We went up to the prison to see what havoc the fire has made with the work shop. The governor is expected soon, and then they will decide what will be done." Thursday, June 26th: "He came and another man with him, to see what will be done. They have not determined yet. The governor's name is Kirkwood; he was formerly from Mansfield, Ohio."

In 1867 Daniel Flint died after a brief illness and was laid to rest in the Ebenezer burying ground by the side of his first wife, Mehitable (Seaward) Flint. After her husband's death, Mary went to Peoria, Illinois, where for twenty years she made her home with her son, Stephen Tripp, often spending months with her daughter, Mrs. Hoover, in Fort Madison, Iowa. In December, 1889, she wrote in her diary, as follows: "My boys have presented me with another diary. I am too old to write very good, but it helps to pass the time.

I make a good many mistakes, but I write without glasses, and am eighty-nine years old." At ninety-two she pieced a silk quilt for one of her grandchildren, which is a much prized possession.

The seven closing years of Mary (Seaward) Flint's life were spent with her daughter, Mrs. Hoover, at whose home she died in 1895, one month before her ninety-sixth birthday. The body was taken to Peoria, Illinois, for burial.

JAMES[6] SEAWARD (Stephen,[5] Noadiah,[4] Ebenezer,[3] Caleb,[2] William[1]), oldest son of Stephen and Lucy (Ingalls) Seaward, born Decatur, New York, January 19, 1802; married Clarissa Barnes, in 1825, at Decatur. To them were born five children:
 I. Lucy.
 II. Mariah.
 III. Lucy (second).
 IV. Stephen.
 V. Delia.

In 1828 this family removed from Otsego county to Franklinville, Cattaraugus county, New York, and settled on a farm. In an early day this section of the country was a vast wilderness. With true pioneer spirit that knew no defeat nor yielded to any discouragement, James succeeded in clearing a large farm and in later years enjoyed the fruit of his labors. In 1832 he with his companion united with the Methodist Episcopal church, of which he remained a member for many years until the church troubles in western New York, when he identified himself with the Free Methodists. In 1876 he took an active part in the erection of the new church at Franklinville, and by untiring zeal and liberal contributions on his part, the church was completed. With the exception of a short time he was steward in the Methodist church for forty-six years.

In February, 1875, he and his wife celebrated their golden wedding and shortly after this event occurred the death of the wife. But not long was he left to journey alone, for just three years from the time of her going, he followed, his death taking place March 10, 1878.

He was an active man, never having yielded to the infirmities of old age until a few days before his death

STEPHEN⁶ SEAWARD JR. (Stephen,⁵ Noadiah,⁴ Ebenezer,³ Caleb,² William¹), fifth child of Stephen and Lucy (Ingalls) Seaward, born January 24, 1804; died November 7, 1824 He was never rugged, his frail condition of health rendering him unable to cope with the sterner realities of life He loved books and spent much of his time in the fields and woods studying nature When about eighteen years of age he went to work for Ezra Williams, a brother-in-law of Samson French, but was unable to continue in his employment, as consumption had fastened itself upon him, and in a few months he was obliged to give up his position and return home He wrote in his diary:

> July 28, 1823. This day attended the funeral of Mrs. Everton, her son and daughter, and Miss Betsey Childs, who were killed on the 27th instant, by the wind blowing down the house which contained them. The Rev Mr. Campbell delivered the funeral sermon from the following words "And behold there came a great wind from the wilderness and smote the four corners of the house and it fell upon the young men and they are dead, and I only am escaped alone to tell thee." Job 1, 19th verse.

About a month before his death he made the last entry in his diary. A short time before his going, he composed an acrostic, which his friend, Lester Houghton, printed, a copy of which was given to each of his sisters

How much he was beloved by his family can be judged from the fact, that each of his brothers and sisters named a son Stephen Seaward, in memory of this young brother, whose death occurred November 7, 1824, and who was laid to rest in the Decatur burying ground by the side of the mother whom he loved so well.

LUCY⁶ SEAWARD, daughter of Stephen and Lucy (Ingalls) Seaward, born January 24, 1806, at Decatur, New York, married Asa

Asa Palmerlee   Lucy Seaward Palmerlee

FRENCH AND ALLIED FAMILIES

Palmerlee (born Litchfield, Connecticut, 1803) in 1824 at Decatur, New York. To them were born eleven children.
- I. Elizabeth; married —— Going. To them were born three daughters:
    1. Mary; married —— Gray.
    2. Villa; married Samuel Snover. Lives at Metamora, Michigan.
    3. Sarah; married Arthur Chapman.

    All living in Lapeer county, Michigan.
- II. Henry; went to Minnesota, where he married Helen Kossulman. To them were born five children:
    1. Franklin D., now of Spangle, Spokane county, Washington.
    2. Lucy Lillian; married Elmer E. Abbott, of Dodge Center, Minnesota.
    3. Efner; died in 1906.
    4. Mary Lodema; married —— Gillies, a Methodist minister, in Minnesota.
    5. Seward. Lives in Dodge Center, Minnesota.
- III. Mary Jane; married Willis Collins Thrall. To them were born nine children:
    1. Hiram Elvin; one child.
    2. Lua Elizabeth; two children.
    3. Lucy Mehitable; two children.
    4. Mina Olive; no children.
    5. William Ernest; four children.
    6. Lois; died when an infant.
    7. Henry Porteus; died aged fifteen.
    8. Stephen Asa; three children.
    9. Mary Effie; two children.

    Four of the above named children of Mary Jane and Willis Collins Thrall are living:

    Lua Elizabeth Evarts, Mantorville, Minnesota.
    Mina Olive Linderman, Hinsdale, New York.
    William Ernest Thrall, Dodge Center, Minnesota.

Mary Effie Alsworth, Arcade, New York.
- IV. Heman; three children:
    1. Charles; lives in northern Michigan.
    2. Mark; Detroit, Michigan. Is mail clerk on railroad between Saginaw and Detroit.
    3. Mary.
- V. Hoel; lived in Michigan. Two sons:
    1. Efner; address, Hunters' Creek, Michigan.
    2. Fred; address, Hunters' Creek, Michigan.
- VI. Stephen; went to Minnesota; married Eunice Kossulman. They were the parents of two children:
    1. Myrtle.
    2. Joseph.
- VII. Roseltha; married Ralph W. Gamsby, in Minnesota; died at Dodge Center, Minnesota. To them were born five children:
    1. }
    2. } Twin boys, who died when young.
    3. Caroline; lives with her father.
    4. Marion; married David L. Printup; lives at Britton, South Dakota.
    5. Lucy; teacher at Clermont, Minnesota.
- VIII. Clymena; married Robert Hutton. To them were born six children:
    1. Lucy; married —— Heminway.
    2. Nannie.
    3. George.
    4. Leah; married Kirk White, Lapeer, Michigan.
    5. Mary.
    6. Millie.
- IX. Albert, born Dodge Center, Minnesota; married —— ——. To them were born four children:
    1. Earl.
    2. Herbert.
    3. James.

4 Helen.
X Lois Permelia; married —— Kingsbury; one son, who died in infancy

The first five children were born at Decatur, the others at Ichsua, Cattaraugus county, New York. Asa Palmerlee and wife, Lucy (Seaward) Palmerlee, moved to Michigan in 1860. Here the husband suffered a stroke of paralysis and died November 7, 1869, the wife living until 1885.

MEHITABLE[6] SEAWARD, seventh child of Stephen and Lucy Ingalls Seaward, born Decatur, New York, July 27, 1808; married Daniel Flint January 13, 1825. To them were born four children.
I Lucy Sharille; married Carp Smith at Iberia, Ohio, in 1848. To them was born one son, Edgar, living in Oskaloosa, Iowa. Sharille Flint Smith died in February, 1861.
II Stephen S.; married Mary J. Brownlee at Iberia, Ohio, in 1858.
III Henry; married Jennie ——. Lives in Minneapolis, Minnesota
IV Sibbel E.; married Allan Coe at Mt. Gilead, Ohio. To them were born four children. Sibbel died about 1902.

In the spring of 1827 Daniel and Mehitable Seaward Flint moved from Otsego county, New York, to Bloomfield, Washington county, Ohio, where they lived until in the spring of the year 1847, when they moved to Iberia, Ohio, where Mehitable died in October, 1847.

SIBBEL[6] SEWARD, eighth child of Stephen and Lucy Ingalls Seaward, born at Decatur, Otsego county, New York, April 15, 1811; married William McNall, March 17, 1829, at Franklinville, Cattaraugus county, New York. To them were born.
I Lucy, born February 2, 1831; married Aaron Skinner October 28, 1849. Two children: Delia and Nillie

II. Almira, born September 12, 1832; married Benjamin Hotchkiss January 8, 1854. She was married three times and was the mother of five children: Vista, Lettie, William, Nellie, and Efner. Almira died in Wisconsin in 1873.
III. Nathan, born June 16, 1834; died March 5, 1857.
IV. Stephen, born February 12, 1836; married Clara Riggs October 12, 1859. To them were born:
   1. Elmer Ellsworth; two children.
   2. Effie Mae; four children.
   3. Luella Eliza; married C. W. Hogue; lives at Franklinville, New York. To them have been born six children — four boys and two girls.
V. Mary, born September 8, 1839; married James Swift December 25, 1861. She was the mother of two children who died in infancy; now living with an adopted daughter at Franklinville, New York.
VI. S. Efner, born February 7, 1841; killed in the Civil War in 1863.
VII. Lois, born February 8, 1844; married Merritt Porter July 4, 1866. To them were born Efner, Ethel, Mabel, Effie, Elmer.
VIII. Charles, born March 22, 1847; died February 23, 1848.
IX. William, born January 19, 1852; died March 15, 1854.

William and Sibbel McNall lived on a farm near Franklinville, New York. Stephen Seaward, father of Sibbel, lived in part of the house until the time of his death. The old farm is still in the McNall family, being the home of Stephen McNall, after the death of his father William, which occurred March 20, 1870, and now being in the possession of William McNall. In 1881 Sibbel McNall visited her sister, Lucy Palmerlee, in Michigan, who at that time was seventy-five years of age; spent some time in the home of the author at Sheldahl, Iowa, going from this place to Chariton, Iowa, where she visited another sister, Alpha Seaward Arnold, who was eighty-six years of age. Turning her face homeward, she stopped at Peoria, Illinois, where Mary Seaward Flint, eighty-one years old, resided. She reached her home at Franklinville April 15, 1882, it being her seventy-first birthday. Elmer McNall, a grandson, met her at the train and took her to the old home where her whole family (twenty-four in number) had gathered in honor of the occasion

She continued to live in the old home for some years, dying April 2, 1891, when eighty years of age.

THE QUEAL FAMILY

First Generation

WILLIAM[1] QUEAL of Wales married Margaret Atchison of Ireland. To them were born seven children — four sons and three daughters, the names of three of the sons being known to the author:

I. Michael
II. John.
III. Robert.

Second Generation

MICHAEL[2] QUEAL (William[1]), son of William and Margaret (Atchison) Queal, emigrated to America some time before 1776 and settled with his family in Oswego county, near Rome, New York. He was a Methodist minister, his license to preach having been signed by Charles Wesley, brother of John Wesley, the founder of Methodism.

There is a tradition in the family that he was a chaplain in the Revolutionary War, but owing to the fact that the chaplains were non-commissioned, there is no record of his service.

A resolution of Congress July 5, 1776, provided for the appointment of a chaplain to each regiment in the Continental army, and an order (published in *American State Papers*, Volume I, page 226), dated at New York, July 9, 1776, directed that the commanding officer of each regiment should procure a chaplain accordingly. A resolution of Congress of May 27, 1777, provided for the appointment thereafter of one chaplain only to each brigade, and that such chaplains be appointed by Congress after having been recommended by the brigade commander and nominated. Nothing has been found of record to show whether or not commissions were issued to any of the chaplains so appointed.

Michael Queal was by occupation a miller, owning a mill near

Rome, New York Of his immediate family but little is known to the author He had one son, Michael.

Third Generation

MICHAEL³ QUEAL (Michael,² William¹), born in Oswego county, New York, in 1800 Married Louisa Moore (born in 1803) in 1822. To them were born seven children.
- I. Araminta; married Otho Williams To them were born two children:
    1 Ida
    2. Willard
- II William Henry, married Mary Moore To them was born one daughter:
    1 Araminta, married Samuel Baker; two children
- III Albert Franklin; married Martha Barber To them were born eight children.
    1. William; died young
    2 Michael; died young.
    3 Frank; died young.
    4 Louisa, married Lewis Tudor, Boulder, Colorado
    5 Philip G ; married Fanny Mickrals, Cincinnati, Ohio, no children; living at Fort Mitchell, Kentucky He is with Gibson & Perin Company, stationers, printers, account book makers, Cincinnati, Ohio
    6 Selina; married William Magee; living at Terrace Park, Ohio
    7 E Barber; never married; is a physician in Boulder, Colorado, and a member of the faculty of the State University.
    8 Anna, born at Boulder, Colorado

    Martha Barber Queal, mother of the above named children, is still living, her home is at Boulder, Colorado.
- IV. John Oscar; married Jennie Buckingham, at Cincinnati, Ohio To them were born two sons
    1 Smith B ; married Emma Coddington (musician) at

Cincinnati, Ohio. He is with the Woman's Home Companion Publishing Company.

    2. William; married —— Davis, Camp Denison, Ohio.

V. Jane; married Dr. Malon Connett. To them were born three children:
1. Albert.
2. Nellie.
3. Ida.

VI. George W.; married Flora Mounts. To them was born one son. George married (second) Katie Jones. They reside at Long Beach, California.

VII. Maria; married Albert Connett. To them were born five children. Their home is at Long Beach, California.

Michael Queal Jr., when eighteen years of age made the journey from Utica, New York, to Cincinnati, Ohio, on horseback. That he was a trustworthy youth is evidenced by the fact that he carried in his saddle bags a large sum of money to friends who had settled in Ohio previous to his coming. He located near Milford, six miles outside the corporation of Cincinnati, where he followed the business of a distiller for many years. In 1840 his distillery was destroyed by fire, and about a year later he removed from Milford to a tract of land which he had purchased in Hamilton county, sixteen miles east of Cincinnati, Ohio, of which tract his son John is the present owner.

When Michael Queal Jr. married, his wife (Louisa Moore) was the possessor of a number of slaves, who remained with her as long as they lived. He (Michael) was a member of the Methodist church when he removed to Ohio and held in his possession for many years a letter of membership, but never united with any church organization in his western home. He was for years a member of the Masonic fraternity. His sons have been successful in business, honorable and upright in their transactions.

Michael Queal Jr. died in 1877, his wife surviving him for more than ten years.

SMITH B. QUEAL
Nephew of Geo. W. Queal

COTTAGE OF GEO. W. QUEAL
Long Beach, California

FRENCH AND ALLIED FAMILIES

Second Generation

JOHN [2] QUEAL (William [1]), son of William and Margaret Atchison Queal, married —— McLean. The names of three of their children are known to the author.
- I Catherine.
- II Mary; married Gilbert Albert of Worcester, New York
- III. William M, born about 1788; came to America with an aunt when about nine years of age and lived with her on South Hill in the town of Worcester. Three years later the parents of William M, John, and —— McLean Queal, emigrated to America and located on a farm on South Hill, where the children were reared

Third Generation

WILLIAM M [3] QUEAL (John,[2] William [1]), married Abbie Smith To them were born four children.
- I. William S
- II. Catherine, died young
- III Jane
- IV. Alexander.

William M Queal and his wife lived on South Hill, owning a large farm on which they spent their married life He died March 21, 1857, his wife surviving him for some years.

Fourth Generation

WILLIAM S.[4] QUEAL (William,[3] John,[2] William [1]), son of William M and Abbie Smith Queal, born July 28, 1821, married Sally Esther Waterman (born December 23, 1824) April, 1844 To them were born seven children.
- I. Mary Estelle, born February 24, 1846; married Charles Cooley of Worcester, Otsego county, New York, January 1, 1865 To them was born one son, James B, born June 18, 1868; died October 28, 1883 Charles Cooley died in 1877 and his widow married (second) David Shelland of Wor-

cester in 1879, who died in 1909. Mrs. Shelland died in Worcester July 6, 1912.

II. John, born April 14, 1848; married Emma Rhodes, who died a few years later. He married a second time and has one daughter, Lena. Lives near Schenevus, New York.

III. Alexander, born at Worcester, New York, in 1850; married Rose DeMars (born in Oswego July 16, 1854) February 9, 1875, in Oswego, New York. They moved to Merced, California, soon after their marriage. To them were born three children:

1. Alexander, born November 9, 1875; married and lives in Alexandria Bay, New York; five children, two boys and three girls.
2. Rose Ella, born August 13, 1885; married T. C. Russell in 1910. They have one son, and live in Syracuse, New York.
3. William N., born August 9, 1887, in Merced, California. His mother died when he was but two years of age, leaving him to the care of her sister, Mrs. C. E. Fields, now living at Alexandria Bay, New York. In 1902 William N. left California and went to Beloit, Wisconsin, where he lived for three years, at the expiration of which time he went to Alexandria Bay.

William N. Queal is an athlete and noted as one of the world's greatest runners. In 1908 he went into a race to fill out a card and won, which good fortune continued to be his for two years, then losing two — through accidents. In 1911 he won a fifteen mile championship race, but the next year lost two fifteen mile races, the distance being too great; but for a distance of five, ten, or twelve miles, has not lost a match race in the four years he has been running. He holds the world's record with Swanberg for fifteen and twenty mile outdoor relay race; twenty and twenty-six mile, 384 yards, indoor relay race (with Holmes) world's record; also one hour running, defeating the best men; as Meadows, Simpson, Longboat, Shrubb, A. Wood, Ted Woods, Swanberg, Hayes, and St. Ives. June 22, 1912, he defeated Woods and Longboat (the Indian) in a five mile race, making a new

WILLIAM N. QUEAL

Anna Queal Starkweather

professional world's record — 24 minutes, 39 2/3 seconds He makes his home in New York City During the indoor season he is coach of the Eighth regiment, and in the spring and fall meets, trainer for Fordham University.

IV Dudley, fourth child of William S and Sally (Waterman) Queal, born in January, 1852; married Alice Waterman August 12, 1877. To them were born three children — George, Fred, and John Dudley Queal died October, 1904 His widow and children are living in Beaudette, Minnesota

V. Henry, born 1854, died 1863.

VI William McLean, born 1856; unmarried

VII Sarah Anna, born November 6, 1861; married Asher Starkweather (born at Worcester, New York, June 20, 1838) April 21, 1881 He graduated from the Madison University (now Colgate) in the class of '62 Taught for many years, and for over twenty years has been school attendance officer in Pittsfield, Massachusetts. To them were born three children·

1 Essa, born August 17, 1886 After graduating from high school attended Pratt Institute, Brooklyn, New York, where she graduated in 1907 She taught normal art and manual training in the schools of Roselle Park, New Jersey, for one year. Married the Rev James Bruce Gilman July 21, 1908 They reside at Nashua, New Hampshire, where he is pastor of the First Baptist Church

2 Morrell A, born July 1, 1888; married Ruth Esmay in April, 1910. To them has been born one child, Helen E, born May 18, 1911 Morrell Starkweather is in the employ of the General Electric Company of Pittsfield, Massachusetts, as die maker

3 Davis Viney, born June 17, 1900

S Anna Starkweather is prominent in the Daughters of the American Revolution, her great-grandfather, John Waterman Sr, having served in the Revolutionary War. She is also identified with the work of the Relief Corps, being wife as well as daughter of a veteran. She was president of Berkshire W. R. C. in 1904 and has been its chaplain for many years. In November, 1911, she was made chaplain of the Department of Massachusetts, W. R. C., auxiliary to the Grand Army of the Republic, with headquarters at Boston.

William S. Queal enlisted in the Civil War and served his country faithfully. His wife, Sally Waterman Queal, died May 6, 1868. He died in April, 1890, at Worcester, New York.

JANE⁴ QUEAL, third child of William M. and Abbie Smith Queal, married James Wade at Worcester, New York. To them were born three children:
   I. Warren; married and has children.
   II. Willis; married Abbie Hanor; two children.
   III. Ardelia; married Orville Gaylord; one daughter.

The descendants of James and Jane (Queal) Wade are still living in Worcester, New York.

ALEXANDER⁴ QUEAL, son of William M. and Abbie Smith) Queal, married Betsey Fox. To them were born one daughter, Celicia, who married Stanley Lewis of Richmondville. They have three sons — Burdette, Herbert, and Dr. A. Lewis of Albany, New York.

Alevander Queal died at Richmondville. His wife survived him many years, dying in March, 1912, aged eighty years.

Second Generation

ROBERT² QUEAL (William¹) was born in Ireland in 1758 and married Elizabeth Conroy in 1777, she having been born in Ireland in 1753. She was the daughter of Luke Conroy, born in Ireland, and Mary Richison, born in England. To Robert and Elizabeth Queal were born six children, two of whom died in infancy.
   I. George C., born in Ireland in 1786.
   II. William C., born August 14, 1788.
   III. Mary, born in 1793.
   IV. Margaret, born in 1795; died in New York City in 1798.

Trunk brought by Robert Queal from Ireland in 1797, now in possession of Author, and said to have contained his private papers

Worcester, Otsego County, New York, showing South Hill

The home of Robert and Elizabeth Queal in Ireland was near the village of Drumsnoh, parish of Anaduff and county of Latrim, from which place they emigrated to America in 1797, sailing from Port Sligo. In Ireland the name was pronounced as though spelled "Quail," to which pronunciation the descendants of Michael still adhere, although the spelling of the name has not been changed from the original — Queal.

Robert Queal and his little family landed in New York City, after their journey of six weeks across the water, and there they resided for two or three years, attending John Street Methodist Episcopal Church and Sunday school. Margaret, their youngest child, died in that city and was buried in the yard of the old John Street Church. From New York City Robert Queal and family moved to Otsego county, New York, and settled on a farm on what is known as South Hill, in Worcester township, located about three miles south of Worcester. The land on which they located was part of a patent granted to Alexander McKee and others, but it is not known how many acres were in the tract, nor the price paid per acre. The first record found is where Robert and Elizabeth Conroy Queal conveyed under date of August 17, 1819, to their son-in-law, Artemas Babcock, and his wife, Mary Queal Babcock, for a certain sum, land on South Hill. On April 20, 1821, Robert Queal and William C. Queal — his son — bought of James Shelland of Decatur, Otsego county, New York, seventy-six and one-half acres of land, for six hundred forty dollars, "money account of the United States," and Robert Queal moved from South Hill to this farm.

On January 16, 1840, he entered into an agreement with his son-in-law, Artemas Babcock of Davenport, Delaware county, New York, by which

> The said Artemas Babcock shall and may have the use, occupation and enjoyment of the farm now owned and occupied by the said Robert Queal, situate in the town of Worcester, during the natural lives of the said Robert Queal and Elizabeth his wife — on the following conditions. that is to say, that the said Artemas Babcock shall move on the said farm and occupy and cultivate the same in a farmer-like manner and provide for, support and maintain, the said Robert and Elizabeth his wife during their natural lives, and during the life of the longest liver of them, and to furnish and provide

for them from time to time all such necessaries as shall be suitable and proper, both in sickness and in health, for their convenience and comfort. The said Robert Queal also reserves the right to keep on said farm seven ewes and their increase, which increase however is not to be kept on said farm only while they are lambs. The said Artemas Babcock agrees to move onto said farm at a suitable time next spring, to commence the spring's work thereon, and he also agrees to make necessary repairs to the dwelling house on said farm, as soon as the same can conveniently be done, in such manner as shall make said house convenient and comfortable for a dwelling house for himself and family, and for the said Robert Queal and his wife. And the said Robert Queal on his part agrees, when said repairs are made to said dwelling house, to give his promisory note to said Artemas Babcock, for the amount of such repairs, which note is not to be paid during the life of said Robert Queal, but it is to be a debt against his estate after his death, and shall not be considered on interest; and whereas, the said Robert Queal has this day made his last will and testament, and thereby devised to his daughter, Mary Babcock and her heirs, the sum of five hundred dollars as and for her portion of the estate of said Robert Queal; now therefore, in order to secure that sum to the said Mary Babcock and her heirs, the said Robert Queal promises and agrees to and with the said Artemas Babcock that if he, the said Robert Queal, shall at any time hereafter revoke, destroy or alter his said last will and testament so as to deprive said Mary Babcock and her heirs of the said sum of five hundred dollars specified in said will, that then and in that case he, the said Robert Queal, hereby agrees to pay the said Mary Babcock, her heirs, executors and administrators the said sum of five hundred dollars, and to be a charge upon his estate in lieu of said sum maintained in said last will and testament aforesaid, in witness whereof we have hereunto set our hands and seals the day and year written.

Signed { ARTEMAS BABCOCK
ROBERT QUEAL

Sealed and delivered in
presence of Schuyler Crippen.

The following shows that everything was satisfactorily settled:

Received of Wm C. Queal six hundred dollars in full of all demands against the estate of Robert Queal deceased, being the amount of five hundred dollars secured to my wife Mary Babcock, by will, and all the demands I hold against the estate of said Robert Queal deceased of every name and nature. (Signed) ARTEMAS BABCOCK
Worcester, March 2d, 1846.

Robert Queal and his wife Elizabeth died in 1840. They were

William C. Queal

buried in the Presbyterian churchyard in Worcester, and years afterward were removed to the Queal lot in the Maple Grove cemetery, where repose the bodies of sixteen of the Queal family

George C Queal, oldest son of Robert and Elizabeth Queal, was born in Ireland in 1786, and came with his parents to America in 1797, he never married He was a quiet man, possessed of a wonderful memory, it having been said of him that he could repeat chapter after chapter of the New Testament, and, upon hearing a passage of scripture quoted, could tell in what part of the Bible it would be found He was an alien until 1840, at which time he became very much interested in politics, and as he could not vote for the man he greatly wished to see elected, went to Cooperstown, New York, and took out naturalization papers, from that time going regularly to the polls, voting with the Whig party After the death of his father he entered into an agreement with his brother, William C. Queal, in which he assigned to him all his right, title, and interest in and to the real and personal estate of their father, Robert Queal, deceased, in consideration of which his brother was to support and maintain him during the remaining years of his life The date of his death, which occurred after months of helplessness and suffering, is unknown

Third Generation

WILLIAM C[3] QUEAL (Robert,[2] William [1]), second child of Robert and Elizabeth Queal, was born in Drumsnoh, Ireland, married Mary Graves February 3, 1814, she having been born in Windham county, Vermont, February 3, 1794, thus becoming a bride on her twentieth birthday. To them were born nine sons and two daughters:

- I Richison, born February 27, 1815; married Harriet Mallory November 3, 1846
- II Atchison, born April 6, 1817; married Lucy Oletha French April 9, 1845
- III John, born November 22, 1818; died April 24, 1822
- IV Martha, born August 28, 1820; married Horatio Flint February 19, 1845

- V. William G, born December 14, 1822; married Lorinda Booth July 3, 1850
- VI Robert F., born July 1, 1825; married Sarah A Houghton in March, 1853, married (second) Kate E Gillespie December 29, 1870
- VII Luke C, born April 2, 1827; married Catherine Klock September 19, 1849, died May 3, 1857 Luke married (second) Sara M Dean April, 1858, died October 18, 1863; Luke married (third) Sarah J Hall, June 30, 1864; died February 25, 1910
- VIII James, born November 21, 1828; died June 13, 1853
- IX Mary, born August 21, 1830, died June 22, 1850.
- X Paul A, born February 4, 1833; died September 19, 1864
- XI Orin H, born April 6, 1837, married Elma A Gillespie September 28, 1875

Reuben Graves, father of Mary Graves Queal, was born in Connecticut in 1776 He was the son of Samuel and Mary (Wolsey) Graves, the family consisting of three children — two sons and a daughter. Reuben Graves married Catherine Nourse (born in 1767) in Connecticut, her parents being —— Nourse and Sarah Walker, of New England She had five brothers and four sisters, her father dying in Illinois in 1839 To the union of Reuben and Catherine (Nourse) Graves were born seventeen children, six of whom died in infancy:

1. Sally Graves, born in 1784 in Vermont; married Charles Bennett in 1806.
2. Reuben, born in 1786 in Vermont; married Lucy Nourse in 1813
3. Samuel, born in 1788 in Vermont; married Sally Larrabee in 1812, died 1818 in Connecticut
4. Amos, born in 1791; married Mary Taggart in 1813
5. Martha, born in 1793; married Daniel Babcock in 1812; died 1831 in New York
6. Mary, born in 1794; married William C Queal in 1814
7. William, born in 1797; married Laura —— in 1821

8. Jesse, born in 1799, married, 1819, Mary Taylor, who died in 1835 Jesse married (second) in 1840
9. Phineas, born in 1801; married Ann Rendal in 1822
10. Orin, born in 1803; married Achsa Farley
11. Daniel, born in 1804; married Electa Babcock in 1827.

This is all the genealogy of the Graves family known to the author

William C Queal came to America with his parents when but a lad His life was devoted to the farm, first in helping clear his father's land, and subsequently in the tillage of the soil for his own remuneration He married when about twenty-six years of age While almost destitute of early educational advantages, he made the most of his opportunities and was always well informed in regard to passing events He was a thoroughly upright, honest man, never practicing deceit or prevarication; in his community he was respected and honored; for some he was a counselor, for others a peace maker, and always a helper to the destitute and distressed

William Queal lived on a farm on South Hill where all his children were born, their early education being obtained in the old log school house which was years ago replaced by a new and modern structure. When about twenty-eight years of age he became a citizen of the United States and thus entitled to all the rights and privileges of such citizenship A copy of the certificate of naturalization which he received at that time follows·

CERTIFICATE OF NATURALIZATION OF WILLIAM C QUEAL

The people of the State of New York by the Grace of God free and independent To all to whom these presents may come or in any wise concern — greeting·

Whereas William C Queal of the town of Worcester in the County of Otsego on this twenty-third day of February, in the term of February, in the year of our Lord one thousand eight hundred and sixteen, in our court of common pleas, in and for our County of Otsego, before the Judges and assistant Justices of the same court, at the court house in Cooperstown, in conformity to the requisitions of the several acts of the Congress of the United States regulating Naturalization, was in due form of law admitted a citizen of the United States of America, and therefore took and subscribed in open court the oath by law prescribed, Now know ye therefore that the said William C Queal is and of right ought to be entitled to all the immunities, powers and privileges of a citizen of the United States of America In faith whereof we have caused the seal of said court of common pleas to be hereunto affixed.

Witness Joseph White Esquire, first Judge of our said court at Cooperstown, the twenty-third day of February in the year of our Lord one thousand eight hundred and sixteen and in the fortieth year of our independence
Per Curiam
S W MORELL Clk of Otsego

William C Queal was a man of business affairs As one of the school trustees for years, it was his duty to examine applicants for the position of teacher, and if found to have the requisite qualifications they were given a certificate That Betsey Bentley taught school in District No. 12, is shown by a receipt given to Ephraim Dunham, William C Queal, and Levi Chase, trustees, for "fifteen dollars in full against all demands of said district" And on February 24, 1827, Laura Bentley received of William Queal and John Essex, trustees for School District No 12, "nine dollars in full for my wages for keeping summer school in 1826." The following bond was given at Worcester January 17, 1827:

We, John Essex and William C Queal, do agree to pay Jacob Stever or bearer the sum of twenty dollars on the twentieth day of June next, in money or grain or both, on condition that Moses Pette, our school teacher, teaches our school till the first of March next, we being trustees of said school in School District No 12, otherwise this bond is null and void, to be delivered at the house of William C Queal
Witness our hands

On March 24, 1831, Stephen Jones received of William C Queal fourteen dollars and eighty-five cents toward his wages for teaching school

There was made out a rate bill for persons liable for teachers' wages in the town of Worcester for the school term ending in February, 1834; tax voted to be raised on real and personal estate The number of days William C Queal had sent children to school was three hundred eighty-nine; he was assessed four dollars and twenty cents Only one man in the district — Barnabas Fuller — paid more, as his children had attended school three hundred ninety-five days, he being assessed four dollars and twenty-seven cents David Stevers' family only attending three days, the sum assessed against him was three cents The entire amount realized from the tax list was twenty-three dollars and fifty-nine cents In addition to his work as school trustee, he transacted the business incident to the office of town supervisor, during the years 1835 to 1837 inclusive

William C. Queal was a member of the Twelfth regiment of Artillery (New York), Third brigade, of which Nicholas Chesbro was captain and John Woodbury, colonel On March 25, 1820, he was appointed first sergeant of said company, of which he remained an active member for fifteen years, at the expiration of which time he received an honorable discharge:

> This may certify that William C Queal has been attached to the Company of Artillery which is now under my command for fifteen years past, and that he has ben in uniform and equiped according to the law and is honorably Discharged from the same ORVA FERRIS
> Capt 10th R Artillery
> Dated at Worcester 1st of Sept 1828

William C. Queal was a member of the Whig party, and a great admirer of Horace Greeley; was a subscriber to the New York *Tribune* from the days of its earliest publication, and every copy which reached his home, was diligently read by his sons and himself This, and the *Northern Christian Advocate* were the papers which helped to shape the lives of his family

New York–17–Mch 1845

Mr W C Queal
  To Greeley & McElrath Dr
For 1 subscription to Weekly Tribune from No 182 to 233 inclusive (Terms $2 00 a year in advance. Your subscription expires with No 233 All papers discontinued at the expiration of the time paid for unless previously renewed) . . $2
  Received payment
    GREELEY & McELRATH
      per J. S Sinclair Jr

The following letter is given as an indication of his prominence as a politician in the community where he lived:

Cooperstown, Oct. 30, 1846.

Mr. Wm C. Queal —

Dr Sir: Again are we called upon as Whigs to exert ourselves in the coming campaign. Our state and Congress ticket can be elected with proper exertions, and if the Whig strength can be rallied we feel sure of electing Shafard and the rest of the Bogey ticket. By all means call out our whole Whig strength. Good faith should prompt us to sustain Shafard and the remainder of the Bogey ticket. The convention yesterday done much for our cause in making the Bogey men more energetic. We request you therefore to take upon yourself the duty of getting our Whig friends out that we may secure to ourselves a glorious victory.

Respectfully yours, &c.

WM NICHOLS
G. W. ERNST
A. M. BARBER
ISAAC K. WILLIAMS
JNO. L. McNAMER
Central Co. Committee.

The postal regulations were very different in those days from the present time, as the following receipted bill shows:

Wm C. Queal for postage at P. O. at Worcester.

Wm C. Queal to H. P. Waterman   Dr for postage on letters and papers.

1 letter Sep 8, 1849	.05
1 letter for James Nov 13, 1849	.05
1 " " Paul Jan. 2, 1850	.05
1 pamphlet for Paul March 26, 1850	.02½
1 letter for Luke Oct 9, 1850	.05
1 " " Paul " 9, 1850	.05
1 letter for Luke's wife Oct. 13	.05
2 " " Paul Nov 22,	.10
1 letter Nov 24, 1850	.05
	.47½

Northern Christian Advocate

from June 20, 1849 to Dec 31, 1849 — 28 papers	.28
The same from Jan. 1, 1850 to Jan 1, 1851, 52 papers	.52

HOUSE BUILT BY WILLIAM C. QUEAL IN 1847 AT WORCESTER, NEW YORK
Showing Rose Bush planted by Mary

HOUSE WHERE ATCHISON QUEAL DIED IN 1859
Morrow County, Ohio

New York Tribune from June 20, 1849,
   to Dec 22, 1849, 26 papers   26

                                              for papers 1 06
                                                   letters   47½

                                                           $1 53½
                      Recd payment
                      H P Waterman P M
                      Jan 7, 1851

    Postmasters were surely not rushed with business in those days, when they could keep track of all letters mailed, and to whom they were sent

    During this period shoemakers were in the habit of going from house to house, in manner similar to the seamstresses of the present day, carrying their tools, and remaining in each home until the family needs in their line were supplied   The bill which is here given was evidently on account of such services rendered:

                                                         October, 1839
    To making five pairs of shoes at 36 cts per pair $1 80
    to making one pair of shoes at   43

                                               making a total of   2.23
    In March 1846, Dr to making one pair of women's shoes   .63

    Shoemaking was surely not a very lucrative business.

    In 1839 William C Queal sold his land on South Hill and bought a farm one and one-half miles north of the village of Worcester   This land was hilly and full of stones, not being easy to cultivate, but by perseverance he was able to make a comfortable living   One of the staple products of that country was hops, but William Queal having strong convictions along temperance lines, would not allow the land to be used for this purpose

    Educational advantages were somewhat limited in this early day in New York state, yet he gave his children all the opportunities the country afforded, and during the winter evenings his boys would choose sides and debate the different questions of the hour, while he acted as judge. Thus they learned to give expression to their thoughts and ideas, while they criticised each other without stint, and although these debates became heated at times, they always ended with every one in good humor.

That he was a man of strong religious principles is shown from the following extract from a letter written to his son, Atchison Queal, under date of October 4, 1836:

> We received your letter of July 29th, which gave us great satisfaction to hear that you were still well, and also created a feeling which none but parents can feel in the absence of a child, when you state your want of a mother's care and assistance. But we hope the time is drawing near when we shall be once more blessed with your company, the absence of which has caused a blank in the family. . . . Your grandfather Queal's folks are as well as usual. Old Mr. Babcock was buried last week. Your grandfather and grandmother Graves have gone to the state of Illinois. They went by land and sent their goods by water, which were all lost or damaged so much that what they received was not worth the cost of transportation.
>
> My dear son, let my advice to you at this time, as I know not but it may be the last I shall ever give you, sink with deep weight upon your mind, for was I possessed of riches, and able to bestow thousands upon you, my experience in life has taught me that my advice to you at this time, if you will be wise and take it, will be worth more to you than all the riches I could bestow without it. I hope that my prayer to the Almighty to enable you to receive it, may be answered. Be wise and virtuous, and remember your Creator in the days of your youth. Be not discouraged in your situation, for God, who is able to make all things work together for good to them that love and keep his commandments, will spread his mantle of love over you. . . . Are your clothes comfortable for the cold weather which is approaching? We are making cloth for you sufficient for a greatcoat and pantaloons. . . .
>
> Your affectionate father
>
> WM. C. QUEAL.

In early life William C. Queal and his wife united with the Methodist Episcopal church on the Charlotteville circuit, in the New York conference, and among the preachers of those days who from time to time were entertained at his home, are the names of John Bangs, Elbert Osborne, Porter Hedstrom, Mathew Van Dusen, A. C. Fuller, and others. William C. and Mary Queal trained their children for

God and Methodism, and so well did they succeed, that of the eleven children who came to adult years, nine were members of the Methodist church, and of the nine, four were ministers of the gospel

Mary Queal died October 10, 1855, after an illness covering many months

On the 21st of October, 1856, William Queal married Mary Ann Judd, who died January 6, 1869 After her death, he went to live with his son William, and died at Milford, Otsego county, New York, March 29, 1872

MARY QUEAL, daughter of Robert and Elizabeth Queal, married Artemas Babcock in Otsego county, New York, in 1818 To them were born five children:

I. Elizabeth, married —— Adkins. One of their sons became a physician and was possessed of considerable literary ability, publishing, among other things, a volume of poems
II. Polly, never married. She was the helper and home-keeper of the family
III Ellinor; never married She was a helpful woman and possessed of great executive ability During the epidemic of yellow fever which visited the South in 1883, she was untiring in her efforts to relieve the distress consequent upon this visitation, and when her friends, anxious for her safety, besought her to go north, she replied that she would do so when those under her care were convalescent Before this time arrived, she too became a victim of the disease and died at Pensacola, Florida
IV. Robert; married and had one daughter
V. Electa, married and lives at Utica, New York

Fourth Generation

RICHISON[4] QUEAL (William,[8] Robert,[2] William[1]), was born February 27, 1815, at Worcester, Otsego county, New York; married

Harriet Mallory November 3, 1846, at Windham, Greene county, New York. To them were born six children:

 I. Rosalie, born ——, 1847; died in infancy.
 II. Mary F., born May 22, 1848; married Charles Newton September 28, 1868. Mary died June 26, 1869.
 III. Isabel, born December 4, 1849; married Allen Keltner, at Ames, Iowa, April 25, 1874. To them were born four children; are living at Ames, Iowa.
 IV. Charles P., born March 27, 1851; married Charlotte L. Davy October 15, 1870, who died September 3, 1904. To them were born seven children, two dying in infancy. Charles P. Queal and family reside in Ames, Iowa.
 V. William N., born February 8, 1853; died February 11, 1884.
 VI. Ellen M., born March 23, 1856; died June 2, 1864.

Richison Queal worked with his father on the farm until he was seventeen years of age, when, becoming discontented with his work and home restraint, he started out for himself, trying various occupations. For some years he drove stage from Prattsville to Catskill, New York. In 1848 he went with his wife and baby daughter to Windham, Greene county, New York, where he worked for a company engaged in the manufacture of paper, remaining in their employ for five years. During their residence in Windham he and his wife united with the Methodist Episcopal church, which fact was a great comfort to his father and mother. Finally, his health failing, he moved his family to Worcester, occupying part of his father's house on the old farm. After some months of suffering he died August 3, 1856.

ATCHISON[4] QUEAL (William,[3] Robert,[2] William[1]), born Worcester, Otsego county, New York, April 6, 1817; married Lucy Oletha French at Decatur, New York, March 9, 1845. To them were born three children:

 I. Hedding H., born January 6, 1847.

II Mary Elizabeth, born January 22, 1849
III John Henry, born August 24, 1851.

Atchison Queal's early life was spent in agricultural pursuits When nineteen years of age he went to Harlem, New York, to teach his first term of school, and after that time spent several years attending school and teaching, in order to have satisfactory equipment for his life work

On July 4, 1835, he received the following certificate

> This may certify that Mr Atchison Queal has this day enrolled himself in a company of Artillery which is now under my command, belonging to the Twelfth Regiment, Third Brigade, Second Division, of New York State Artillery, according to law   JOSHUA CHAMPION Capt
> Dated Worcester, July 4, 1835

This was the year before he went to Harlem to teach and it is not known how long he remained a member of this artillery company

In 1840 Atchison Queal taught in Worcester, receiving ten dollars per month for his services, and attended school at Homer, New York, in the summer. In September of that year he went to Waterloo, New York, where he taught four months, receiving sixteen dollars per month. Not being in the best of health, he thought the western climate might prove beneficial, and accordingly, in August, 1843, went to St Charles, Illinois, where he taught a three months' term of school, at the conclusion of which he returned to Mt. Vernon, Indiana, where he taught a select school At this place, on March 4, 1844, he was given license by the Methodist church to exhort He wrote to his intended wife, telling her that he felt the Lord of the harvest was calling him to labor for souls, and asking if she thought she could become the wife of a minister She replied, as follows:

> This is not as I had made my calculations, but it has occupied the most of my thoughts since hearing from you and has been to me a subject of some prayers and some tears I feel that it is a hard life, but if you think it is your duty to be a minister of the Gospel, do it in the fear of God, and you shall have my prayers for your success I would say to you, act as you feel it your duty to, and I will try and do my part Be faithful, and let your example be as becometh a minister of Christ

Atchison Queal returned home in May of that year, giving up the idea of settling in the West, as had been his expectation when going to Illinois. The same fall he went back to Waterloo, New York, and taught four months of school at eighteen dollars per month. In the spring of 1845 he returned to Worcester and on April 9th married Lucy Oletha French, at the home of her father, in Decatur, New York. At the following session of the Oneida conference, he was received into its ranks. Methodist ministers at that time never remained longer than two years on a charge, and often were moved every year. He preached at Bainbridge, Otsego county, one year; Mt. Upton, Chenango county, one year; Fly Creek, two years; Exeter, two years; Westford, one year; Otego, two years, and Plymouth, one year. It was in the last mentioned place that his health failed, and he was obliged to give up his work in the ministry. In 1853, the first year he preached at Otego, he received three hundred fifty dollars as salary, and sixty dollars for house rent. The same year, the missionary collection on this charge was thirty-two dollars and four cents, three dollars and fifty cents of this amount being given by Atchison Queal and family.

From his father he inherited some inventive genius, and while in Plymouth completed a waterwheel on which he obtained a patent.

In the spring of 1856 Atchison Queal removed with his family to Morrow county, Ohio, where he left them in the care of his wife's father and went to Kansas to seek a home. The border ruffians were the terror of that country at the time, and as he felt unwilling to have his family surrounded by such conditions, returned to Ohio, where he moved them into a one-room log cabin, on a farm which he purchased, where they lived for more than two years.

In the winter of 1856-57 he taught school about one mile from his home, and two of his children — Hedding and Mary — were among his pupils. Until about one year before his death, he hoped that he might again take up his chosen work — the ministry — but such was not God's plan. He died July 6, 1859, leaving a wife and three children. He was buried in the Ebenezer burying ground, in Morrow county, Ohio, but some years later his remains were removed to Des Moines, Iowa, where they now rest in Woodland cemetery.

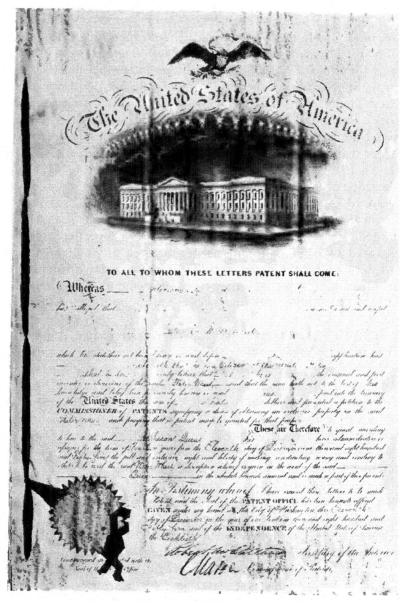

FAC-SIMILE OF LETTERS PATENT ISSUED TO ATCHISON QUEAL

Lucy Oletha French, wife of Atchison Queal, was born at Decatur, New York, February 16, 1821, at which place she grew to womanhood She was educated in the common branches of learning, as taught in the district schools of that day, and was trained in habits of industry and economy in household affairs, receiving the discipline in early years that enabled her to do her life work well Being the second child and eldest daughter in a family of thirteen children, many of the duties and responsibilities of the home fell upon her shoulders, and consequently but little opportunity was given for play At one time in her young girlhood she became the proud possessor of a rag doll, which a girl in the neighborhood made for her, painting the cheeks red and making the hair and eyes with ink However, she was not long permitted to enjoy the only doll she ever owned, for her brother Thomas in a spirit of mischief placed it in the watering trough, and pumping water over it destroyed all the beauty it ever possessed

Every girl in those days was taught to knit, and later on to spin the yarn from which the stockings and mittens were made for family use As Lucy grew older, she became an expert in the knitting of these articles, and every fall would have a number of pairs to sell. These her father took with him when he went to Albany (to which place he journeyed about twice each year) and exchanged them for something she wished to possess One time he brought her a pair of the glass candlesticks then in fashion, one of which is in her daughter's possession at the present time

Some time after her engagement to Atchison Queal and when thinking of her "setting out," her father told her that a cabinet maker in the neighborhood was owing him, and if she wished she might have some furniture made for the new home she was planning She immediately embraced the opportunity, and had made a number of pieces of furniture — among them a chest of drawers or bureau In the meantime some busybody in the community wrote to Atchison Queal, who at this time was away attending school, that Lucy was preparing to marry a young man in the neighborhood, was having her furniture made, and was very busy getting her linen ready for housekeeping. For some time after the receipt of this news the young man failed to write as had been his custom, and when he did so, she could read between the lines that something was wrong. Upon insisting that an explanation was her due, and must be made, the cause of the long silence and its following coldness was revealed, and a happy termination of the affair was reached. The bureau — which was an innocent party to the misunderstanding — is now in the possession of her grandson, John H. Beyer, and is a highly prized article of furniture in his home.

Lucy French was known among the members of her own family and in the community as well, as a peacemaker, and all the children in the neighborhood counted her as their friend. She was never too weary to do an act of kindness or lend a sympathizing ear in times of misfortune. In her early girlhood she united with the Methodist church, of which her mother was then a member, and amid these surroundings the sweet spirited girl grew to be a gentle, lovely woman, slow to take offense; not given to disparagement in speaking of others, often saying, "If you can say no good of people, say nothing."

About one year before their marriage, Atchison Queal felt that he was called to work in the Master's vineyard. Lucy had some doubts as to her ability to fulfil the duties and responsibilities incident to life in a parsonage home, but as in every other undertaking so in this, she determined by God's help to do her best and decided to keep her promise and become the wife and helpmeet of the young Methodist minister. She was married to the Rev. Atchison Queal April 9, 1845, at her father's home in Decatur, New York, and took up the duties which fall to the lot of a preacher's wife. After eleven years of faithful service, the health of the husband failed and he was obliged to give up the ministry and seek a permanent home. Hoping that he might be benefited by the change, they moved to Morrow county, Ohio, in the spring of 1856, whither the French family had gone in 1847. Atchison Queal went farther west, but finding no more favorable location, decided to remain in Ohio, where he bought forty acres of land from his father-in-law, Sampson French, giving in payment five hundred dollars in cash, and securing the remaining five hundred dollars by mortgage on the place. The first two years they lived in a log cabin which was on the farm, but in the summer of 1858 Atchison Queal built a house, doing much of the work himself, and in November of that year they moved into what seemed to them a palatial residence as compared with the one-roomed cabin which they vacated

It is a matter of record that, on the 5th of June, 1859, there came a killing frost which did widespread damage throughout the whole country. The children in this home were sent into the garden to cover the beans so that they might be kept from freezing, and on completing this task went into the house, their fingers stinging with pain, the mother finding it necessary to put their hands in cold water to relieve their suffering

On July 6, 1859, Atchison Queal died, after two weeks of great suffering, leaving a widow and three children. Hedding H, aged twelve, Mary E, aged ten, and John H, aged eight. The widow was advised by some to find homes for her children, and to give up the place, but her answer was a demonstration of her firm, steadfast character: "Not until I have tried to keep a home for them, fulfilling my duty as a mother, and failed, shall I separate my children from me, and with God's help that time will never come."

She took up the work of the farm where her husband left it, and after the death of her father, in 1861, was able to pay off the mortgage, selling the forty acres two years later for fourteen hundred dollars. Purchasing a farm of ninety-six acres, near Iberia, for three thousand dollars, the payment of the difference became her great ambition. On this farm was a large number of oak trees, which she had sawed into wood, selling the bark to a man who owned a tanyard. Accumulating stock as rapidly as possible, she was able, with the assistance of hired help and what her boys could do, to not only make a living but meet the payments on the farm as they became due

In 1871 Lucy French Queal sold this property and removed to Ames, Iowa, near which place she bought a farm of one hundred twenty acres

In the spring of 1864 her oldest son enlisted in the War of the Rebellion, with the "one hundred day" men, and the mother heart was sorely tried as this new experience came to her. Many of these men never returned, but her boy, although broken in health, was spared to the family circle.

In 1879 a great sorrow came to this home, in the death of Hedding — the first born, and shortly after, the family removed to Sheldahl, Iowa, then to Ames, and finally in the spring of 1884 to Des Moines, where after more than a year's illness, Lucy French Queal died at the home of her daughter, Mary Queal Beyer, March 15, 1885. To her children she gave the best of her thought and strength, and none ever had a more careful, loving mother. She was a loyal sister, a devoted wife, an affectionate mother, and all the relations of life she well fulfilled.

Fifth Generation

HEDDING H.[5] QUEAL (Atchison,[4] William,[3] Robert,[2] William[1]), oldest son of Atchison and Lucy French Queal, was born January 6, 1847, at Mt. Upton, Chenango county, New York, and went with his parents to Ohio in the spring of 1856. His father was a great admirer of Bishop Hedding of the Methodist church, and it was in his honor that his first born son was named. School privileges were constantly being improved, and Hedding made the most of the opportunities offered, never failing to come to his classes with lessons perfectly prepared. After the death of his father he worked on the farm, often performing tasks which he was physically unfitted to do, that his mother might be spared the necessity of hiring help she could illy afford.

In September, 1862, when David Tod, governor of Ohio, called on the minute men of the state, and the "Squirrel Hunters" — as they were designated — enlisted by thousands in response to the summons, Hedding went with the company which his uncle, Oscar French, organized. After his return home he constantly wished he were old enough to go to the war as a regularly enlisted soldier; when seventeen years of age and the call was made for one-hundred day men, he enlisted at Iberia in the One Hundred Thirty-sixth regiment, Ohio

Hedding Queal

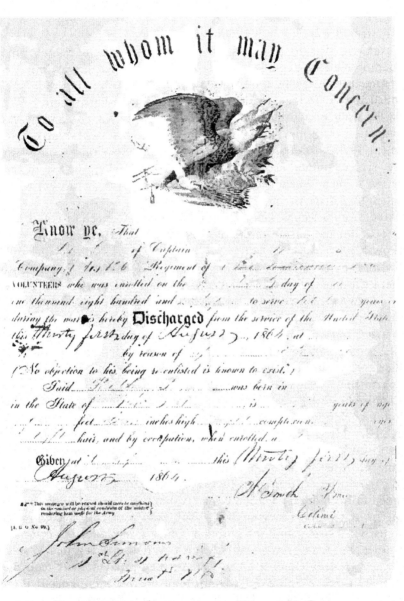

DISCHARGE FROM SERVICE GIVEN TO HEDDING H. QUEAL

Volunteer Infantry, James McPeak, captain. They were sent to Alexandria, Virginia, and stationed at Fort Lyon, at which place Hedding contracted malarial fever so that his health was impaired for some time after his return to his home. The following year he attended Iberia College, two miles distant, and boarded at home. During vacation he worked on his mother's farm, but not finding this occupation congenial, he went to Chicago in 1866, where he entered the employ of his uncle, Robert F. Queal, a lumber merchant of that city. He continued in this position until 1870, when his health failing, he went to Minnesota, spending the winter at St. Cloud, where he taught a three months' term of school.

Hedding united with the Trinity Methodist Church of Chicago in 1875, under the pastorate of the Rev. W. F. Crafts, and died in its fellowship.

In the spring of 1871 Hedding's mother removed to Ames, Iowa, where she had purchased a farm about two miles from the village and for two summers the son worked for her at this new home, teaching school during the winter months. In 1873 his health being somewhat improved, he went to Chicago, took the examination, and became a mail carrier. In 1875 he was given a clerkship in the post-office and at the time of his death was in charge of the dead letter department. One very cold night in February, 1879, the Chicago postoffice building was destroyed by fire and while working in frozen clothing, Hedding Queal contracted a cold from which he never recovered. He married Nettie Ross April 9, 1879, and on May 1st was given leave of absence from the office. He went to his mother's home at Ames, where he remained for three weeks, returning to Chicago at the expiration of that time, but after two weeks again returned to his mother's home with a six months' leave of absence. In August of that year he started for Colorado overland, accompanied by his wife, sister, and her husband. For a few days he seemed to improve, but soon grew steadily worse. When they reached Waconda Springs, near Cawker City, Kansas, they pitched their tents and decided to remain in this place until some change should occur in his condition. His brother, John H. Queal, came to assist in his care, and nothing that willing hands could do or loving thought suggest, was lacking to make the last days and hours as comfortable as possible, but the end came September 6, 1879, and the burial took place at Cawker City, Kansas. Years afterward his remains were removed to Des Moines, Iowa, and buried in the family lot in Woodland cemetery. In 1884 his widow married Frank Kegley, and they removed to Princeton, Illinois, at which place she died some years later.

JOHN HENRY[5] QUEAL (Atchison,[4] William,[3] Robert,[2] William[1]) was born at Exeter, Otsego county, New York, August 24, 1851. He moved with his mother to a farm near Ames, Iowa, in April, 1871, remaining there until 1873, when he went to Chicago, where he was employed by his uncle, Robert F. Queal, a lumber merchant of that city, of the firm of R. F. Queal & Co., which firm later sold their lumber business in Chicago and removed to Pensacola, Florida. John H. Queal remained in Chicago and was employed by Mendsen & Winter and the T. Wilce Company of that city as traveling salesman, and later traveled for C. Lamb & Sons of Clinton, Iowa. He was married to Jennie Nelson in 1875. She died in February, 1906, and he married (second) April 23, 1907, Alice Henshaw Nigh of Huntington, West Virginia.

In 1879 John H. Queal, with his brother-in-law, Jackson Beyer, bought a small lumber yard at Sheldahl, Iowa, where the foundation of the business was laid, the firm name being J. H. Queal & Co. They later opened yards at Cambridge and Madrid, Iowa, and bought a lumber yard from C. Lamb & Sons located at Ames, Iowa. About this time he gave up traveling and devoted his energies to the business of J. H. Queal & Co.

In 1883 John H. Queal moved to Des Moines and started a yard at East Fourth and Locust streets, now located at East Second street and Grand avenue. The lumber merchants at Des Moines, not wanting more lumber yards than were already there, tried various methods to keep the company from establishing their business, finally having

John H. Queal

them arrested for maintaining a lumber yard within the fire limits; but as all the other yards in the city were maintained under the same condition, the suits were of no avail and the business was established. He moved to Minneapolis, Minnesota, in 1889, and the main office of the company was located in that city. The firm of J. H. Queal & Co. own a line of yards in Iowa, Minnesota, and South Dakota, and are also interested in timber lands in Oregon and California.

For the past seven years John H. Queal has divided his time between McCloud, California, and Minneapolis. At the present time he is president of the McCloud River Railroad Company and the McCloud National Bank, and quite heavily interested in the corporations mentioned, besides being a director in other national banks and timber companies. His residence is at Minneapolis, Minnesota.

Fourth Generation

MARTHA QUEAL, daughter of William C. and Mary (Graves) Queal, born August 28, 1820; married Horatio Flint February 19, 1845. Being the oldest daughter in the family and for ten years the only one, she early acquired habits of industry, thus being of great assastance to her mother in the care of the younger children. As soon as old enough she was taught to spin, thus relieving her mother of this important labor for the household. She spun the wool from which the clothing for her father and brothers was made; she was also taught how to make butter and cheese. In those days there was not much time for play, either for boys or girls, as every child was given some definite task to do. During the winter evenings two candles were lighted and some member of the family would read aloud while the mother patched or darned, as the necessity demanded, while Martha, with her knitting, listened and learned. She united in early life with the Methodist Episcopal church. On May 19, 1844, she wrote to her brother William, who was attending school at Cazenovia, New York, and among other items of interest, said:

> There is quite an excitement prevailing in Decatur and vicinity in the Methodist church concerning Mr. Turble using his bass viol in the church, to assist in singing. Some of the members are very much in favor of it, and some are decidedly opposed to the "big fiddle" as they term it. It is uncertain

> how it will terminate, but I fear for the result. As for my own part I can see no inconsistency in using the viol, as there are very few bass singers, and I believe that if the heart is right in the sight of God, that he will not be displeased with the viol or the use of it. They will destroy much of the good feeling which has existed among them, if it does not amount to a division of the society, as both parties are very strenuous in their opinions concerning it.

Quite a general dissatisfaction resulted from the use of the bass viol and it was years before harmony was restored in the church.

Horatio Flint bought fifty acres of William Queal's farm, upon which he built a house for his bride, only a short distance from the home of her mother, and on their wedding day took possession of their new residence which they were not permitted to long enjoy, as the wife became ill with that dread disease, consumption, and died February 13, 1847.

WILLIAM GRAVES[4] QUEAL (William,[3] Robert,[2] William[1]), was born in Worcester, Otsego county, New York, December 14, 1822; he married Lorinda L. Booth (born March 6, 1831) July 3, 1850, at Oxford, New York. To them were born three children:

I. Martha Amelia, born July 14, 1851.
II. Alice, born September 23, 1856; married George Benedict; died August 23, 1905.
III. William Booth, born January 26, 1864; died of diphtheria in Salem, Pennsylvania, December 20, 1875.

William Graves Queal, like his brothers, was reared on a farm. As a child he was conscientious and studious; he remained in the family home during his boyhood days, attending school when he could be spared from work and studying at home as opportunity offered. In this way he gained an education sufficient to enable him to pass an examination, and before he was seventeen years of age he commenced teaching during the winter months and attending school in the summer. At nineteen he entered Cazenovia Seminary, which he attended two or three terms. While there he wrote to his brother, Atchison Queal, as follows: "I met a Mr. Moore a few days since, and he told me that he once had an introduction to you, although he concluded we were not brothers, as your name was *Queal.* He pronounced my name Quail."

William united with the Methodist Episcopal church, and early felt the call to preach the gospel. In 1846 he was received into the Oneida conference. He remained in the ministry for thirty-eight years, when he retired from active service and lived at Norwich, New York, where he purchased a home, afterwards moving to Bethlehem, Pennsylvania. His gentle, sympathetic nature endeared him to all his friends. He was noted for his simplicity and for his sincerity. In business affairs he was honest and true — a man whose word was as good as his bond. Though of decided ability, he never pushed himself to the front to the crowding out of others. Ever ready to give place, he never shrank from duty, nor did he lack the courage of his convictions. He was possessed of excellent judgment, hence his counsel was often sought. His strength of purpose, purity of life, kind, sympathic heart, and maturity of judgment distinguished him as a rare man, out of, as well as in the church. He was honored by being twice elected delegate to the General Conference of the Methodist Episcopal church, and once as reserve delegate. His sermons, essays, and other writings showed much thought and study; the books he wrote display scholarship and ability.

In January, 1888, he went to visit his brother Orin, who was living in Kansas City, Missouri, and from that city went to San Diego, California, accompanied by his nephew, Irving Queal of Kansas City, and Jackson Beyer of Des Moines, Iowa. The trip was in the interest of business as well as pleasure. On the return journey he was taken very ill, and upon reaching Pueblo, Colorado, was removed from the train to a hotel, in the evening, and died at 7 o'clock the following morning. His wife, on receipt of the telegram that he was seriously ill, took the first train to reach his bedside. Another message arrived the following morning, telling of his death. Every effort possible was made to reach her, but all proved futile until just before she arrived at a junction near Kansas City, Missouri. Here a telegram was delivered to her with instructions to leave the train at the next station, where she was met by friends returning with the body of her husband, and the sad and weary journey was made back to the home in Norwich, New York.

William Graves Queal died in Pueblo, Colorado, February 26, 1888. After his death, his widow resided with her daughter Martha, in whose home in Oneonta, New York, she died November 6, 1908.

MARTHA AMELIA QUEAL, daughter of William and Lorinda (Booth) Queal, married Bradley Meaker August 17, 1881. To them was born one child, Robert Queal Meaker, December 2, 1884, who died January 20, 1902. Bradley Meaker was a teacher in the Lehigh University, at Bethlehem, Pennsylvania. On the 6th of November, 1885, while in the university gymnasium, where he had gone to take exercise, he suddenly fell to the floor and expired before assistance reached him. Following this sad event, Martha Meaker and her son went to reside with her parents at Norwich, New York, remaining with them until after the death of her father, William Graves Queal, when, accompanied by her mother, she and her son removed to Carbondale, Pennsylvania, where she became a kindergartner, teaching in this capacity for some years. After her son's graduation from high school at the age of sixteen, she moved to Syracuse, New York, where he entered the university the following year. At the age of eighteen he returned to Carbondale to visit an uncle and attend the commencement exercises of the high school. His mother and grandmother were soon to follow. He and a companion were sprinting close beside a switch track of the railroad, when an engine was seen backing toward him. The boy who was with him, noting his imminent danger, tried to warn him. Robert, hearing the call, sprang aside, but unfortunately, the wrong way, and the engine passed over his body. His mother received a telegram that Robert was badly injured, but before the departure of the first train for Carbondale, the papers at Syracuse were being sold on the streets telling of Robert Meaker's death. This was a terrible blow to his mother, from which she never fully recovered.

Five Children of William C. and Mary Graves Queal

Robert F. Queal Mary Queal Rev. James Queal
Capt. Paul A. Queal   Orin H. Queal

Rev. Atchison Queal

Rev. William G. Queal

Rev. Luke C. Queal

Old "French School House" at Decatur, New York, where Reverend Atchison Queal, Reverend William G. Queal, and Reverend Luke C. Queal each preached His First Sermon

On April 9, 1908, Martha Meaker married Nathan M. Briggs of Oneonta, New York, and at this home her mother died the following November. In October, 1909, while in Norwich, where she had gone to settle some business affairs in connection with her mother's estate, she received a telegram, stating that her husband was dangerously ill. Taking the first train, she arrived at her home shortly after his death, which was caused from hemorrhage of the brain. Martha was again a widow.

In January, 1912, Martha married Frank Ives, an old time friend, whose home was in Los Angeles, California. At the beginning of their journey to that city, she was suddenly stricken with paralysis, and was removed from the train at Binghamton, New York, a few days later being taken to her home in Oneonta, where she still lives, though a sufferer from the stroke.

ALICE, daughter of William Graves and Lorinda (Booth) Queal, was born September 23, 1856; married the Rev. George Benedict of Plymouth, New York, August 17, 1881. To them were born three children:
1. Mabel; married Wendel Morgan, July, 1910, at Oneonta, New York; one child, born in May, 1911.
2. Fannie H.; a teacher in Porto Rico.
3. George Barnard; lives with his father in Porto Rico.

George and Alice Benedict in 1892 went as missionaries to South America, where they remained six years, at the expiration of which time they returned to the United States. In 1900 they were sent to the mission field in Porto Rico. Owing to ill health, Alice returned on July 9, 1905, and five weeks later died very suddenly while visiting in the home of her husband's brother at South Plymouth, New York. George Benedict married a second time, and died in September, 1912, while a missionary in Porto Rico.

ROBERT F.[4] QUEAL (William,[3] Robert,[2] William [1]), was born July 1, 1825, in Worcester, Otsego county, New York; married Sarah

Cook Houghton in March, 1853. To them was born one son, Irving Queal. Sarah Houghton Queal died in 1856. Robert F. Queal married (second) Kate Gillespie, of Schenectady, New York, December 29, 1870. Kate Gillespie Queal died in 1889.

Robert F. Queal received his education in the common schools, supplemented by a course of reading in a law office. In his youth he was teacher, clerk, and merchant. Though disliking the first named occupation, he nevertheless taught a number of terms of school. When nineteen years of age, while clerking in a store in Worcester, he wrote to his brother who was attending school in Cazenovia, as follows:

> My time has been uninterruptedly given to the concerns of *profit making* for my employers, which I think is not exactly adapted to the development of man's moral and intellectual nature, but one after all that furnishes a diversified field fit for a *Shakesperean*; and let me say, as the result of my observations, I believe although men may be cold and selfish and their exterior frigid as the chain which girds the ice-bound pole, yet within the human heart worlds of feeling live, and far beneath the reach of human ken, in human souls exist principles which prove man's author a living God, stamping him a living candidate for immortality.
>
> The world I find very different from what my boyish imaginings had fancied it. In my leisure I have studied *politics*, and have had many sharp conflicts with the opposition, together with some squibbings in the papers, but I find there is little confidence to be placed in political leaders; still there are great questions which involve the destiny of our Republic, to be decided upon in the coming election, prominent among which are the tariff, and annexation of Texas. My motto is, *Annexation never*. And I am sorry to find that I fear Mr. Clay (trembling lest he should lose votes in the South) has abandoned the ground for the party, in a recent letter published in Alabama, and come out for ultimate annexation, slavery and all, when the consent of Mexico and the several United States is obtained. Still, the war must go on, for on one side is arrayed those who say, "Texas immediately," on the other, those who mainly say, "Texas never," whose candidate says, "Texas when certain things are secured," which I believe never can be. . .
>
> You refer in your letter to Abolition movements. I think their efforts should be more rational, if they would oppose the extension of slavery in an available way instead of wasting their influence and votes on a condition morally certain of defeat.

In the spring of 1857 Robert Queal went to Chicago where he built up an extensive lumber business. He was a representative man in the Methodism of that city. To him the marvelous reconstruction of that church's institutions after the great fire gave large opportunity for relaying its foundations. He was fitted to the demands of the hour, and by his liberal contributions and wise counsels did a great work. With suggestions that commanded the approval of the wisest men, he could easily secure the concurrence of the young men in the churches by his strong sympathies with them. His own large contributions to the relief fund at the very start gave it the weight of his convictions, and secured success for it in the end.

Robert Queal was for years a trustee of the First Methodist Church of Chicago and of the Northwestern University, where his influence was much felt. He was a member of the board of education for the city, and one of the first trustees of the Chicago Public Library, in all of these places being preëminently a working member. His church also selected him as an honored member of the General Conference of 1876.

Robert Queal had rare literary taste and marked ability. He read with delight the best authors and kept abreast of the literary world. He was familiar with the atmosphere and traditions of the worthy authors, both at home and abroad, and was especially fond of the writings of Robert Burns. In spite of his heavy burdens in business life, he was the author of some sweet and stirring poems; was also a good critic, giving his literary instincts the mastery over his personal friendships. He was a liberal man and bore the burdens of many, caring for and giving a loving Christian home to two children, whose mother gave up her life in the work of the Woman's Foreign Missionary Society. He was commanding in his presence, judicial in his mind, wise in his arguments, happy in his language, faithful in his friendships, and unimpeachable in his motives.

After disposing of his business interests in Chicago, Robert Queal went to Pensacola, Florida, and there started an extensive business in lumber and milling. In 1883 he contracted a malarial disease in the South, although the more serious symptoms did not present themselves until he neared his home in Evanston, Illinois, at which place he died three days later, November 2, 1883, in the fifty-eighth year of his age. His body was taken to the home of his boyhood, and rests in Maple Grove cemetery at Worcester, Otsego county, New York.

The following verse is from a poem written by Robert Queal, and read at the service for the consecration of this burial ground on June 7, 1865:

> And why repine? This tangled skein
> Of hope and joy and grief and pain
> That we call life, — this unknown state
> Of death, that we call human fate,
> Shall be made plain in God's own time,
> Parts of a plan, complete, sublime;
> And through these realms a trumpet call
> Shall reach these people, great and small —
> Death's power shall yield, his fetters break,
> And earth's long tenants shall awake.

I. Irving, son of Robert F. and Sarah (Houghton) Queal, born September 23, 1855, Worcester, New York; married November 25, 1880, Lucy Bannister (born Cazenovia, New York, January 15, 1855) at Evanston, Illinois. To them were born four children:
1. Robert F., born July 14, 1882, Story City, Iowa; died March 29, 1889.
2. Harry B., born November 10, 1883, Kansas City, Missouri; married Nellie Wheeler, Beresford, South Dakota, March, 1905; two children; lives at Kewanee, Illinois.
3. Ralph W., born August 25, 1886, Kansas City, Missouri, where he still resides.
4. Lucy Mary, born July 10, 1889, Kansas City, Missouri.

After the death of his mother, Irving Queal lived with an aunt, Louise Albert, in Worcester, New York; later he went to Chicago, spending part of his time with his father, attending school in Evanston, Illinois. For some years he was in the employ of J. H. Queal & Co. at Story City, Story county, Iowa, from which place he removed to Kansas City, Missouri, where he found employment in the office of his uncle, Orin H. Queal. His health becoming impaired, he went to South Dakota, taking up a quarter section of land, where he

Lot in Maple Grove Cemetery, Worcester, New York, where Sixteen of the Queal Family are buried

still resides The daughter, Lucy Mary, graduated from the high school at Kansas City, in home economics, and taught for two years in that city, then entered Columbia University, New York City, where she is taking the regular course in her chosen work. After her graduation she expects to take a government position in the Philippine Islands

LUKE C.[4] QUEAL (William,[3] Robert,[2] William [1]), was born at Worcester, Otsego county, New York, April 2, 1827; married September 19, 1849, Catherine Klock (born November 30, 1825), at Seward, Schoharie county, New York To them were born two children·
 I. Mary Matilda, born May 28, 1852, at Worcester, New York Mary has never married; lives in Elmira, New York For years she has devoted herself to the work of the Woman's Foreign Missionary Society of the Methodist Episcopal church; has been conference secretary of Central New York conference for thirteen years, for four years was also field secretary for the states of New York and New Jersey; has been twice a delegate to the general executive meeting, and was a delegate to the world's missionary conference in Edinburgh, in June, 1910 The cause of missions has received much inspiration from this gifted woman, who has gone up and down this great land of ours, urging upon the people, with voice and pen, the needs of those of our less favored sisters whose lives are spent in spiritual darkness
 II Alice, born October 27, 1855; died March 8, 1857

Luke C Queal married (second) Sara M Dean of Milford, Otsego county, New York, April 22, 1858 Two children were born of this union:
 III Arthur Dean, born August 23, 1861, in West Eaton, Madison county, New York; married Alice Hubbel, of Troy, New York, November 10, 1885. To them was born one child:
  1 Katharine M , born December 21, 1886, Kansas City, Mis-

souri; married August 1, 1912, Dr. John Gould of the Eleventh Cavalry, U. S. A.

Arthur Dean Queal died in London, England, in April, 1890. His widow married August 2, 1894, and is living in Des Moines, Iowa.

IV. Kittie Sara, born November 6, 1862; died October 31, 1863.

Luke C. Queal married (third) Sarah J. Hall, at Cazenovia, New York, June 30, 1864. To them were born two sons:

V. James Hall, born July 27, 1865, Norwich, New York; married Susie Gifford of Scipioville, New York, in July, 1895. He has been for some years engaged in newspaper work; is now living in New York City.

VI. Herbert Paul, born at Cazenovia, New York, May 17, 1867; married Minnie E. Davis in August, 1902, at Buffalo, New York. He is a very successful lawyer, handling large estates. Office, No. 42 Broadway; residence, 929 West End avenue, New York.

Luke C. Queal's boyhood life differed but little from that of his brothers. He worked on the farm, attended school and taught school — at one time teaching for some months for eleven dollars and fifty cents per month. He was coached for his first teacher's certificate by his brother Robert, who, becoming discouraged at his slow progress, wrote to his brother William: "Luke, while bright in other ways, seems dull when it comes to book learning." He studied medicine and practiced a short time before commencing to preach. He did not have a college education, but because of his natural ability, his eloquence, his force of character, and his strength as a debater, Hamilton College in 1870 conferred upon him the degree of doctor of divinity. When he was twenty-seven years of age he entered the Oneida conference and when the conferences were divided became a member of the Central New York conference, while membership in Wyoming conference fell to the lot of his brother William. As a pastor Luke C. Queal served the largest city churches of his conference, and was prominent in connection with Syracuse University, being a member of the board of trustees for many years. For seventeen years Doctor Queal performed the duties of presiding elder, and at the time of his death was one of the trustees of the Central New York conference He was seven times elected to the general conference, and elected to two ecumenical conferences, one held in Baltimore, Maryland, the other in Washington, D C

The physical characteristics of Doctor Queal well expressed his moral attributes He was a man of large make in every particular, and his fighting qualities won for him no less his bodily, than his mental and spiritual triumphs Doctor Queal did not fight for himself alone, but for everyone who needed his strong championship in a righteous cause. But the spirit of the warrior was not the only spirit that animated the noble heart of Luke C. Queal He knew all the depths of devotion of which a man is capable The sorrows of the poor, and the trials of man's lot appealed to him strongly, while the ties of blood were strong as steel. He feared no foe and would sacrifice himself before he would desert a friend As a speaker he had few equals To him was given what few people are blessed with — power to think faster than he could speak. He was counted one of the strongest debaters on the floor of the general conference; a wise parliamentarian possessed of a keen legal mind He was a fearless preacher and a plain-spoken man, in as well as out of the pulpit Without egotism but with authority, he declared his own convictions, which beliefs he also taught to others

After a lingering illness, he died at Moravia, New York, on January 2, 1898, and was buried in Maple Grove cemetery, Worcester, New York His widow, Sarah Hall Queal, died at Binghamton, New York, February 26, 1910.

JAMES[4] QUEAL (William,[3] Robert,[2] William[1]), son of William and Mary (Graves) Queal, was born November 21, 1828, at Worcester, Otsego county, New York. Being one of the younger children of the family, James missed some of the hardships which naturally fell to his older brothers. He was educated in the common schools, and later taught school to earn the money with which to pay for a better education. At the age of thirteen he united with the Methodist Episcopal church, and when little more than a boy he felt the call to work in the Master's vineyard, fully deciding this to be his life work when about twenty-two years of age. He joined the Troy conference, but was not long permitted to engage in his chosen work. Although delicate in health, he continued to perform the arduous duties assigned him with acceptability until December, 1852, at which time it became evident that he was suffering from tubercular trouble. Very reluctantly he gave up his labors and returned to his former home, where he hoped to regain strength to enable him to resume his pastoral duties. All efforts made toward the restoration of his health were unavailing, and on June 13, 1853, he died, at Worcester, Otsego county, New York, and was buried in Maple Grove cemetery.

MARY, daughter of William and Mary Graves Queal, was born August 21, 1830, at Worcester, Otsego county, New York, where she grew to young womanhood much beloved by a large circle of friends as well as the immediate family. During her childhood, being of delicate health, she was an object of solicitude to her parents, and the constant companion of her mother.

In the spring of 1848, while visiting her brother Atchison at Fly Creek, New York, Mary engaged to teach a three months' term of school, for which she received fourteen dollars per month. She returned to her home in the fall and was ill for the greater part of the following year. In the spring of 1849 she set out a rose bush in the front yard of her home, watching and nourishing its growth during that summer, and the next spring was delighted to see that it lived and grew rapidly, and when the first bud burst into bloom, rejoiced that she had been permitted to pick a blossom from her own bush. She died June 13, 1850, in her twentieth year. As long as the family lived on the farm, "Mary's rose bush" was carefully covered in winter and nourished during the summer. When the property was sold to a friend of the family, the story of the bush was repeated to the purchaser, and now, after more than sixty years, the rose bush still

Captain Paul A. Queal

lives and blooms It has been trimmed back and carefully looked after during this time, and many members of the Queal family who were not born at the time of Mary's death, have gathered roses from this historic bush

PAUL A[4] QUEAL (William,[3] Robert,[2] William [1]), son of William and Mary Graves Queal, was born February 4, 1833, at Worcester, Otsego county, New York. His childhood and youth were spent on his father's farm, his academic education being received at Carlisle and the New York Conference Seminaries When eighteen years of age he engaged in the manufacture of paper at Windham Center, New York Evidently the business proved unsatisfactory, for after a few months it was discontinued and he entered the seminary at Charlotteville, New York. In July of that year he wrote his brother as follows·

> I have passed through one of the ordeals of improvement in public speaking, having had the honor of representing in connection with two other speakers, the Wesleyan Association One of the speakers delivered an oration, and another with myself debated a question I spoke for about half an hour before nearly one thousand persons and was fortunate enough to gain the question. If you were ever in the same situation, you can imagine about where my pulse was when I came on the stage

Being forceful in argument, Paul Queal concluded to become a lawyer, and commenced his professional reading for the law in the office of General Burnside, in Worcester, New York Before its completion in 1857 he removed to the west, taking up his residence at Toledo, Tama county, Iowa, where he remained one year Having been admitted to the bar, he located at Nevada, the county seat of Story county, Iowa, where he speedily acquired a good practice and a high reputation politically and professionally A history of Story county states: "Paul A Queal was a brilliant young lawyer, and bade fair to take a leading place at the bar."

The legislature of Iowa decided in March, 1858, that there should be established a State Agricultural College within its borders; Paul Queal with others, convinced that Story county would be a suitable place to locate such an institution, worked toward that result. The first meeting of the board of trustees, consisting of eleven members, took place in Des Moines, January 10, 1859. Proposals for the sale of lands for the college farm were issued at this meeting and circulated over the state, to be acted upon at the meeting of the board the following June. At that time, propositions were received from the counties of Hardin, Polk, Marshall, Tama, Jefferson, and Story; committees were appointed to visit the various sites offered, and a spirited but good natured contest ensued. The record shows that at one time Hardin county had seven votes and Polk county four; it is said that a speech made by Paul A. Queal decided the question and the location was awarded to Story county. On the 20th of June, 1859, the board located the farm in the western part of Story county, buying a tract of six hundred forty-seven and one-half acres of unimproved land in one body for five thousand three hundred eighty dollars. On July 4, 1859, the citizens of Boone county turned out en masse to visit the college grounds, while the people of Story county gladly extended the hand of welcome to their guests on this auspicious occasion. The Declaration of Independence was read by Paul A. Queal, and later, while at dinner, he responded to the toast — "The Heroes of the American Revolution."

Paul A. Queal was a delegate to the Republican state convention which met in Des Moines January 18, 1860, and selected the delegates to the Chicago convention which nominated Abraham Lincoln for the presidency. In the summer of 1861 he assisted in raising a company of volunteers for the Second Iowa Cavalry, of which organization he was appointed the original first lieutenant, on July 30th. The regiment was organized with Major Elliott of the regular army as colonel, and mustered into the service at Davenport, Iowa, August 31, 1861. The regiment after leaving Davenport was first ordered to St. Louis, and was subsequently sent to the field under General Pope, sharing in the service of the army which captured New Madrid and Island Number Ten.

After these victories, the regiment was ordered to join the army in west Tennessee. Apart from the usual duties of scouting and skirmishing, the first desperate field service to which it was called was in the battle of Farmington, Mississippi Here they were ordered to charge a consecutive line of batteries, heavily supported by infantry. In the teeth of an appalling fire (ninety horses being shot in their regiment) they charged to the muzzles of the guns, striking down and driving the gunners from their positions at the point of the saber. Correspondents of the press and early historians of the war describe it as equal in daring to the most famous military exploits of modern times Lieutenant Queal received open mention in the report of this battle, for his coolness and bravery, as will be shown by the following. "The daring of Lieutenant Queal, commanding Company B, was conspicuous, cheering his men to the very muzzle of the enemy's guns."

On April 15, 1862, Lieutenant Queal was promoted to captain The Second Iowa Cavalry, under the command of Colonel Elliott, together with the Second Michigan cavalry, left Farmington and marched rapidly by a circuitous route for the purpose of deceiving the enemy as to the object of the expedition The second morning they appeared before Boonville, the forces of the enemy which had been left to guard the town falling back with but little resistance The railroad depot was filled with commissary stores, ammunition, etc. Upon entering the town the telegraph wires were cut thus preventing speedy communication with the enemy Shortly after, Colonel Elliott was promoted to the rank of brigadier general

On the morning of July 1, 1862, the enemy was discovered in strong force approaching the camp of the Second Iowa, whose pickets reported a number of rebels in sight Colonel Hatch (who succeeded Colonel Elliott) by a strategic movement overcame the superior force by which he was opposed The entire strength of his command was less than eight hundred men From this small force he detached four companies, two from each regiment, with orders to move rapidly and gain the rear of the approaching foe He then posted his remaining force in a strong position and awaited the attack of the enemy, whose number was estimated to be not less than four thousand. The two cavalry regiments were splendidly armed and mounted, and had absolute confidence in their leaders, which confidence was not misplaced, as the result proved. The attack of the enemy was met by such a heavy fire that they fell back in disorder, only to be charged upon by the detachment which had been sent to attack them in the rear, resulting in their being driven from the field with heavy loss. In his official report, written the following day, Colonel Sheridan describes in detail the different movements of his command and those of the enemy during the engagement. He makes special mention of the gallantry and good conduct of Colonel Hatch, Majors Coon and Hepburn, and Captains Gillett and Queal.

On November 12th the army began its march southward, the cavalry brigade commanded by Colonel Hatch taking the advance, the scouts keeping well out in front and on the flanks. The enemy's cavalry was alert and watchful, and skirmishing occurred frequently. At Coffeeville, after a hard fought engagement, the Union cavalry found themselves greatly outnumbered and were compelled to retreat. The loss of the Second Iowa in this encounter was twenty-two men killed and wounded. As our forces were gradually being driven back, Captain Queal's horse was shot under him, he being slightly scratched by a shell.

Again, the Second Iowa Cavalry participated in the expedition under Grierson in his great raid, but was withdrawn after two days to make a diversion of the enemy's forces. On February 21, 1863 (the engagement in which the Second Iowa was most conspicuous), among those who distinguished themselves for coolness and bravery, stands prominent the name of Paul A. Queal, captain commanding the second battalion. Major Coon was detailed to take the Second Cavalry and a battalion of the Sixth Illinois, and hold the enemy in check until the large transportation train could get safely under way. Instead of falling back, Major Coon requested the brigade commander, Lieutenant Colonel Hepburn, to let him make a standing fight. Hepburn's reply was that the orders of General Smith must be obeyed. There was nothing left but for the rear guard to continue to slowly retire, protecting both its front and flanks as best it could against the persistent attacks of the enemy. The battalions, under Captains Queal and Horton, dismounted and fought from behind trees with their Colt's revolving rifles, inflicting heavy loss upon the enemy

In the summer of 1863 Captain Queal was with his regiment except for a few weeks while reorganizing and in command of an Iowa regiment of cavalry During that summer while separated from his command he was taken prisoner, but was soon after exchanged These are some of the leading features of his service in the field, but they imperfectly represent the fatiguing marches, privations, exposures, and wearing service to which the cavalry in west Tennessee and northern Mississippi were subjected during the war, on a field and over a region which was the theater of continuous raids and many battles. In the fall of 1863 Captain Queal was appointed judge advocate on the staff of General Veitch, commanding the district of Memphis, Tennessee, where he remained for several months, discharging with ability the important and responsible duties of the position General Veitch being ordered to the field, Captain Queal rejoined his regiment, participating in the expedition under General Smith, early in the spring of 1864, to Tallahatchie The march was laborious, and the fighting hard, but for bravery and gallantry he received the warm commendation of General Smith in person, and special honorable mention in his report This was his last field service He, with his regiment came north in the month of April on furlough, spent three happy weeks in Iowa with his friends, visited his brothers in Chicago, and returned in May to Tennessee Soon after he was detached to perform judge advocate duties in Memphis, in which service he was engaged until his death On Friday, September 16, 1864, he was occupied all day in court, conducting the defence of a friend on trial for disobedience of orders During the night following he was taken violently ill, grew rapidly worse, and in spite of the best medical skill of both army surgeons and eminent physicians of the city, after two days of intense suffering, he died in the arms of Lieutenant Stratton, sending his last messages to his regiment and his friends His term of enlistment was about to expire, and after three years of service in the army he was anticipating a speedy return to civil life He was to have been married in a few weeks, and it was his intention to engage anew in his profession.

Paul A. Queal was possessed of those excellencies and attractions of character which brought to him many friends, who had predicted for him a brilliant career. His death occurred September 19, 1864; his remains were taken by his brothers back to the old home in Worcester, Otsego county, New York, and laid to rest in Maple Grove cemetery.

ORIN H.[4] QUEAL (William,[3] Robert,[2] William[1]), youngest child of William C. and Mary Graves Queal, was born at Worcester, Otsego county, New York, April 6, 1837. He married Elma Gillespie September 28, 1875. To them were born:
    I.   Sheldon Gillespie, born August 28, 1877.
    II.   Irving Wyatt, born October 4, 1878; married Francis Gradwohl December 12, 1907, at Kansas City, Missouri. To them has been born one child:
        1. Josephine Elma, born February, 1909.
    Irving enlisted in April, 1898, in the Spanish-American War, being a member of the Third Missouri regiment; was in the service but five months when the regiment was mustered out. The family are living at Fort Worth, Texas, where he is engaged in the lumber business.

The boyhood of Orin, like that of his brother, was spent on the farm. At the age of sixteen he taught a three months' term of school and the following year attended school at the academy at Richmondville, New York, for four months, teaching the following winter. At the age of nineteen he went to Ohio and taught in what is known as the Flint district, making his home with his brother, the Rev. Atchison Queal. In 1857 he went first to Galesburg, Illinois, and in the fall to Young America (now Kirkwood), Warren county, Illinois, working on a farm during the summer and teaching during the winter months, receiving for his services thirty dollars per month. Two years later he taught the same school, engaging to teach ten months for thirty dollars per month In a letter to his brother, he says:

> A good many of the settlers here are from the South, and they are pretty good examples of southern life and character There are large girls attending my school, of this stock, and they read and write with difficulty There are many Eastern people here too, who are intelligent and enterprising It is this class that makes this part of the world move

Orin only taught five months of his school year, as he was seized with the Pike's Peak fever, and the first of April, 1860, in company with ten others, started on a journey to the gold regions of Colorado They crossed Iowa, stopping at Nebraska City, where they purchased their provisions, and the 22d of April started on the journey across the plains They were outfitted with ox teams and one pony team, and about five weeks later reached Denver, Colorado On the night of May 7th while on the plains they experienced a very severe storm, ten inches of snow falling before morning; it became exceedingly cold, and a cloth tent proved a very insufficient shelter Some cattle, belonging to parties camping near, strayed away Their owners started out in the morning in search of them, and four men were frozen to death within a mile of camp They were buried without coffins, and men unused to weeping, stood around their graves in tears

Orin Queal and his companions reached their destination about the first of June They stopped near the head waters of the Platte River and went to prospecting, spending six weeks in traveling about on the Blue, Arkansas and Platte rivers, searching for gold but without success In a letter written home, he says:

> Before leaving civilization, I was dreaming of gold — gold — gold With prophetic vision I then looked into the future and saw myself the possessor of houses and lands, of horses and carriages, of dogs and guns etc , etc But alas for my prophecy, these things have not come to pass

In July Orin and his companions turned their faces homeward, just as the rainy season was beginning It rained every day; the bolts of lightning fell thick and fast about them, and the road across the plains was lined with the graves of men who had met death in this violent manner They returned to Illinois about the first of September, and soon afterward Orin went to Iowa and later to Wisconsin, transacting business for his brother, Robert F. Queal. Returning to Chicago, he attended the "Seward meeting," where, as he remarked afterward, "I heard Republicanism explained and justified."

During the following year Orin Queal was employed by his brother Robert in the lumber business in Chicago. In 1862 he enlisted in the Chicago Mercantile battery, Volunteer Light Artillery, which left that city about the 6th of November, their destination being Memphis, Tennessee. Leaving the latter city thirty thousand strong, they started south to coöperate with General Grant in "clearing out" General Price. But the old general burned his army stores and left with most of his army for Grenada before the northern forces arrived. The enemy destroyed the ferry at Wyatt, so the Union army was obliged to construct a bridge before it could proceed.

In August, 1863, Orin Queal was taken ill while in camp in Vicksburg, and was sent to St. Louis where he was in the hospital for some time; he was later transferred to Chicago and remained several weeks in the hospital in that city. He was unable to reënter the service and for years was much impaired in health. The battery to which he belonged was not engaged in the siege of Vicksburg, although it was on the field and in line of battle for five days.

In later years Orin Queal became prominently engaged in lumber interests, first in Chicago and later in Pensacola, Florida. In 1885 he removed with his family to Kansas City, Missouri, and engaged in the real estate business. In 1895 he was elected county recorder of Jackson county, Missouri, which position he held for four years, being the first Republican ever elected to that office in the county. His health failed and for two years he was unable to attend to the affairs of a business life. About two months before his death, longing to be near his old home, and hoping for beneficial effects from the pure spring water to be found there, Orin returned with his wife and son Sheldon, to Worcester, New York, at which place he died on December 7, 1906 — the last of the family of eleven children born to William C. and Mary (Graves) Queal. He was laid to rest in the family lot in Maple Grove cemetery, where lie the other members of a family known at home and abroad for real worth, and who lived for what is worth while.

THE BEYER FAMILY

THE Schwenkfelders — so called — received their name from Caspar Schwenkfeld, a Silesian nobleman, born in 1490 He was educated at Cologne, but spent several years at other universities, where theology attracted his attention, and the writings of the church fathers were his favorite study. Despite the fact of his inclination to study along these lines, he carried out his original intention and fitted himself for knighthood While a young man, he entered the service of the Hussite king of Bohemia, and the doctrines as received in that court made a deep and lasting impression upon his mind, and no doubt gave direction to his future life and labor. He met many theologians who were drifting in the way of reformation Luther had now withdrawn from the Church of Rome, and his preaching engaged the attention of Schwenkfeld and inspired him with a more intense zeal for the service of the divine Master He renounced the Roman Catholic Church to become an evangelist, and for thirty-six years with voice and pen, exhorted men to repentance and godliness His followers were called Schwenkfelders in derision (a name which they accepted), and were stigmatized by almost every appellation that was supposed to convey a reproach.

The persecution continued until it became unbearable and the Schwenkfelders resolved to escape from the country at all hazards The exodus began in February, 1726, when they went to Holland, where they lived for eight years in a state of uncertainty as to their future. About this time they found that application had been made to the proper authorities for their enforced return to Silesia, they being permitted to remain in Holland until spring Two families, however, determined to seek a new home in a new land, and accordingly emigrated to America, arriving in Philadelphia, Pennsylvania, September 18, 1733. Their report of the country was so favorable that about forty families determined to follow them, one hundred eighty-four persons settling in Pennsylvania in 1734. Many others came in 1736, among them Abraham Beyer and wife, Rosina Yeakel, who with their children, Abraham, Andrew, Anna Rosina, and Anna Maria, arrived on October 19, 1736 (old style), and settled in Worcester, Montgomery (then Philadelphia) county.

First Generation

ABRAHAM[1] BEYER was born in Silesia, Germany, July 28, 1690; married Rosina Yeakel (born June 11, 1699). To them were born:
  I. Abraham, born October 4, 1721; married November 8, 1750; died March 6, 1796.
  II. Andrew, born in 1733; married Philipina Weyand.
  III. Anna Rosina; married David Schultz October 29, 1745.
  IV. Anna Maria; married Abraham Yeakel October 19, 1748.
  V. George, born July 13, 1739; died September 19, 1744.
  VI. Susanna; married Durk Casselberger November 1, 1762.

Abraham Beyer lived in Worcester, Montgomery (then Philadelphia) county, Pennsylvania, where in March, 1737, he bought ninety-four acres of land near the present Worcester meeting house. He died October 30, 1754, aged sixty-four years, two months and two days. His widow, Rosina, died July 31, 1770, aged seventy-one years, one month and twenty days.

Anna Rosina, third child of Abraham and Rosina (Yeakel) Beyer, was born in Germany, coming with her parents to this country in 1736. She married David Schultz October 29, 1745, and they established their home in Goshenhoppen, Upper Hanover. While away from home performing the duties of his office as surveyor, he left his wife with a German servant whom he employed to carry on the work of the farm. This servant was a "Redemptioner"; that is, one who had to reimburse the shipping company or private individual (as the case might be) who had paid his passage from the old country. This servant had been brought over by Abraham Beyer, father of Anna Rosina, and given to his daughter for whom he was to work out his obligation. On June 13, 1750, while David Schultz was absent from home on a surveying expedition, his wife was murdered by this "Redemptioner," who was apprehended, convicted for the crime on October 22, 1750, and hung the 14th of the following November — the first murderer to be sentenced and hung in this community

Second Generation

ANDREW [2] BEYER (Abraham [1]), second son of Abraham and Rosina (Yeakel)) Beyer, was born in 1733; married Philipina Weyand November 7, 1758. To them were born

I Susanna, born August 2, 1759; died June 4, 1764
II Abraham, born October 8, 1760; married Catherine Rickerd; died August 8, 1832
III Jacob, born February 14, 1762; married Rachel Metz (born July 26, 1763). Jacob Beyer died August 23, 1846, Rachel Beyer died July 5, 1855
IV. Wendel, born December 9, 1763; died December 17, 1779
V. Daniel, born November 6, 1765; married Rebekah ——
VI Rosanna, born April 27, 1769.
VII. Andrew
VIII. David.
IX Anna Maria.

Andrew Beyer died April 19, 1773, aged nearly forty years

Third Generation

JACOB [3] BEYER (Andrew,[2] Abraham [1]), third child of Andrew and Philipina Beyer, was born February 14, 1762; married Rachel Metz (born July 26, 1763) To them were born·

I Catharine, born September 14, 1783; married Jacob Bean
II. Andrew, born July 24, 1785, married Catharine Bean
III Christiana, born October 20, 1787; married Michael Van Fossen.
IV. Joseph, born November 17, 1789; married Hannah Bean.
V. Margaret, born April 13, 1794; married Samuel Kline in February, 1813.
VI Rachel, born February 12, 1796; married Daniel Rittenhouse September 10, 1820.

VII. Jacob, born April 19, 1798; married Magdalena Boorse in 1822.
VIII. Mary, born July 4, 1800; married Joseph Metz September 11, 1821.
IX. Elizabeth, born January 5, 1806; married John Metz January 6, 1828.

Jacob Beyer died August 23, 1846; Rachel, wife, died July 5, 1855.

Fourth Generation

JACOB[4] BEYER (Jacob,[3] Andrew,[2] Abraham[1]), seventh child of Jacob and Rachel (Metz) Beyer, was born April 19, 1798; married Magdalena Boorse in 1822. To them were born:
 I. Samuel, born February 13, 1823; married Hannah Brunner in 1844. To them were born:
   1. Mary Ann, born January 1, 1846; married Geo. Pennick.
   2. Martha Jane, born June 1, 1847.
   3. Emily, born January 18, 1849; married John Baker.
   4. Elizabeth, born September 15, 1850; died November 13, 1851.
   5. Franklin, born March 23, 1852.
   6. Cyrus, born April 7, 1855; married Susan Miller in 1875.
   7. Lydia, born January 29, 1857.
   8. Amanda, born December 10, 1862.
   9. Eva, born April 7, 1866.
   Samuel Beyer died March 29, 1867.
 II. John, born April 8, 1824; married Sarah Schwenk in 1850. To them were born:
   1. Theodore, born April 14, 1852; died June 22, 1852.
   2. Margaret Schwenk, born October 20, 1853.
   3. Sarah Jane, born December 31, 1854; married Edwin Bean November 24, 1878.
   4. Sophia H., born June 9, 1856.
   5. Elizabeth, born October 16, 1860.
   John Beyer died August 22, 1898.

Adam Beyer

Jacob Beyer Homestead

- III Jesse, born September 13, 1825; married Hannah Dettra in 1851 To them were born.
  1. Louise Ann, born November 19, 1853
  2. Mary Magdalene, born May 20, 1855
  3. William, born June 4, 1858
- IV Adam, born August 24, 1827; died November 18, 1911
- V Elizabeth, born October 31, 1828; married David Kook September 10, 1853 To them were born.
  1. Franklin, born June 3, 1854
  2. Angeline, born August 31, 1857
  3. Jacob, born November 24, 1859.
  4. Sarah Elizabeth, born July 15, 1863
  5. Catherine Ann, born May 15, 1867
- VI. Daniel, born June 27, 1830; married Catharine Oberholtzer in 1853 To them were born:
  1. Ellen J, born December 21, 1856
  2. Elizabeth, born March 4, 1860, died February 20, 1861
  3. William N, born December 20, 1862; married Mary Huber.
  4. Emma K, born July 8, 1868.
  5. Alvin D, born November 8, 1872, married Mary Yost

  Daniel Beyer died December 26, 1883
- VII Albert, born January 8, 1832, died January 5, 1851
- VIII Jacob, born June 21, 1834; married Carolina Haas in 1855 To them were born
  1. Amelia, born October 8, 1856; died July 23, 1859
  2. Abraham, born November 5, 1858, died in 1904
  3. John, born July 26, 1860; died March 11, 1878
  4. Elizabeth, born September 23, 1862; married John Pfleiger.
  5. Mary Ann, born July 15, 1865, died December 28, 1865

  Jacob Beyer died in July, 1910
- IX. Benjamin, born March 4, 1836; died April 23, 1849
- X. James, born October 29, 1838; married Elizabeth Dettra in 1864 To them were born.

1. James Irwin, born November 28, 1869.
2. May Ella, born January 3, 1872.
3. Vernon, born July 29, 1874.

James Beyer died May 8, 1906.

XI. Franklin, born June 28, 1840; died April 16, 1852.
XII. Charles, born April 30, 1842; died January 18, 1848.
XIII. Sarah, born April 13, 1844; married James U. Bean January 28, 1865. To them were born:
1. Ida Jane, born November 26, 1865; married John Groff.
2. James Wilson, born October 16, 1867.
3. Mary Catharine, born April 24, 1870; married John Wagner.
4. Sarah Elizabeth, born September 14, 1872; married Henry Brunner.

James Bean died July 14, 1912.

Magdalena, wife of Jacob Beyer, died March 30, 1848. He married (second) Elizabeth Oberholtzer in 1855.

Jacob Beyer died in 1886.

Fifth Generation

ADAM [5] BEYER (Jacob,[4] Jacob,[3] Andrew,[2] Abraham [1]), fourth child of Jacob and Magdalena (Boorse) Beyer, was born in Montgomery county, Pennsylvania, August 24, 1827. He married Mary, daughter of Frederick and Lydia (Umstead) Brunner (born September 25, 1828) in 1852. To them were born five children:

I. Amelia, born in 1852; died August 10, 1853.
II. Jackson, born in Montgomery county, Pennsylvania, December 28, 1853; married Mary Elizabeth Queal, at Ames, Iowa, November 30, 1876.
III. Jefferson, born in Montgomery county, Pennsylvania, August 2, 1855; married Ida H. Detwiler (born July 17, 1859) January 23, 1883.
IV. Wesley B., born April 4, 1857, in Montgomery county, Pennsylvania; married Addie Thomas (born September 11, 1855) at Norristown, Pennsylvania, April 6, 1881.

JACKSON BEYER

Mary Queal Beyer

HOME OF AUTHOR, AT 1027 DES MOINES STREET, DES MOINES, IOWA

V Harry Brunner, born in Montgomery county, Pennsylvania, August 27, 1858; married Jennie Elizabeth McElyea (born in Lee county, Illinois, November 5, 1861) April 19, 1882, at Ames, Iowa.

Mary (Brunner) Beyer died December 19, 1866.

Adam Beyer married (second) Elizabeth, daughter of Charles Hendricks, in 1870 To them was born one son·

VI Irwin, born February 20, 1871 He was a soldier during the Spanish-American War; is living (1912) in Philadelphia, Pennsylvania.

Adam Beyer was a carpenter by trade, and lived in Norristown, Pennsylvania, for many years He was one of the charter members of the Reformed Church in that city, of which church he remained a communicant during his life. After the death of his second wife, he made his home with his son, Jefferson Beyer, where he died November 18, 1910.

Sixth Generation

JACKSON [6] BEYER (Adam,[5] Jacob,[4] Jacob,[3] Andrew,[2] Abraham [1]), second child of Adam and Mary (Brunner) Beyer, was born in Montgomery county, Pennsylvania, December 28, 1853; married Mary Elizabeth Queal November 30, 1876 To them were born two children:

I Lucy J , born in Ames, Iowa, April 11, 1878; married Ellis R Engelbeck September 8, 1898

II John Hedding, born in Sheldahl, Iowa, March 18, 1883; married Lila Elizabeth Beard December 24, 1906

After the death of his mother in 1866 Jackson Beyer lived on a farm with his grandfather, Frederick Brunner, for three years, at the expiration of which time he went west, arriving at Nevada, Story county, Iowa, August 7, 1869, where he remained until the following spring, going from that place to Ames, Iowa, where he worked on a farm In 1876 he rented the Queal farm, which he worked for three years; then entered into partnership with his brother-in-law, John H Queal, in the lumber business at Sheldahl, Iowa In the spring of 1884 he moved with his family to Des Moines, Iowa, where J H.

Queal & Company had opened a lumber yard. Jackson Beyer is a member of the Masonic fraternity, being a thirty-second degree Mason; he is also a member of the order of Knights of Pythias. He has now been a resident of Des Moines for more than twenty-eight years, where he is still looking after the business affairs of J. H. Queal & Co.

Mary Elizabeth, second child of Atchison and Lucy Oletha Queal, was born at Fly Creek, Otsego county, New York, January 22, 1849; married Jackson Beyer at Ames, Iowa, November 30, 1876.

Fly Creek, the birthplace of Mary Queal Beyer, is a beautiful village, four miles from Cooperstown, New York. Here is standing today the parsonage home in which she was born, the only change being in the addition of a porch across the front and a kitchen in the rear of the building. The house was sold some years since, and is now occupied by a Mr. Simons and his family. A new parsonage has been built by the side of the church, but the church stands today as it was in 1849, with the exception of new windows which have replaced the old ones, and the removal of the gallery.

Mary went with her parents to Morrow county, Ohio, in 1856. Her education was gained in the district school of the neighbrohood, with the exception of one year, which was spent in attending the school at Iberia. Three terms of school were taught by her before removing with her mother to Ames, Iowa, in 1871. Here she taught five consecutive terms in the same school, living at home.

After the marriage of Mary Queal and Jackson Beyer, they remained on the farm for three years, removing in the fall of 1879 to Sheldahl, Iowa, where her brother, John H. Queal, and Jackson Beyer entered into a partnership in the lumber business, which is known as J. H. Queal & Company. In the spring of 1883 the family went to Ames, where they remained one year, removing to Des Moines, Iowa, in 1884, in which city they still reside, at 1027 Des Moines street, in the home built by them in 1893.

JEFFERSON[6] BEYER (Adam,[5] Jacob,[4] Jacob,[3] Andrew,[2] Abraham[1]), third child of Adam and Mary (Brunner) Beyer, was born in Mont-

PARSONAGE AT FLY CREEK, NEW YORK, WHERE AUTHOR WAS BORN

CHURCH AT FLY CREEK, OSTEGO COUNTY, NEW YORK, WHERE
ATCHISON QUEAL PREACHED, 1848-50

Mrs. Jennie McElyea Beyer

gomery county, Pennsylvania, August 2, 1855; married Ida Detwiler (born July 17, 1859) January 23, 1883 To them was born:
    I   Hiram Weldon, born November 22, 1884; married Anna Haas December 26, 1905 To them has been born one child·
        1   Lester Haas, born October 4, 1908

Jefferson Beyer was for many years a farmer, then moved to Norristown, Pennsylvania, where he engaged in the grocery business, the son, Hiram Weldon, remaining with his father until 1910, when he engaged in the same line of business for himself.

WESLEY B[6] BEYER (Adam,[5] Jacob,[4] Jacob,[3] Andrew,[2] Abraham[1]), fourth child of Adam and Mary (Brunner) Beyer, was born in Montgomery county, Pennsylvania, April 4, 1857; married Addie Thomas July 6, 1881. To them were born two children·
    I   Charles, born June 11, 1884, is a civil engineer at Norristown, Pennsylvania
    II.   Etelka, born December 14, 1889; living with her parents in Norristown, Pennsylvania

Wesley B Beyer has been for years and is at the present time secretary for the corporation of R S Newbold & Son Company, founders, machinists, and boilermakers, at Norristown, Pennsylvania

HARRY BRUNNER[6] BEYER (Adam,[5] Jacob,[4] Jacob,[3] Andrew,[2] Abraham[1]), fifth child of Adam and Mary (Brunner) Beyer, was born August 27, 1858, married Jennie Elizabeth McElyea April 19, 1882, at Ames, Iowa To them were born three children·
    I   Harriet Newell, born March 28, 1886, at Rock Valley, Iowa, married Dr Charles H Stange, dean of the veterinary division, Iowa State College, at Ames, Iowa, October 20, 1909
    II   Genevieve Brunner, born November 10, 1887, at Rock Valley, Iowa; died October 25, 1902

III. Winifred Belle, born September 12, 1890, at Rock Valley, Iowa; died June 10, 1908.

Harry Brunner Beyer removed to Iowa from Pennsylvania in 1877, and worked for his brother Jackson on the farm. He was later employed by the firm of J. H. Queal & Co. and went to Rock Valley in December, 1885, where he died February 28, 1892. His widow, Jennie McElyea Beyer, resides in Ames, Iowa.

Seventh Generation

JOHN HEDDING[7] BEYER (Jackson,[6] Adam,[5] Jacob,[4] Jacob,[3] Andrew,[2] Abraham[1]), second child of Jackson and Mary (Queal) Beyer, was born at Sheldahl, Story county, Iowa, March 18, 1883; married Lila Elizabeth Beard, daughter of Joseph and Alice (Briar) Beard, December 24, 1906. To them have been born:

I. Jean, born October 16, 1909.

II. Jack, born September 8, 1912.

John Hedding Beyer holds a responsible position in the office of J. H. Queal & Co., at East Second street and Grand avenue, Des Moines, Iowa.

John Hedding Beyer

THE COOPER AND ENGELBECK FAMILIES

WILLIAM and SARAH COOPER lived in Boughton, Kent, England. Here Sarah Cooper died, and in 1841 her husband emigrated with his family of four sons and two daughters to America, finding a home in Monroeville, Ohio, where the last years of his life were spent in the home of his daughter, Maria Day, where he died at the age of eighty-four years

CALEB, son of William and Sarah Cooper, was born in England August 17, 1820, and came with his father to America, also locating in Monroeville At the breaking out of the Mexican War he enlisted as a soldier, serving his country with credit, and at its close located at Plaster Bed, Ohio, on the north shore of Sandusky Bay Here he followed the cooper's trade

At Banff, Scotland, on January 15, 1829, Jeannette McDonald first saw the light of day, and when but four years of age this little Scotch lassie came to America with her parents, where she grew to womanhood, met and married Caleb Cooper November 17, 1849 Of this union were born four children:

I   Sarah Elizabeth, born October 13, 1851; married George P Engelbeck January 4, 1870
II   William A, born June 22, 1853; married Eliza Howard To them were born four children William A Cooper and wife live in Riverside, California, where they own a fine orange grove.
III   Ranald, born July 10, 1857; married Addie LaBour; two sons They are living in Salina, Kansas
IV   Margaret M., born January 10, 1859; married John Lightner; lives in Danbury, Ohio

In the early part of the year 1851 Caleb Cooper bought a farm near Gypsum, Ohio, to which they removed when their first child was but six months old, and where the wife, Jeannette (McDonald) Cooper, died March 16, 1888, the husband surviving his wife nine years — dying January 14, 1897.

HARMON ENGELBECK was born in Ompt, Saven, Germany, kingdom of Hanover, June 15, 1801. He married Caroline Fitchther (born Pathen Bone, Middle States, Prussia, January 15, 1811). To them were born nine children:
    I. William, born August 12, 1835.
   II. Hermon W., born December 23, 1837; married Nancy Wornell of Gypsum, Ohio.
  III. John R., born September 9, 1839.
  IV. Henry J., born October 10, 1841.
   V. Kathlyn C., born August 10, 1843; married William Slackford of Gypsum, Ohio.
  VI. Joseph W., born July 10, 1845.
 VII. George P., born February 20, 1849.
VIII. Antoinetta, born February 20, 1850; died September 11, 1851.
  IX. Margaret, born February 20, 1850; died September 18, 1851.

Harmon Engelbeck came with his wife to America from Germany, arriving in this country March 10, 1833, and making his home in New York until November, 1835, when they removed to Ohio and located on a farm in Ottawa county, near Port Clinton, when that section of the country was new and the land unimproved. Here they spent the remainder of their days, Caroline the wife, dying January 29, 1874, her husband surviving her less than three months, his death occurring April 26, 1874.

GEORGE P., seventh child of Harmon and Caroline Engelbeck, was born February 20, 1849; married Sarah Elizabeth, daughter of Caleb

Harmon Engelbeck, born 1801

Caroline Engelbeck, born 1811

and Jeannette (McDonald) Cooper, at Gypsum, Ohio, January 4, 1870 To them were born four sons.
- I. George, born April 7, 1872; died October 18, 1873
- II. Ellis Ranald, born April 5, 1874; married Lucy J Beyer, at Des Moines, Iowa, September 8, 1898 To them have been born two children:
  1 Elizabeth, born October 3, 1899
  2 Ranald Beyer, born August 6, 1904
  Ellis R Engelbeck is employed by J H Queal & Co. as manager of one of the lumber yards owned by the firm in the city of Des Moines, Iowa.
- III Arthur C, born July 18, 1876; married Bessie Thomas in 1895 To them has been born one child
  1. Ruth, born February 4, 1898
- IV. Claude E, born September 20, 1878; married Clara Hahnen September 20, 1907 To them has been born one child:
  1 Katherine, born February, 1909

The older sons of Harmon and Caroline Engelbeck served as soldiers in the War of the Rebellion, but because of his youth George P Engelbeck was obliged to remain at home, where he assisted his father in carrying on the work of the farm After his marriage in 1870, he removed to Victor, Iowa, where the family resided until 1889, when they made their home in Des Moines. George P Engelbeck died September 5, 1910; his widow resides in Des Moines, Iowa

THE ARMITAGE AND BEARD FAMILIES

JOHN ARMITAGE, born July 24, 1798; married Elizabeth Harrold, daughter of Christopher Harrold and Martha Cable (born March 2, 1802) January 21, 1819. To them were born eleven children:

    I. John Harrold, born December 21, 1819; died March 16, 1872.
    II. Washington, born April 2, 1821; died October 21, 1833.
    III. Elizabeth, born November 23, 1822; died March 30, 1898.
    IV. Christopher, born August 14, 1825; died January 25, 1855.
    V. Theodore, born October 29, 1827.
    VI. Hiram, born February 6, 1830; died 1907.
    VII. Evans, born January 31, 1832; died November 2, 1892.
    VIII. Henry, born January 25, 1834.
    IX. Susannah, born January 26, 1836; died June 12, 1888.
    X. Harrison, born July 9, 1840; died during War of Rebellion.
    XI. Joseph, born January 31, 1842; died October 18, 1849.

Elizabeth, third child of John and Elizabeth Armitage, married Edward Barnett Beard (born September 10, 1819) March 26, 1845, near Athens, Ohio. To them were born:

1. Mary Elizabeth, born at Athens, Ohio, January 19, 1846; died April 20, 1900.
2. Emily Jane, born October 4, 1848, Athens, Ohio.
3. Christopher Armitage, born October 15, 1854, at Elwood, Iowa.
4. Joseph Harrold, born October 15, 1854, at Elwood, Iowa.
5. David Moore, born October 7, 1858, at Elwood, Iowa.
6. Abraham Lincoln, born January 21, 1861, at Elwood, Iowa.

7   Schuyler Colfax, born April 1, 1867, at Elwood, Iowa
    Joseph Harrold Beard, born October 15, 1854, married Alma Mae Briar, daughter of John and Elizabeth Eicher Briar (born March 28, 1857) March 28, 1882, at Sigourney, Iowa   To them were born:
    1. Lila Elizabeth, born April 26, 1883
    2 Clarke Briar, born November 29, 1884

Index

INDEX

Abbott, Elmer E., 259
Abbott, Joshua, 46
Abbott, Lucy Lillian, 259
Abbott, Thomas, 23
Adams, Almaretta, 249
Adkins, Elizabeth, 291
Albert, Gilbert, 269
Albert, Louise, 316
Albert, Mary, 269
Alderman, Etta, 147
Alderman, Helen French, 147
Alderman, Judson, 147
Alderman, Newell, 147
Allen, Andrew, 221
Almy, Georgianna, 187
Alsworth, Mary Effie, 260
Amherst, Jeffry, 103
Anderson, Anna, 66
Anderson, Kenneth French, 66
Appleseed, Johnny, 102, 163
Appleton, Lieut Francis H, 37
Armitage, Christopher, 358
Armitage, Elizabeth, 358
Armitage, Evans, 358
Armitage, Harrison, 358
Armitage, Henry, 358
Armitage, Hiram, 358
Armitage, John, 358
Armitage, John Harrold, 354
Armitage, Joseph, 358
Armitage, Susanna, 358
Armitage, Washington, 358
Arnold, Alpha, 245, 249, 262
Arnold, David, 245, 248
Arnold, Edward, 249
Arnold, Harry, 248
Arnold, Mary, 249
Arnold, Samuel, 248
Arnold, Stephen, 248, 249
Ashley, Samuel, 228

Atchison, Margaret, 264
Atherton, John, 77
Atkinson, Theodore, 100
Auger, Edmund, 34

Babcock, Artemas, 277, 278, 291
Babcock, Daniel, 282
Babcock, Eleanor, 291
Babcock, Electa, 29, 283
Babcock, Mary, 277, 278
Babcock, Polly, 291
Babcock, Robert, 291
Baker, Araminta, 265
Baker, Emma, 181
Baker, John, 336
Baker, Samuel, 265
Baldwin, John, 46
Baldwin, Jonathan, 26
Baldwin, Thomas, 27
Ballard, Samuel, 52
Ballou, Alpha, 235
Ballou, Eliza, 232, 235
Ballou, Ellis, 232
Ballou, Henry, 232
Ballou, Jacob T, 232
Ballou, James, 224, 230, 231, 236
Ballou, Mehitable, 231
Ballou, Orrin, 232
Ballou, Phoebe Tanner, 232
Ballou, Thomas, 230
Bancroft, Roger, 84
Bangs, John, 290
Bannister, Lucy, 316
Barber, A M, 286
Barber, Martha, 265
Barfoot, Susan, 157, 177
Barnard, David, 65
Barnard, Joseph, 66
Barnard, Louisa M, 65
Barnard, Sarah F, 65

Barney, Martha, 241
Barnes, Clarissa, 245
Barrett, Elizabeth, 221, 222
Barrett, William, 29, 30
Barron, Elizabeth, 26
Bates, Andrew, 66
Bates, Eleanor French, 79, 83, 84
Beale, Samuel, 68
Beale, William, 68
Bean, Catharine, 335
Bean, Edwin, 336
Bean, Hannah, 335
Bean, Jacob, 335
Bean, James U, 340
Bean, Joseph, 97
Bean, Mary Catharine, 340
Bean, Sarah, 340
Bean, Sarah Elizabeth, 340
Beard, Abraham Lincoln, 358
Beard, Christopher Armitage, 358
Beard, Clarke Briar, 359
Beard, David Moore, 358
Beard, Edward Barnett, 358
Beard, Emily Jane, 358
Beard, Joseph Harrold, 358
Beard, Lila Elizabeth, 345, 350, 359
Belcher, Gov, 34
Bell, Hezekiah, 242
Bell, Sabina, 242
Benedict, Fannie H, 313
Benedict, George, 308, 313
Benedict, George Barnard, 313
Benedict, Mabel, 313
Bennett, Charles, 282
Bentley, Betsey, 284
Bentley, Laura, 284
Benton, Loren, 242
Benton, Sarah, 242
Bird, Rev Samuel, 98, 99, 100

INDEX

Bisemore, Nettie, 66
Bishop, Catherine, 147
Bishop, Jane, 143, 155
Bishop, Samuel, 143
Bitnar, William, 221
Blanchard, Elizabeth, 87
Blanchard, Grace, 87
Blanchard, James, 75
Blanchard, John, 68, 74
Blanchard, Joseph, 98, 99
Bloggett, Thomas, 34
Bonnell, Lydia, 22
Boorse, Magdalena, 336
Booth, Lorinda, 282, 308
Bordman, William, 29
Bostacke, Thomas, 28
Bowen, James B., 205
Boynton, Alpha, 172, 236
Boynton, Amos, 235
Boynton, Harriet, 235
Boynton, Henry Ballou, 235
Boynton, Phoebe, 235
Boynton, Silas, 235
Brackett, John, 27, 53
Brackett, Mary, 53
Briar, Alma Mae, 359
Briar, John, 359
Briggs, Nathan, 313
Brockway, Reed, 157
Brooks, Delia, 109
Brooks, Dr. P. B., 114
Brown, Nathaniel, 242
Brown, Orpha, 242
Brown, Sarah, 25
Browne, Will, 51
Brownlee, Mary J., 261
Brunner, Frederick, 340, 345
Brunner, Hannah, 336
Brunner, Henry, 340
Brunner, Lydia Umstead, 340
Brunner, Sarah E., 340
Buckingham, Jennie, 265
Bulson, Ichabod, 157
Burrage, Hannah, 22
Burrage, John, 22
Bushnell, Lydia, 240, 241
Butterfield, Catherine, 85
Butterfield, Esther, 86
Butterfield, John, 85, 86, 89

Butterfield, Jonas, 85, 86
Butterfield, Leonard, 85
Butterfield, Olive, 85
Butterfield, Rebecca, 86
Butterfield, Sarah, 85
Beyer, Abraham, 334, 335, 339
Beyer, Adam, 339, 340, 345, 349
Beyer, Albert, 339
Beyer, Alvin D., 339
Beyer, Amanda, 336
Beyer, Amelia, 339, 340
Beyer, Anna Maria, 335
Beyer, Anna Rosina, 334
Beyer, Andrew, 334, 335
Beyer, Benjamin, 339
Beyer, Charles, 340
Beyer, Cyrus, 336
Beyer, Daniel, 335, 339
Beyer, David, 335
Beyer, Elizabeth, 336, 339
Beyer, Ellen, 339
Beyer, Emma K, 339
Beyer, Emily, 336
Beyer, Etelka, 340
Beyer, Eva, 336
Beyer, Franklin, 336, 340
Beyer, Genevieve Brunner, 349
Beyer, Harriet Newell, 349
Beyer, Harry Brunner, 345, 349, 350
Beyer, Hiram Weldon, 349
Beyer, Irwin, 345
Beyer, Jack, 350
Beyer, Jackson, 304, 309, 340, 345, 346, 350
Beyer, Jacob, 335, 336, 339, 340
Beyer, James, 339, 340
Beyer, James Irwin, 340
Beyer, James Wilson, 340
Beyer, Jefferson, 340, 346, 349, 350
Beyer, Jennie McElyea, 350
Beyer, Jesse, 339
Beyer, John, 336, 339
Beyer, John Hedding, 298, 345, 350
Beyer, Joseph, 335
Beyer, Lester Haas, 349
Beyer, Lila Elizabeth, 350

Beyer, Louise Ann, 339
Beyer, Lucy J., 345, 357
Beyer, Lydia, 336
Beyer, Margaret Schwenk, 336
Beyer, Martha Jane, 336
Beyer, Mary, 349
Beyer, Mary Ann, 336, 339
Beyer, Mary Brunner, 345
Beyer, Mary Magdalene, 339
Beyer, Mary Queal, 300, 340, 346, 350
Beyer, May Ella, 340
Beyer, Rachel, 335, 336
Beyer, Rosanna, 335
Beyer, Samuel, 336
Beyer, Sarah Jane, 336
Beyer, Sophie H., 339
Beyer, Susanna, 335
Beyer, Theodore, 336
Beyer, Vernon, 340
Beyer, Wesley B., 340, 349
Beyer, William, 339
Beyer, William N., 339
Beyer, Winifred Belle, 350
Burnside, Gen., 325

CALDWELL, Harriet N., 65
Caldwell, Jefferson, 65
Caldwell, Myra A., 65
Campbell, James, 224
Cane, Christopher, 34
Capron, Capt. Oliver, 228
Carmer, Jessie, 20
Carpenter, Sybil, 223, 224
Cary, Walter, 155
Casselburger, Durk, 334
Casselburger, Susanna, 334
Chawick, John, 52
Chamberlain, Belle, 158, 197
Chamberlain, Wm., 40, 46, 59
Chamm, Sam'l, 46
Champion, Joshua, 293
Champney, Daniel, 59, 60
Champney, Mary, 25, 27
Champney, Richard, 25
Chapman, Arthur, 259
Chapman, Jonathan, 163
Chapman, Sarah, 259
Chase, Levi, 284

INDEX

Cheavers, Thomas, 52
Cheseboro, Edwin, 157
Chesbro, Nicholas, 285
Childs, John, 28
Childs, Hannah, 60
Cipperly, David, 157
Clapp, John, 235
Clark, Alva, 227, 228
Clark, Angeline, 228
Clark, Daniel, 235
Clark, Edwin, 227
Clark, Eliza, 228
Clark, Eliza Cram, 227
Clark, Elizabeth, 228
Clark, Eunice, 228
Clark, Harvey Cunning, 227
Clark, James Stone, 227, 228
Clark, Jesse, 227
Clark, Laura, 232
Clark, Luna, 227
Clark, Sarah Louisa, 227
Clark, Sebra, 227
Clark, Stephen, 227
Clement, Sarah, 96, 98
Clevenger, Mary, 158, 184
Clogston, Paul, 104
Coddington, Emma, 265
Coggan, Abigail, 22
Coe, Allan, 261
Coe, Sibbel, 261
Cole, Bell, 147
Cole, Mary, 224
Collin, John, 21
Combs, Jonathan, 88
Comstock, Lovina, 248
Connett, Albert, 268
Connett, Edward, 268
Connett, Ida, 268
Connett, Malon, 268
Connett, Maria, 268
Conroy, Elizabeth, 274
Conroy, Luke, 274
Convers, Mary, 27
Converse, Josiah, 53, 55, 56
Covington, Ella, 250
Cook, Ellen, 110
Cook, James, 224
Cooke, Captaine, 34
Cooke, Colonel Geo, 37

Cooke, Joseph, 37
Cooley, Charles, 269
Cooley, James B, 269
Cooley, Mary Estelle, 269
Cooper, Caleb, 353
Cooper, Eliza, 353
Cooper, Sarah, 353
Cooper, Sarah E, 354
Cooper, William, 353
Cowles, William, 147
Crafts, E G, 152
Crafts, Rev W F, 303
Crane, Della, 228
Crane, Eliza, 228
Crane, Evan Joseph, 228
Crane, Florence, 228
Crane, George, 228
Crane, Marion, 228
Crane, Rosetta, 228
Crocker, Minnie, 248
Crockett, Moses, 65
Croe, John, 41
Crosby, Joseph, 28
Crosby, Josiah, 25
Crosby, Sarah, 60
Crosby, Simon, 51, 52, 55
Cummings, Addie, 66
Cummings, Easter, 85
Cummings, Elizabeth, 78, 84, 87
Cummings, Elizabeth French, 85
Cummings, Isaac, 68
Cummings, James, 86
Cummings, John, 62, 68, 71, 74, 78, 84, 85, 86, 87, 88
Cummings, Jonathan, 88
Cummings, Katy, 86
Cummings, Lucy, 86
Cummings, Molly, 86
Cummings, Nathaniel, 88
Cummings, Olive, 85
Cummings, Rebecca, 85
Cummings, Sarah, 27, 62, 68
Cummings, Thomas, 68
Curtis, Mrs Mary, 25

DANF, Francis, 221
Danforth, Jacob, 46
Danforth, Jonathan, 40, 43, 46, 48, 51, 53, 56

Danforth, Rhoda, 84
Danforth, Sarah, 25
Danforth, Samuel, 97
Danforth, Thomas, 30
Davis, Elizabeth, 85
Davis, Jefferson T, 181
Davis, Minnie, 320
Davy, Charlotte, 292
Day, Calvin, 242
Day, Maria, 353
Day, Sarah, 242
Day, Steeven, 29
Dean, Sarah M, 282, 319
De Mars, Rose, 270
Deltra, Elizabeth, 339
Deltra, Hannah, 339
Detwiler, Ida H, 340, 349
Devanpeck, Charles, 157
Dickinson, Castor, 104
Doolittle, Col Ephriam, 228
Downe, William, 97
Dudley, Thomas, 34
Dunham, Ephriam, 284
Dunklin, Mary, 60
Dunklin, Nathaniel, 28
Dustin, Hannah, 78
Dutro, Mrs Rufus, 232

EASTON, Della C, 250
Easton, Otis M, 250
Eaton, John, 222
Eaton, Ruth, 222
Eicher, Elizabeth, 359
Elder, Lydia, 158, 197
Eliot, John, 39
Eliot, Robert, 22
Elliott, Major, 327, 328
Ellis, Benjamin, 224
Ellis, Elizabeth, 53
Ellis, Rebecca, 231
Ellis, Richard, 53
Engelbeck, Antoinnetta, 354
Engelbeck, Arthur C, 357
Engelbeck, Bessie Thomas, 357
Engelbeck, Caroline, 357
Engelbeck, Claude E, 357
Engelbeck, Elizabeth, 357
Engelbeck, Ellis R, 357
Engelbeck, George, 354

INDEX

Engelbeck, George P., 353, 354, 357
Engelbeck, Harmon, 354, 357
Engelbeck, Henry J., 354
Engelbeck, Hermon, 354
Engelbeck, John R., 354
Engelbeck, Joseph W., 354
Engelbeck, Katherine, 357
Engelbeck, Margaret, 354
Engelbeck, Ranald, 353, 357
Engelbeck, Ruth, 357
Engelbeck, Sarah Elizabeth, 353
Engelbeck, William, 354
Ernst, G. W., 286
Esmay, Ruth, 273
Essex, John, 284
Estabrook, Mary, 83, 84
Estabrook, Sarah, 65
Evans, Emily, 232
Evarts, Lua Elizabeth, 259

Farley, Achsa, 283
Farley, George, 40, 43, 44, 46, 48
Farnum, Sarah, 221
Farwell, Henry, 67, 68, 91
Ferris, Eliza, 143
Ferris, George, 143, 155
Ferris, Hannah, 143, 155
Ferris, Lucy Jane, 143, 155
Ferris, Marah, 144, 156
Ferris, Nancy, 143, 151, 156
Ferris, Orva, 285
Ferris, Philo, 144, 156
Ferris, Phoebe, 144, 156
Ferris, Polly Lodema, 144, 156
Ferris, Watson, 144, 156
Ferris, Wesley, 143, 155
Fitchther, Caroline, 354
Fields, Mrs. C. E., 270
Fletcher, Catherine, 86
Fletcher, Elizabeth, 86
Fletcher, Isaac, 86
Fletcher, James, 25
Fletcher, Joseph, 86
Fletcher, Lucinda, 86
Fletcher, Molly, 86
Flint, Betsey, 241
Flint, Daniel, 161, 197, 245, 253, 254, 261

Flint, Henry, 261
Flint, Horatio, 281, 307, 308
Flint, Jacob, 242
Flint, Mary, 236, 237, 255, 262
Flint, Mehitable, 245, 253
Flint, Sharille, 178
Flint, Stephen S., 178, 161
Foster, Thomas, 48, 55
Fowler, Jane A., 67
Fowler, Laura, 242
Fox, Betsey, 279
Foxcroft, Ira, 73

French, Aaron, 96, 106, 125, 155, 156
French, Abbie, 197
French, Abigail, 23, 27, 28
French, Alice (Octave Thanet), 28, 67
French, Alice Gertrude, 202
French, Alta, 144
French, Alva, 155, 158, 168, 197, 198, 201, 203, 214
French, Amanda, 144
French, Anna E., 66
French, Augusta E., 113
French, Augustus, 86
French, Bayard Taylor, 184
French, Benjamin, 24, 66, 86 93
French, Belle, 188
French, Betsey, 24, 86, 110
French, Bridget, 84, 87
French, Calvin D., 158, 168, 201, 202, 203, 204, 216
French, Carson, 113
French, Charles E., 109
French, Charles Jefferson, 65
French, Charlotte, 62, 86, 119
French, Chauncey, 147, 151, 152, 155, 201
French, Cidney E., 187
French, Clara, 116, 119, 131, 135
French, Clare Vernon, 158
French, Clarence Walters, 187
French, Clement, 106, 114, 115, 116, 123, 131, 134, 135, 136
French, Cordelia J., 67
French, Dallas A., 147
French, David, 24, 26, 87, 96

French, Dewitt Clinton,
French, Dwight, 106, 115
French, Ebenezer, 25, 62, 65, 67, 71, 80, 81, 87
French, Ebenezer Smead, 110, 113, 116
French, Edward, 22
French, Edward Beecher, 65
French, Eleazer, 62, 82
French, Elizabeth, 21, 22, 23, 24, 25, 27, 30, 33, 47, 62, 84, 85, 93, 94, 96, 97, 116, 156, 168, 175, 179, 184, 187, 245
French, Ellen, 109
French, Ellen W., 66
French, Emma, 109
French, Ephraim, 24
French, Estella J., 67
French, Esther, 26, 86
French, Francis, 22, 109
French, Franklin, 106
French, Frederick, 87
French, Garfield, 187
French, George M., 65
French, Gilbert, 178
French, Gilbert Edward, 177
French, Gordon R., 187
French, Hannah, 23, 24, 27, 28, 33, 47, 56, 59, 62
French, Harriet, 147, 187
French, Harry G., 176
French, Harriet Gilberta, 178
French, Harry Seward, 177
French, Hebzibeth, 110
French, Helen Beatrice, 187
French, Helen Melissa, 147
French, Henry, 135
French, Henry S., 65
French, Herbert George, 187
French, Hiram, 144, 151, 155
French, Howard A., 187
French, Ira, 105, 106, 109, 115
French, Jabez, 26
French, Jacob, 24, 25, 27, 33, 52, 53
French, James M., 67, 147
French, James Thomas, 157, 158, 168, 176, 177
French, Jane, 109

INDEX 367

French, Jared A, 144
French, Jefferson, 65
French, J. Fred, 178
French, Jerrymya, 22
French, Joel, 24
French, John, 21, 22, 23, 24, 26, 33, 53, 62, 65, 66, 67, 71, 81, 88, 155, 168, 178
French, John M, Dr., 68
French, Jonathan, 24, 25, 26, 67, 96, 133
French, John Seward, 157, 177
French, John William, 65
French, Joseph, 22, 24, 25, 26, 62, 84, 85, 87, 88, 91, 93, 96, 97, 99
French, Josiah, 84, 86, 105, 123, 125, 126
French, Julia, 119, 144
French, Katherine, 86
French, Katherine May, 202
French, Laura Alfaretta, 184
French, Leslie Ray, 187
French, Leslie Russell, 168, 176, 177
French, Lewis M, 201
French, Lucius, 110
French, Lucy, 26, 87, 106, 109, 130
French, Lucy May, 187
French, Lucy Olettra, 157, 161, 293, 294, 297, 298
French, Lusannah, 119, 124, 143
French, Lydia, 26
French, Malinda Keech, 187
French, Marcena, 147
French, Marietta, 143
French, Marshall, 155
French, Martin M, 194, 197
French, Martin V, 147, 155
French, Marvin, 158, 194
French, Mary, 21, 22, 26, 28, 33, 47, 56, 66, 109, 113, 147, 158, 176, 179, 180
French, Mary Clevenger, 184
French, Mary Suzanne, 178
French, Mehitable, 24
French, Molly, 84
French, Nancy Almeda, 147, 155, 156
French, Nancy M, 147

French, Nathaniel, 24
French, Nehemiah, 24
French, Nellie, 110, 177
French, Nettra, 187
French, Nicholas, 26
French, Olive, 110
French, Oliver, 26
French, Orin, 113
French, Orva Martin, 201
French, Oscar L. R., 155, 158, 184, 188, 189, 193, 203, 214, 300
French, Polly, 157
French, Priscilla, 26
French, Rebecca, 85, 105, 147
French, Rhoda, 65
French, Richard, 67
French, Richard Calvin, 201
French, Root, 109, 115
French, Rose, 110
French, Sadie, 67
French, Salphronius, 68, 106, 113, 114, 115, 116, 120
French, Sampson, 86, 93, 96, 97, 98, 99, 100, 103, 119
French, Samson, 105, 113, 116, 119, 120, 123, 124, 125, 128, 134, 135, 136, 143, 151, 155, 156, 157, 158, 161, 162, 163, 164, 165, 166, 167, 168, 171, 175, 179, 184, 201, 245, 253, 298
French, Samson Babb, 187
French, Samuel, 26, 27, 62, 67, 68, 71, 72, 73, 74, 75, 77, 78, 80, 81, 84, 87, 88, 93
French Sarah, 23, 24, 26, 27, 28, 33, 47, 56, 59, 62, 65, 66, 67, 84, 105, 126
French, Sarah Elizabeth, 65
French, Seldon, 178
French, Seward H, 201, 202
French, Sherman Queal, 187
French, Silas, 26
French, Stephen, 24
French, Stephen Henry, 157
French, Submit, 105, 106, 130
French, Susan, 65, 66, 178, 179
French, Susannah, 84
French, Sydney J, 147
French, Tabitha, 24

French, Thelismar, 144, 155
French, Theodore, 84
French, Thomas, 21, 22, 84, 86, 87, 105, 123, 128, 129, 133, 143, 144, 146, 148, 151, 152, 155, 156, 157, 161, 246
French, Timothy, 26
French, Walter H M 67
French, Wendell P., 187
French, William, 22, 23, 24, 25, 29, 30, 53, 66, 71, 72
French, Lieut William, 22, 27, 28, 32, 34, 37, 38, 39, 40, 43, 44, 45, 46, 47, 48, 51, 52, 60, 62, 71
Frost, Benjamin, 21
Frost, Edmond, 34
Frost, Elizabeth, 24
Frost, Joseph, 23
Fuller, A C., 290
Fuller, Barnabus, 285
Fuller, John, 52
Fuller, Jonathan, 62
Fuller, Joshua, 52
Fuller, Samuel, 223

GAINSBY, Caroline, 260
Gainsby, Ralph W, 260
Gainsby, Roseltha, 260
Garfield, Abram, 232, 235
Garfield, Eliza, 172, 232, 236, 237
Garfield, James, 172
Garfield, James Abram, 235, 236, 237, 238
Garfield, Mary, 235
Garfield, Mehitable, 232
Garfield, Thomas, 232
Gaylord, Orville, 274
Gibbs, George H, 250
Gibbs, Jennie V, 250
Gier, Casander, 228
Gifford, Susie, 320
Gill, Elizabeth, 248
Gillespie, Edna A, 282, 330
Gillespie, Kate E, 282
Gillies, Mary Lodema, 259
Gilman, James Bruce, 273
Gilmore, Frank, 246
Gloner, Mrs, 34
Going, Elizabeth, 259

INDEX

Goodenough, Giles, 157
Gookinge, Capt., 47, 61
Goold, John, 68
Goold, Samuel, 68, 78
Gould, John, Dr., 320
Graves, Amos, 282
Graves, Catherine, 282
Graves, Daniel, 283
Graves, Jesse, 283
Graves, Martha, 282
Graves, Mary, 281, 282
Graves, Orin, 283
Graves, Phineas, 283
Graves, Reuben, 282
Graves, Sally, 282
Graves, Samuel, 282
Graves, William, 282
Gray, Mary, 259
Green, Hen., 52
Gregory, Caroline, 227
Groff, Ann, 176
Groff, Ida Jane, 340
Groff, John, 340

Haas, Anna, 349
Haas, Caroline, 339
Hadden, Katherine, 34
Hahnen, Clara, 357
Hall, Samuel, 366
Hall, Sarah J., 282, 320
Halley, Mary Littell, 201
Hallock, Mrs., 157
Hamblet, Susanna, 62
Hand, Joseph, 239
Hanor, Abbie, 274
Harper, Jane, 232
Harrington, Cynthia, 113
Harrington, Sally, 106, 109
Harvard, Rev. John, 38
Hassell, Joseph, 68
Hatch, Col., 327, 338
Hawks, Dr., 114
Hawks, Elizabeth, 106
Hawley, Martin, 136
Hedges, Col. Sidney M., 338
Hedstrom, Porter, 290
Hellinger, George, 184
Heminway, George, 260
Heminway, Lucy, 260

Heminway, Mary, 260
Heminway, Millie, 260
Heminway, Nannie, 260
Hill, Elizabeth, 25
Hill, Joanna, 25
Hill, Ralph, Jr., 40, 44, 46
Hill, Ralph, Sr., 40, 43, 46, 48, 51
Hill, Patrick, 56
Hendricks, Charles, 345
Hendricks, Elizabeth, 345
Hepburn, Major, 328
Hiscock, Polly, 105, 143, 148
Hoag, Solomon, 242
Hogue, C. W., 262
Hogue, Luella Eliza, 262
Holmes, Sarah E., 66
Hooker, Rev., 33
Hoover, Mary Elida, 252, 254, 255
Hoover, Stephen Delbert, 250
Hoover, William H., 252
Hoover, William O., 252
Hosmer, Susan, 65
Hotchkiss, Almira, 262
Hotchkiss, Benjamin, 262
Houghton, Sarah, 282, 314
Howard, Portia, 224
Howe, John, 240
Howland, Frank, 113
Howland, Isaac, 113
Howland, Nellie, 113
Howland, William, 113
Huber, Mary, 339
Hudson, J. S., 147
Hudson, Rebecca, 155
Hutton, Clymena, 260
Hutton, Robert, 260
Hurd, Jacob, 52
Hurd, Mary A., 109
Hutchinson, John, 98
Hyde, Jonathan, 22, 53

Ingalls, Abram, 224, 232
Ingalls, Alithea, 223
Ingalls, Alpha, 227
Ingalls, Ann, 220, 222
Ingalls, Candace, 224
Ingalls, Ebenezer, 223, 224

Ingalls, Edmund, 220, 223
Ingalls, Eliza, 227
Ingalls, Elizabeth, 221, 223, 224
Ingalls, Faith, 221
Ingalls, Francis, 220
Ingalls, Frederick, 223
Ingalls, Hannah, 224
Ingalls, Henry, 219, 221, 223, 224, 228, 229, 230, 245
Ingalls, Hiram, 224
Ingalls, Isaac, 224
Ingalls, James, 232
Ingalls, John, 221, 222
Ingalls, Lois, 223
Ingalls, Lucy, 227, 242, 245
Ingalls, Mary, 222, 224
Ingalls, Mehitable, 223, 224, 230, 232
Ingalls, Olive, 224
Ingalls, Robert, 219, 221
Ingalls, Roxey, 224
Ingalls, Rufus, 224
Ingalls, Ruth, 224
Ingalls, Sabia, 224
Ingalls, Samuel, 222
Ingalls, Sarah, 221
Ingalls, Sebra, 227
Ingalls, Sybil, 227, 230
Ives, Frank, 313
Ivory, William A., 177

Jackman, Luthera, 65
Jeffrey, James, 81
Jeifts, Henry, 40, 46, 59
Jewett, David, 85
Jewett, Elizabeth, 85
Jewett, Jacob, 85
Jewett, James, 85
Jewett, John, 85
Jewett, Leonard, 85
Jewett, Lucy, 85
Jewett, Ralph Winslow, 85
Johnson, Dolly French, 143, 155
Johnson, George, 148
Johnson, Sally, 106
Jones, Katie, 268
Jones, Libbie, 158, 201
Jones, Margaret, 76
Judd, Mary Ann, 291

INDEX

Keayne, Robert, 37
Keech, Cidney Ellen, 158, 184
Keeler, Mina, 113
Kegley, Frank, 304
Kelley, Carmi, 184
Kelley, Lucy May, 184
Kelley, Rhoda, 242
Keltner, Allen, 292
Keltner, Isabelle, 292
Kelton, James, 223
Kelton, Daniel, 29
Keyes, Barney, 204
Kidder, Ephraim, 24
Kidder, Thomas, 46
Kingsbury, Lois Permelia, 260
Kirk, John, 250, 251, 254
Kirk, Lucy Helen, 250, 251
Kirk, Stephen Efner, 250
Kittredge, Dr John, 23
Kline, Margaret, 335
Kline, Samuel, 335
Klock, Catherine, 282, 319
Knapp, Theodore, 176
Kook, Angeline, 339
Kook, Catherine Ann, 339
Kook, David, 339
Kook, Franklin, 339
Kook, Jacob, 339
Kook, Sarah Elizabeth, 339
Kossulman, Helen, 259
Kresinger, Frank, 202

La Bour, Addie, 353
La Moree, Phoebe, 106
Landers, Capt Frank, 115
Larrabee, Marenas, 235
Larrabee, Sarah, 282
Lathrop, Thomas, 28
Lee, Alamanson, 147
Lee, Charles, 155
Lee, Daniel, 155
Lee, Edwin, 147
Lee, Harriet, 152, 155
Lee, Morris, 150, 155, 156
Lee, Nathaniel, 105, 126
Lee, Parley, 133, 136
Lee, Polly, 135, 136, 155, 156
Lee, Polly Jane, 148

Lee, Roland, 135
Lee, Sarah, 136
Leppere, A Hamilton, 65
Lewis, Benj, 47
Lewis, Cyrus, 342
Lewis, Dr A, 274
Lewis, Burdette, 274
Lewis, Herbert, 274
Lightner, John, 353
Lightner, Margaret, 35
Linderman, Mina Olive, 259
Littlefield, Francis, 23
Littlefield, Mary, 23
Lolendine, John, 68
Loomis, B N, 152
Loomis, Frank, 152
Loomis, Ida, 147
Lovejoy, W Luzerne, 66
Lovewell, Caty (Honey), 84
Lovewell, John, Jr, 68, 78, 88
Lovewell, Jonathan, 100
Lovewell, Joseph, 68
Lovewell, Mollie, 86
Luddin, Eunice, 223
Lund, Thomas, 68, 80
Lyon, Hepsibah, 106

McDonald, Jeannette, 353, 354, 357
McElyea, Jennie Elizabeth, 345, 349
McKenzie, Alexander, 33
McIntyre, Chauncey, 144, 155
McIntyre, Ebenezer, 144, 155
McIntyre, Franklin, 144, 155
McIntyre, Marcena, 144
McIntyre, Polly, 144, 155
McIntyre, Thomas, 144, 155
McNall, Charles, 262
McNall, Effie Mae, 262
McNall, Elmer, 262
McNall, Elmer E., 263
McNall, Nathan, 262
McNall, S Efner, 262
McNall, Sibbel, 245, 262
McNall, Stephen, 262
McNall, William, 245, 261, 262
McNamer, John L., 286

McPeak, Henry, 303
Mace, Priscilla, 24
Magee, Selina, 265
Magee, William, 265
Mallory, Harriet, 281, 292
Man, William, 34
Mann, Mary, 224
Manning, Benjamin, 26
Manning, William, 27
Marshall, John, 46
Mason, John, 98
Meade, John, 21
Meaker, Bradley, 310
Meaker, Martha (Queal), 310, 313
Meaker, Robert Queal, 310
Merchant, Phineas, 106
Merchant, Submit (Mrs), 136
Metz, Elizabeth, 336
Metz, John, 336
Metz, Joseph, 336
Metz, Mary, 336
Metz, Rachel, 335
Mickrals, Fannie, 265
Miller, Grace, 201
Miller, Susan, 336
Minor, Callie, 250
Mitchell, Jonathan, 33
Mooar, Mrs Mehitable, 25
Mooar, Priscilla, 26
Mooers, Edmund, 103
Moon, Julia, 242
Moore, Louisa, 265, 268
Moore, Mary, 265
Morgan, Festus, 105
Morgan, Wendel, 313
Morrell, S W, 284
Morrill, Abraham, 29
Morton, Adelgetha, 66
Morton, Chandler, 66
Morton, Charles Frank, 66
Morton, Eudora, 66
Morton, Henry, 66
Morton, Howell, 66
Morton, Naamah, 66
Mounts, Flora, 268
Mounts, Karah, 197
Mowat, Anna, 251

INDEX

Mowat, Guy, 251

NEEDLES, Thomas, 227
Neff, Mary, 78
Nelson, Jennie, 304
Newton, Charles, 292
Newton, Mary, 292
Nichols, Ferd, 197
Nichols, John D., 37
Nichols, William, 286
Nigh, Alice Henshaw, 304
Norton, Grace, 239
Norval, Agnes, 110
Nourse, Catherine, 282
Nourse, Lucy, 282

OBERHOLTZER, Catherine, 339
Oberholtzer, Elizabeth, 340
Orcutt, Ina M., 178
Osborne, Elbert, 290
Osgood, Christopher, 47
Osgood, John, Jr., 103
Osgood, Mary, 221

PAGE, Julius, 136
Palmerlee, Albert, 260
Palmerlee, Asa, 245, 259, 260
Palmerlee, Charles, 260
Palmerlee, Earl, 260
Palmerlee, Efner, 259, 260
Palmerlee, Franklin D., 259
Palmerlee, Fred, 260
Palmerlee, Helen, 260
Palmerlee, Heman, 260
Palmerlee, Henry, 259
Palmerlee, Herbert, 260
Palmerlee, Hoel, 260
Palmerlee, James, 260
Palmerlee, Joseph, 260
Palmerlee, Lucy, 245, 260, 262
Palmerlee, Mark, 260
Palmerlee, Mary, 260
Palmerlee, Myrtle, 260
Palmerlee, Seward, 259
Palmerlee, Stephen, 260
Parker, Benjamin, 23
Parker, James, 40, 46
Parker, John, 40, 43, 44, 46, 48

Parker, Lucinda, 105
Parker, Lucy, 248
Parker, Robert, 40
Parker, Sally, 245
Parks, Mary E., 67
Parmalee, Caroline, 242
Parris, Robert, 68
Passmore, Jacob, 231
Passmore, Lydia, 231
Patterson, James, 46
Patten, Mehitable, 23
Pattin, William, 40, 46
Paul, David, 246
Paul, Delilah, 247
Peabody, Wallace, 66
Peake, Jonathan, 24, 53
Peake, Sophia, 242
Pfleiger, John, 339
Pendell, Frank, 113
Pendell, Nellie, 96, 124
Pennick, George, 336
Perrin, 30
Perry, Obadiah, 68, 74
Pette, Moses, 282
Phillips, Julia, 155
Phillips, Levi, 144
Pierce, D., 99
Pierce, Eliza, 65
Pike, Rosella, 65
Pope, General, 326
Pope, Olive, 106
Porter, Lois, 262
Porter, Merritt, 262
Prentice, Jno., 52
Prentice, Thomas, Jr., 62
Prentice, Thomas, Sr., 52
Price, Matilda J., 232
Printup, David, 260
Printup, Lucy, 260
Printup, Marion, 260
Proctor, Robert, 68
Proctor, Sarah, 62

QUEAL, Abbie Smith, 269, 274
Queal, Albert F., 265
Queal, Alice, 308, 313, 319
Queal, Alice Hubbel, 319
Queal, Alexander, 269, 270, 274

Queal, Anna, 265
Queal, Arthur, 319
Queal, Atchison, 157, 162, 184, 281, 290, 292, 293, 294, 297, 298, 299, 300, 308, 330, 346
Queal, Catherine, 269
Queal, Charles P., 292
Queal, Dudley, 273
Queal, E. Barber, 265
Queal, Elizabeth, 274, 281
Queal, Ellen M., 292
Queal, Frank, 265
Queal, Frances Gradwohl, 330
Queal, Fred, 273
Queal, George, 273
Queal, George C., 274, 281
Queal, George W., 268
Queal, Harry B., 316, 320
Queal, Hedding H., 292, 294
Queal, Herbert Paul, 320
Queal, Irving, 309, 314, 316
Queal, Irving Wyatt, 330
Queal, James, 282, 321
Queal, James Hall, 320
Queal, Jane, 268, 269, 274
Queal, John, 264, 269, 270, 273
Queal, John Henry, 293, 299, 303, 304, 307, 316, 345
Queal, John Oscar, 265
Queal, Josephine Elma, 330
Queal, Kate Gillespie, 314
Queal, Katherine M., 319
Queal, Kittie Sara, 320
Queal, Lena, 270
Queal, Lucy French, 155, 281, 292, 299, 300, 346
Queal, Lucy Mary, 316, 319
Queal, Luke C., 282, 319, 320, 321
Queal, Margaret, 274, 275
Queal, Margaret Atchison, 269
Queal, Martha, 281, 307
Queal, Martha Amelia, 308, 310
Queal, Martha Barber, 265
Queal, Mary, 274, 281, 290, 291, 294, 298, 321, 322, 323, 332
Queal, Mary Elizabeth, 293, 345, 346
Queal, Mary Graves, 281, 308

INDEX

Queal, Mary Matilda, 319
Queal, Michael, 264, 265, 268
Queal, McLean, 269
Queal, Orin H, 282, 309, 316, 330, 331, 332
Queal, Paul A., 282, 320, 325, 326, 327, 329, 330
Queal, Philip G, 265
Queal, Ralph W., 316
Queal, Richison, 281, 291
Queal, Robert, 264, 274, 277, 278, 281
Queal, Robert F, 282, 303, 304, 313, 314, 315, 316, 332
Queal, Sally Waterman, 274
Queal, Sarah Anna, 273
Queal, Sarah Hall, 321
Queal, Sarah Houghton, 314
Queal, Sheldon Gillespie, 330
Queal, Smith B, 265
Queal, William, 264, 265, 268, 269
Queal, William Booth, 308
Queal, William S, 269, 274
Queal, William G, 282, 307, 308, 309, 310, 320
Queal, William Henry, 265
Queal, William McLean, 269, 273
Queal, William N, 270, 274, 292
Queal, William C, 269, 274, 277, 278, 281, 282, 283, 284, 285, 286, 289, 290, 291, 307, 308, 321, 322, 323, 332

Reed, Christopher, 68
Remington, Jonathan, 93, 96
Rendall, Ann, 283
Riggs, Clara, 262
Richardson, Jonathan, 24
Richardson, Sibil, 84
Richison, Mary, 274
Rickerd, Catherine, 335
Rittenhouse, Daniel, 335
Rittenhouse, Rachel, 335
Rhodes, Emma, 270
Robinson, Dee, 251
Robinson, Virginia, 251
Rogers, John, 23
Rogers, John H, 205

Rogers, John, Sr, 46, 48, 55
Rogers, Mary, 23
Rogers, Priscilla, 55
Root, Lusannah, 105, 120, 255
Rose, Dorothy, 241
Ross, Nettie, 303
Rudolph, Lucretia, 235
Rule, Frank, 184
Rule, Harry Hamilton, 184
Rummel, Albert C, 188
Rummel, Robert French, 188
Russ, Samuel, 157
Russell, Alice, 248
Russell, John, 65
Russell Rose Ella, 270
Russell, T. C, 270

Sanders, Amanda, 155
Schwenk, Sarah, 336
Schwenkfeld, Casper, 333
Schultz, David, 334
Scranton, John, 239
Seaward, Alpha, 247, 248
Seaward, Caleb, 239, 240
Seaward, Catherine, 242
Seaward, Damaris, 241
Seaward, Daniel, 240
Seaward, David, 245, 246
Seaward, Delia, 255
Seaward, Delilah, 245, 246
Seaward, Ebenezer, 239, 240, 241
Seaward, Electa, 246
Seaward, Eliphalet, 241
Seaward, Elizabeth, 143, 157, 158, 171, 175
Seaward, Emily, 246
Seaward, Ephraim, 240
Seaward, Hannah, 239
Seaward, James, 255
Seaward, Joel, 241
Seaward, John, 239, 241, 242
Seaward, Joseph, 239
Seaward, Lucy, 245, 249, 255, 256
Seaward, Lucy Ingalls, 261
Seaward, Lydia, 240
Seaward, Mariah, 255
Seaward, Mary, 249
Seaward, Mehitable, 161, 261
Seaward, Noadiah, 240, 241, 245

Seaward, Porter, 241
Seaward, Samuel, 239
Seaward, Sarah, 241, 242
Seaward, Sarah Swain, 241, 245
Seaward, Sibbel, 261
Seaward, Stephen, 148, 227, 231, 239, 242, 245, 246, 247, 249, 255, 256, 261, 262
Seaward, Swain, 242
Seaward, Thomas, 240
Seaward, William, 239
Sell, Adam, 164
Seward, Anna, 110
Shannon, Rose, 248
Sharp, Mary, 56
Shed, Daniel, 23
Shed, Nathan, 23
Shed, Zachariah, 55
Shelland, David, 269
Shelland, James, 277
Shelland, John, 157
Sheppard, Thomas, 52
Shildon, John, 46
Skinner, Aaron, 261
Skinner, Delia, 261
Skinner, Lucy, 261
Skinner, Nillie, 261
Slackford, Kathlyn, 354
Slackford, William, 354
Smith, Abbie, 269
Smith, Ada S, 181
Smith, Carp, 261
Smith, Edgar Frank, 261
Smith, Elroy, 187
Smith, Joseph (Capt), 103
Smith, Lafayette, 181
Smith, Louis N, 181
Smith, Lucy Sharille, 261
Smith, Mary, 168, 181, 182, 183, 184, 197
Smith, Nathan (Dr), 158, 180, 181, 182, 183, 184
Smith, Pelatiah, 52
Smith, Polly, 155
Smith, Stella, 181
Smith, Susanna, 235
Smith, Viola, 181
Smith, William L, 181
Snover, Samuel, 259

INDEX

Snover, Villa, 259
Snow, Joseph, 97
Snyder, Amelia, 251
Snyder, Edna, 187
Snyder, Edward, 187
Snyder, Helen, 187
Stanford, Henry Martin, 110
Stanford, Rosa Olivia, 113
Stange, Charles Henry, 349
Stange, Harriet Beyer, 349
Starkweather, Asher, 273
Starkweather, Davis Viney, 273
Starkweather, Essa, 273
Starkweather, Morrell, 273
Starkweather, Sarah Anna, 273
Stearns, Mary, 28, 47
Steedman, John, 30
Sternes, John, 40, 46
Sternes, Isaac, 55
Sternes, Samuel, 55
Stevenson, Andrew, 34
Stever, Calvin, 242
Stever, Charles, 242
Stever, David, 143, 285
Stever, Dorothy, 242
Stever, Emmeline, 242
Stever, Jacob, 284, 285
Stever, Jesse, 242
Stever, Marietta, 143, 152, 155
Stever, Olive, 242
Stever, Robert, 242
Stever, Seneca, 242
Stever, William, 143, 155, 242
Sparrowhawk, Nathaniel, 34
Spaulding, Elizabeth, 65
Spencer, Allen, 110
Spencer, Amanda, 109
Squire, James, 113
Stickney, Daniel, 46
Stickney, William, 46
Stone, Gregory, 34
Stone, James, 227, 235
Stone, John, 33
Stoner, Clarence Birch, 187, 188
Stoner, Helen Constance, 188
Stoner, Lowell French, 187
Stoner, Lucy (French), 187
Swain, Sarah, 241
Swift, James, 262

Swift, Mary, 262

Taggart, Mary, 282
Talmage, Chloe, 241
Talmage, Joseph, 241
Tanner, Phoebe, 231
Tarboll, John, 47
Tay, Will, 44, 46
Taye, Nathaniel, 55
Taylor, Mary, 283
Tedman, Rachel, 242
Temple, Alenda, 144
Temple, Christopher, 68
Temple, James, 144
Temple, Polly, 144
Thomas, Addie, 340, 349
Thomas, Anna, 177
Thomas, Bessie, 357
Thompson, Annie, 65
Thompson, Deacon, 62
Thompson, Joseph, 53, 56
Thorne, Ann, 235
Thrall, Henry Portens, 259
Thrall, Hiram Elvin, 259
Thrall, Lois, 259
Thrall, Lucy Mehitable, 259
Thrall, Stephen Asa, 259
Thrall, Willis Collins, 259
Thrall, William Ernest, 259
Tod, David, 300
Treat, Calphurna, 157, 176, 177
Treat, Dolly, 242
Treat, Thomas W., 242
Tripp, Almaretta Adams, 250
Tripp, Amelia, 259
Tripp, Charles, 250
Tripp, David Henry, 250, 251
Tripp, Edwin, 250
Tripp, Ella, 250
Tripp, Emma, 250
Tripp, Hannah, 253
Tripp, Henry, 178
Tripp, Jennie, 251
Tripp, Lucy, 253
Tripp, Mary, 252, 253
Tripp, Mary B., 250
Tripp, Minnie, 250
Tripp, Nathan, 245, 249, 250, 252
Tripp, Polly, 253

Tripp, Robert Edwin, 249, 253
Tripp, Sidney, 250
Tripp, Stephen H., 250, 254
Tripp, Stephen Seaward, 251, 252
Tripp, William K., 257
Trowbridge, Stephen, 232
Trull, John, 46
Tudor, Lewis, 265
Tudor, Louisa, 265
Tuffs, Henry, 59
Turner, John, 224
Tustin, John, 239
Tuttle, Harry, 119
Tuttle, Michael, 106, 119
Tyng, Eleazer, 73
Tyng, Jonathan, 68, 74, 78
Tyng, Mary, 68

Underwood, Emily, 65
Usher, Robert, 68

Van Alstine, Marietta, 155
Van Dusen, Matthew, 290
Van Fossen, Christianna, 335
Van Fossen, Michael, 335
Venner, Mary Jane, 65

Wade, Ardelia, 274
Wade, James, 274
Wade, Jane, 274
Wade, Warren, 274
Wade, Willis, 274
Wagerley, George H., 207, 214
Wagner, John, 340
Wagner, Mary C., 340
Waldo, Cornelius, 68, 74
Waldo, Daniel, 68
Walker, Joseph, 55
Walker, Sarah, 282
Walker, William, 76
Walters, Lue Lincoln, 184, 187
Warner, Samuel, 68
Washburn, Olive, 242
Waterman, Alice, 273
Waterman, Amanda, 144
Waterman, H. P., 286, 289
Waterman, John, Sr., 273
Waterman, Sally Esther, 269
Watters, Carrie, 187

INDEX

Weld, Thomas, 68, 74, 75, 78, 91
Wells, Sarah, 241
Wentworth, Gov Benning, 99, 100
Weyand, Philipina, 334, 335
Wheeler, Elizabeth, 223
Wheeler, Joseph, 68
Wheeler, Nellie, 316
Wheeler, Rachel, 223
Whitaker, John H , 110
White, John, 24
White, Joseph, 84
White, Kirk, 260
White, Leah, 260
Whiting, Rev Samuel, 43, 44, 45, 46, 53, 55, 78
Whittemore, Nathaniel, 25
Williams, Araminta, 265

Williams, Arthur, 119
Williams, Charlotte French, 119
Williams, Daniel, 119
Williams, David, 119
Williams, Ezra, 115, 256
Williams, Ida, 265
Williams, Isaac, 286
Williams, Otho, 265
Williams, Willard, 265
Winnie, Fred, 157
Winship, Edward, 38
Winthrop, Gov , 37, 38
Wiswall, Ebenezer, 52
Wolsey, Mary, 282
Woodbury, John, 285
Woodruff, Lena, 201
Wood, Carrie, 197
Wood, Charles, 110, 197

Wood, Chauncey, 197
Wood, Ellsworth, 197
Woods, Isaac, 62
Woods, Nathaniel, 67
Woods, Oliver, 67
Wornell, Nancy, 354
Wright, Abijah, 86
Wright, Asahel, 85
Wright, Eliza, 66
Wright, Pomeroy, 242

YATES, B F , 251
Yates, Edward, 156
Yates, Joseph C , 156
Yates, Mary Edna, 251
Yeakel, Abraham, 334
Yeakel, Rosina, 334
Yost, Mary, 339

CPSIA information can be obtained
at www.ICGtesting.com
Printed in the USA
LVOW13s0608270917
550233LV00009B/102/P